W9-CJN-799

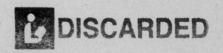

LEADERSHIP IN WAR 1939-1945

Defence Is Our Business

Before the Dawn (Dunkirk and Burma)

The Only Enemy (autobiography)

Sandhurst

The Story of the Victoria Cross

The Story of the George Cross

In This Sign Conquer: The Story of the Army Chaplains

The Valiant

The Will to Live

Percival and the Tragedy of Singapore

Leadership in War

1939-1945

THE GENERALS IN VICTORY AND DEFEAT

Brigadier The Rt Hon
Sir John Smyth, Bt, VC, MC

DAVID & CHARLES

NEWTON ABBOT   LONDON
VANCOUVER

0 7153 6600 9

Set in 11 on 13 Baskerville
and printed in Great Britain
by John Sherratt and Son Ltd
for David & Charles (Holdings) Limited
South Devon House Newton Abbot Devon

Published in Canada by Douglas David & Charles Limited 3645 McKechnie Drive West Vancouver BC

Contents

Illustrations

All photographs reproduced by courtesy of the Imperial War Museum

Introduction

It is a remarkable fact that, in the latter half of the twentieth century, and when World War II is already far away, the public should be so interested in military history and the biographies of the politicians and the generals who have made it. Books on World War II are followed by books on World War I; and recently new books have appeared on such great commanders as Wellington, Napoleon and Marlborough. It is as though the eternal questions—What makes a general? Why did one general fail whilst another succeeded? How does one general compare with another? What constitutes leadership in battle?—still remain unanswered and perennially fascinating. And how big a part do prime ministers and governments play in the conduct of military operations?

There is also the important question as to how much continued strain and ill-health can affect the judgement of a high commander in battle. General Wavell was a case in point. He had undergone a tremendous strain in his North African campaigns and when he was replaced by General Auchinleck he was very badly in need of a long rest. The Chief of the General Staff Sir John Dill knew this and so did Wavell himself. Dill begged Winston Churchill not to send him as commander-in-chief in India, knowing that war with Japan was almost certain. But Churchill insisted that Wavell should go to the India Command and 'sit under the pagoda tree'. Very soon Wavell became involved as generalissimo of the ABDA Command in the hectic and disastrous operations which led to the loss of Malaya and Burma. Then on 10 February 1942,

just as he was departing from Singapore in his flying boat, he
had a serious accident in the blackout breaking two bones in
his back. He was unconscious and should certainly have been
hospitalised. But who can insist on a commander-in-chief
going to hospital if he himself refuses to go? And it was in the
next few weeks that Singapore and Burma were lost and the
remnants of Burma Army nearly went into the bag. During
this short time everyone who saw Wavell remarked on how ill
he looked and some of the decisions he made and the extraordinary signals he sent out (as recorded by his biographer
John Connell) were far from being those he would have made
had he been in full health.

Another thing which has always interested me is this: how is
military history written? I can speak on the latter subject with a
certain amount of personal experience. The reading public
think that the historian must always be right: that an official
military history must be gospel truth. I am not insinuating that
the historian is not telling the truth as he sees it—but how does
he come to see it in the first place? The historian, coming along
many years after the events about which he is to write, becomes
circumscribed by all that has already been written—and
spoken—about them. He does his best to arrive at the truth
from a mass of documents; but, however unbiased he may try
to be, and however many different opinions he may examine,
he must be influenced by two overriding factors; these are the
commander-in-chief's despatches and the political interpretation put upon them. The despatches are naturally
influenced by what the commander-in-chief has been told by
the commander of the forces engaged. If, for some reason, he
was given a wrong picture in the beginning, the distortion in
the despatch becomes the accepted fact for subsequent writers.

I was to have a vivid example of this which is quite in-
controvertible. The Sittang Bridge disaster in Burma on
23 March 1942 was (quite rightly) described by both Wavell
and Winston Churchill as the operation which lost Burma.
The immediate report of the incident given to Wavell and
Churchill was, however, basically untrue; yet, as it appeared in

both Wavell's despatch and in Churchill's book on World War II, it had been so widely accepted that it became part of the history of the war long before the history was actually written. Later, the war historian was forced to have second thoughts because of information which was subsequently brought to light and he had to alter the previously accepted story in several vitally important particulars. Fortunately this was able to be done, but this has not always been the case.

The autocrats of the battlefield are the commanders-in-chief, the prime minister and, finally, the war historians, all of whom are prone to error. It is no wonder that the more junior generals sometimes hardly recognise their battles when they come to read of them in the history books. Within his own sphere the commander-in-chief in the field is supreme as few other people in authority ever are; and the higher he is, the further away he is, and the more important the operation he is conducting, the more supreme he is. He can sack anyone in his command and they have no redress whatever—and the higher they are the harder they fall. Years afterwards the war historian may try to pick up the pieces but usually not all the King's horses nor all the King's men can put Humpty Dumpty together again. A case in point is that of General Gough, commanding the Fifth Army in France in March 1918, though he, in fact, did live long enough to have something of his reputation restored.

The commander-in-chief or chief of staff can of course be sacked by the prime minister, as Wavell, Dill and Auchinleck were by Winston Churchill. Prime ministers, however, unlike commanders-in-chief, are responsible to their governments and have to have a good majority in the House of Commons. Lloyd George in World War I never had this or he would have sacked Douglas Haig. Winston Churchill was more fortunate in this respect in World War II—although he was not a great sacker of generals. But in his position as Minister of Defence Winston did influence the military conduct of the war to a greater extent than any other prime minister has ever done. His political grip of the whole world war situation was masterly, and a great strength to the Allied cause, but his interference with operations at a lower level was often unfortunate and most exasperating to the Chiefs of Staff and the fighting generals. Both Lloyd George and Winston Churchill wrote their memoirs fairly soon after their respective wars—and it was not easy for a war historian to refute or disregard them.

So much for history. Now for the generals who played such a large part in its making. And let me say at once that I have the highest admiration for most of the generals about whom I shall be writing. No one becomes a general unless he has shown outstanding qualities of knowledge and leadership. The interesting thing is how different generals then stand up to different conditions—which rise to the big occasion and which fail to do so; and all the time the imponderable factor of luck plays its very important part. The generals about whom I shall be writing in this book are British generals of World War II, many of whom I have known, served under or written about. And it is because of this personal knowledge which I have of so many of these men that I feel competent to write this book in the way I have.

Between the wars I was for five years at the Staff College Camberley, the school for generals, where most of the generals of World War II were either my teachers, my pupils or my fellow teachers. They included Ironside, Gort, Dill, Alan Brooke, Wilson, Adam, Dempsey and Gott—and the two Canadians, Vanier and Crerar. I was brought up in the Indian Army with Auchinleck and Slim—the former being several years senior to me and the latter two years junior. I served under Auchinleck as a battalion commander in the Mohmand Expedition of 1935, in which Alexander (with whom I was at Sandhurst) was one of the brigadiers. Two years later Alex came up to stay with me on 'the roof of the world' whilst I was commanding Chitral Force.

General (later Field-Marshal) Sir John Dill was Commandant of the Staff College at Camberley during the whole of my three years as an instructor, from 1931 to 1933. He obtained for me a brevet lieutenant-colonelcy in my last year and asked me to recommend a suitable successor for this Indian Army appointment. I recommended one Major Slim of the 6th Gurkhas.

Bill Slim duly arrived to take over from me and we remained close friends until the day of his death on 14 December 1970. On 14 June 1962, when he was Master of the Clothworkers Livery Company and I was Master of the Farriers, he invited me to be the Guest of Honour at his Court dinner. In the course of his speech he said he wanted to disclose something he had never told anyone before. 'For the whole of my first year as a teacher at the Camberley Staff College,' he said, 'I gave off Jackie Smyth's lectures without altering a word of them!' When he died the obituaries in the national newspapers referred to his appointment at Camberley as the stepping-stone to his career.

When World War II started Lord Gort got me over from India—where I was a lieutenant-colonel commanding the 45th Sikhs—to command a brigade in his British Expeditionary Force. However, when Auchinleck became commander-in-chief in India he insisted on my returning to India to command a division. I raised the 19th (Dagger) Division and then commanded the 17th Division in the disastrous First Burma Campaign of 1942—after which I had a considerable period of sickness, following which I became a military correspondent, a Member of Parliament and an author.

During the last three years of the war I was military correspondent to a number of newspapers in the Kemsley Group, including the *Sunday Times* and *Daily Sketch*, and I was writing several articles a week on the war. I also wrote extensively for the Ministry of Information and when the invasion of Europe was pending I was engaged by the National Broadcasting Company of America to talk to New York on the progress of the Normandy landings. So I was in close touch with all that the generals were doing on the various battlefronts.

After the war both Montgomery and Alexander gave me invaluable assistance over several of my books. Montgomery wrote the forewords to my book on Sandhurst and the Life of

'Bolo' Whistler, one of his best and most valued brigade and divisional commanders. Monty was also most interested and helpful over my book, *In This Sign Conquer: The Story of the Army Chaplains*, and arranged for me to go and stay with the Dean of Ripon, who had been his senior chaplain in North Africa and Normandy and later became chaplain-general to the Army. Alexander was also most interested in this book and got his favourite Army Chaplain (when he had been commanding the 1st Battalion Irish Guards), the Rt Reverend Abbot J.R. (Dolly) Brookes, the representative of the English Benedictines at the Vatican, to get in touch with me and afterwards to come over and see me in London. Alexander also wrote the foreword to my book, *The Story of the Victoria Cross*.

On Wednesday, 15 February 1967, I was asked by the BBC to broadcast on 'What Makes a General'. I began my broadcast with these words:

> 'Many people who have studied military history have asked themselves this question but nobody seems to have produced an answer which would satisfy everyone—least of all the generals themselves, who may perhaps be unable to see themselves as others see them. There are generals and generals— ancient generals and modern generals, staff generals and fighting generals. But there is no perfect general whom one could use perhaps as a prototype for all occasions and all campaigns.'

Leadership is of course the most important quality which every successful battle general must have. Many people have tried to define leadership but few of them have agreed— except that a leader is someone whom men will follow. In victory—yes; in defeat? For better or for worse? Or what? These are the questions.

It is of course an advantage for a leader to look the part and have a distinguished appearance and a striking personality. But that won't get you very far if you don't know your job— or you haven't got courage, both physical and mental. It is

easy enough to be a general whom men will follow when you
have the big battalions—on whose side God is always supposed
to be—and everything is going your way. But the real test of
leadership comes when you are up against it, you are outgunned
and outnumbered and 'England's far and honour a name'.

Most of the generals I shall be writing about in this book
made their reputations in the mud and blood of World War I,
when they were comparatively junior officers; and they
emerged from that cauldron really knowing what leadership
meant from the bottom up—and then put their knowledge to
good effect when they gained high command.

I am therefore writing this book from a personal knowledge
of many of the military leaders of my lifetime and as a critic of
some of the things which historians and others have written
about them—and sometimes which they have written about
themselves.

Finally there is the all-important problem of generalship—
which must come first in every military operation—and that
is the making of the plan. In World War II Montgomery and
Slim were the great planners. Alexander left most of it to his
chief of staff, although he always liked to have two or three
alternative plans put forward for his consideration—from
which, by means of his keen intuition, he almost invariably
chose the right one.

Various distinguished military writers and theorists have
sought to define certain principles of war which can be taken
as a guide for all situations. Perhaps the most distinguished of
them was the late Sir Basil Liddell Hart, for whom I had a
great admiration. Amongst other things we were two of the
originators of the 'Military Commentators Circle' in the latter
part of World War II. Liddell Hart's strategy of 'The Indirect
Approach' as applied to World War I in France had a considerable vogue. In brief, the precept which he preached was
'to avoid what is strong and to strike what is weak'. I do of
course agree with this thesis when the circumstances permit.
Bill Slim was a firm believer in it in his final successful campaign
in Burma. The Japanese were almost impossible to shift by

means of a frontal attack. But in the situation which existed in World War I in France, there was no obvious weakness which could be exploited until the continuous front of strong trench systems, protected by acres of barbed wire, flanked by the Vickers machine gun, the Queen of the Battlefield, had been broken.

In the two great amphibious operations in our history, Gallipoli and Overlord (the landing in Normandy in 1944) the best places for landing were naturally the most heavily defended. The crust had to be broken by the application of overwhelming force, which Montgomery planned and applied in Overlord and Ian Hamilton failed to do in Gallipoli because, firstly, he was pressed by the War Cabinet to make the landing much too soon, and secondly, he just didn't have the weapons which were essential to destroy the underwater wire and give cover to the assaulting troops.

The Japanese ensured the success of their invasion of Malaya in December 1941 by overwhelming air superiority over the whole area of operations. The British defence plan was also based on the same idea—the only trouble was that the first-line aircraft couldn't be supplied to implement it.

Surprise, of course, remains the all-important principle in every operation of war, which every commander seeks to achieve; but in World War I it was very difficult. Perhaps the Germans had it over the first use of poison gas in April 1915 and later the British, in their first use of tanks: but both sides missed the bus because they were not able to exploit their initial success.

Many years ago I converted to military purposes the much-quoted dictum of that famous American industrial management consultant, Mary Parker Follett, which was: 'The law is in the circumstances.' Military leaders have often had to play the hand which has been dealt to them, even though they may realise that it contains very few winning cards. They are often then blamed for the plan and their means of implementing it—though they had no responsibility for either. Douglas Haig was much blamed for the Somme battle. But he had been all against fighting the battle at that time. Most of his troops were the newly arrived 'Kitchener Army' divisions, whom he would have preferred to initiate more gradually into battle conditions. But the necessity to relieve pressure on the French at Verdun forced Haig into the blood-bath of the Somme. It may be that he continued the battle for too long; but he had to fight it. Auchinleck in North Africa, again, would have liked much more time to train his troops with their tanks before committing them to battle. But the circumstances of the war as a whole, and the political pressure brought to bear on him, forced him to attack much sooner than he thought right. With the passage of time, however, these things are apt to be forgotten.

But it was in the early campaigns of World War II, with Britain completely unprepared, that the law of the circumstances applied most dramatically. And Dunkirk, Singapore and the First Burma Campaign of 1942 were the graveyards of military reputations. The commanders of those days just had to 'make do and mend' with what they had. And that was generally precious little.

J.G.S.

CHAPTER ONE

Dunkirk and the Battle of Britain

The two years which immediately preceded World War II found Britain with some extremely capable top-ranking generals competing for the two most coveted appointments in the Army. These were Chief of the Imperial General Staff at the War Office and the command of the British Expeditionary Force in the war against Germany which all informed military opinion considered inevitable. It appears now quite incomprehensible that, by 1937, these two appointments had not been decided upon at the highest level—even though the latter appointment could only be in embryo until war had actually been declared.

There had, however, been a change of prime minister in the early half of 1937, Stanley Baldwin being replaced by Neville Chamberlain; and, still more important from the Army's point of view, the appointment of a new secretary of state for war, Mr Leslie Hore Belisha. The latter was a new broom as a minister and very much more so as a war minister since the Army was something about which he knew nothing. He had many virtues as a politician, being an eloquent speaker with a quick brain, a hard worker and a zealous reformer, with a determination to accept nothing at its face value. He suffered no fools gladly and was inclined to class all those who disagreed with him in that category. He was by nature intolerant

17

of generals and civil servants and, as Neville Chamberlain had told him that the Army required a new broom, he at once looked round for something to sweep. He somehow felt that if he asked for advice from one of his official advisers in the War Office he would get a dusty answer—and dust was just what he wanted to get rid of. He therefore looked for outside advice and found it in Liddell Hart, a well-known and much respected writer on military matters, who was at that time Military Correspondent of *The Times*.

Hore Belisha would have gained valuable knowledge from that quarter had he used it circumspectly; but he almost immediately began circulating Liddell Hart's treatises to his senior generals and staff officers—particularly the paper which maintained that they were all much too old. There may have been some truth in that but, despite the frustrations which had existed amongst young regular officers who had distinguished themselves greatly in World War I and then had found their promotion retarded, the system had thrown up some very fine generals such as Dill, Brooke and Ironside, who were vying for the top positions in the Army.

What the British Army was suffering from at this time was not so much a paucity of ideas as lack of money. It was the dead hand of the Treasury which had kept Britain from developing the tank, which had been her own invention and which it was well known was being made the basis of Germany's new model army. However, the two generals then at the top, Montgomery-Massingberd, Chief of the Imperial General Staff, and Sir Cyril Deverell, who was due to succeed him, were certainly on the old side—particularly in view of the fact that Britain was soon likely to be involved in another war.

Hore Belisha had heard good accounts of Lord Gort, VC, from Liddell Hart, but had not actually met him until, in 1937, he had collided with him on the ski slopes in Switzerland. Gort was then Commandant of the Camberley Staff College, where Hore Belisha visited him and, after lunching with him in London, at once invited him to accept the post of Military Secretary at the War Office. In this capacity Gort would be the principal adviser to the Secretary of State on the appointment of senior officers. Gort would much rather have been given command of a division and, in the light of after events, this would probably have been a better appointment for him, as he had had no experience of the command of troops since World War I. On the other hand, he would not have occupied one of the seats of the mighty, which led to his even higher preferment. However, Gort and Hore Belisha between them got rid of Deverell and the hunt for a new CIGS was on.

Gort was as straight as a die and no thought of himself entered into this dismissal. The one job he did want was the command of troops—preferably, of course, command of the British Expeditionary Force. Nearly all the senior British generals at this time put Dill as the outstanding choice for CIGS. Brooke, Alexander and Montgomery were all emphatically in support of him for this appointment. He had every possible qualification for it—except perhaps one. There was a doubt as to whether he was robust enough for such a demanding task. In his book *Man of Valour: Field-Marshal Lord Gort* J. R. Colville says that Liddell Hart had told Hore Belisha that Dill had been slow in recovering from a serious accident. It is doubtful, however, whether Dill would have been allowed to go out to France with the BEF in command of a corps if he had been physically unfit to fill the more sedentary position of CIGS. Hore Belisha, however, realised that he would never have got on with Dill: they would have been like oil and water.

Ironside too was very much in the running for CIGS, though he hated the idea of it. The job he wanted was Commander-in-Chief of the BEF, for which he was strongly supported by Winston Churchill and many others. What a great effect personalities have on the course of events! Had Dill been appointed CIGS at that time, as he so nearly was, neither Ironside nor Gort would have attained their high positions at the outbreak of war.

However, Gort it was who, at the age of only fifty-one, got the top appointment of CIGS, with General Sir Ronald Adam as his Deputy. If it had to be Gort there was no one who could support and advise him better than Adam. Although Gort's appointment was well received by the Army as a welcome change from the elderly previous incumbents, he did not feel happy about it himself, nor did he have a happy or distinguished tour of office, though it was fortunately brief. He was, however, promoted to full general and thus went over the heads of Dill, Wavell and Alan Brooke—and this fact was to have repercussions later.

The Secretary of State's increasing dependence on Liddell Hart now caused the greatest antagonism in the higher ranks of the Army—most of all in Gort himself, until he and Hore Belisha became hardly on speaking terms. It is curious that Prime Minister Neville Chamberlain was so uninterested in military affairs that he failed to take cognisance of this lamentable state of affairs. General Sir John Kennedy, Director of Military Operations, in his book *The Business of War* comments: 'Gort's unsuitability for the post [of CIGS] soon became apparent to all. In the War Office this fine fighting soldier was like a fish out of water.'

With the worsening of relations between Gort and Hore Belisha it did not appear very likely that Gort would obtain his heart's desire of command of the British Expeditionary Force. However, when I was home on leave from India in the summer of 1938 he asked me to come to see him. He told me then that he expected to become Commander-in-Chief of the BEF and in that event he would like me to command one of his brigades. He also said that no troops or officers of the Indian Army were being brought over to the Western Theatre but that if I could manage to be home on leave when the war started he would be able to 'requisition' me. As I was then only a lieutenant-colonel in command of the 45th Sikhs in Allahabad I was naturally much flattered. But how it was going to be managed I didn't quite know. However, with the help of Gort himself and his Deputy CIGS, General Ronald Adam, it was. I also lunched with Dill on 31 May 1938 whilst I was in London. He had been a very good friend to me and I liked and admired him very much; but I deemed it politic not to say anything about Gort's plans for me—or for himself.

Early in 1939 discussions took place between the British and French military authorities with regard to some joint planning for the direction of operations in the event of war with Germany, which was now generally considered to be inevitable and indeed imminent. Colonel Hastings Ismay, who had succeeded Hankey as Secretary of the Committee of Imperial Defence, was despatched to Paris to discuss matters with General Gamelin, the French Commander-in-Chief, and military conversations then took place between Gort and Gamelin in Paris.

As the British were to contribute such a small part of the total Allied forces it was agreed unanimously that the British Expeditionary Force should be concentrated in the Le Mans area as requested by Gamelin and come under command of General Georges, with adequate rights of appeal to the British Government. This was the system which had been adopted between Foch and Haig in 1918. These plans were sanctioned by the British Cabinet, and British staff officers were then sent over to France to make detailed plans for the movement of a British Expeditionary Force to France.

The quite extraordinary situation was that, although operational plans had been continuing for some time, and the French commanders had all been appointed, no commander of the British Field Force had been selected. Naturally there was much speculation as to who would get this highest command. The strong favourite appeared to be Sir John Dill, who had been GOC Aldershot Command and had then relieved Wavell (who had been appointed Commander-in-Chief Middle East) as GOC Southern Command. Liddell Hart was of course consulted by Hore Belisha and Ironside was brought back from Gibraltar so as to be on the spot if selected. There were rumours and counter-rumours and General Dill was led to believe that he had the job in his pocket. He was certainly bitterly aggrieved and disappointed when he didn't get it, as was Alan Brooke, who had the greatest admiration for him.

General Sir Ronald Adam, the Deputy Chief of the General

Staff, was the man who knew more about what was going on at the War Office at this particular time than anyone else. I therefore wrote to him on the subject in January 1972 and received the following reply, dated the 31st of that month:

> I am very interested to hear that you are writing a book on leadership in battle and am certain that you will do it very well. In answer to your query, the choice of CIGS, GOC British Expeditionary Force and the two Corps Commanders was left very late except that Dill and Brooke were in the positions in peace which one would have expected them to be in to be chosen as Corps Commanders. Dill, I know, was very disappointed at not being chosen as GOC of the BEF. I think he must have been commencing the illness from which he eventually died (anaemia). Brooky was undoubtedly a great commander, as he showed in his handling of II Corps throughout the retreat. Alex and Monty made their names during the retreat and I do not think were considered for the job [of GOC] and I am certain that I was not. Gort wanted me as Chief of Staff but was not allowed to take me. Ironside expected the job. In the circumstances Gort did the job very well; he saved the BEF and the decision was entirely his. I (as III Corps commander) was at the other end of the phone when he made up his mind, as I had to give orders for my reconnaissance parties to start south and I had rung up to tell Jack [Gort] that in my opinion my attack was not on. Brooky did not think much of Gort, I know; he did not approve of the advance into Belgium and he thought Jack bothered too much about details but in the circumstances he did a great job.

This is an invaluable comment and can be taken with that of General Sir John Kennedy, who was Director of Military Operations at the War Office at the time. In *The Business of War* (p 16) he wrote as follows (my italics):

On the 3rd September the Cabinet had decided that Gort

was to be Commander-in-Chief of the Field Force and Ironside was to replace him as CIGS. Adam [Deputy CIGS] told me this news at dinner in the Club. These appointments were a complete surprise to us all. I was sorry on personal grounds that Gort was to leave the War Office. Gort's appointment as Commander-in-Chief must have seemed to the Cabinet a good solution politically in view of the strained relations between him and Hore Belisha; and possibly as good a solution as any other militarily. *The Army after all had at that time no single soldier with war experience of high command.* Gort had been very much in the public eye and had been 'built up' in the Press.

I think now [1957] that the appointment of Gort to be Commander-in-Chief may be regarded as one of those strokes of great good luck which came our way more than once in the course of the war. Under any other commander the Field Force might, for quite good reasons, have been manoeuvred differently, and in such a way as to be cut off from the sea when the French Army collapsed—a disaster from which it would have been difficult to recover . . .

I believe Gort as CIGS had advised the appointment of Dill as Commander-in-Chief. Lelong, the French Military Attaché, said the French would prefer Dill to Ironside as Commander of the Field Force, and so did Colonel Petitbon of Gamelin's staff. But Dill was comparatively unknown to the British public—as opposed to the Army; and if he had been appointed the problem of Gort's disposal would still have remained.

Ironside's appointment as CIGS was well received. He was much in the public eye at the time, was *persona grata* with the Prime Minister and was strongly backed by Churchill. Had Ironside not been brought back by Hore Belisha from Gibraltar, a year or so earlier, to be Inspector-General of the Forces, it is probable that he would never have been considered for a high command—and almost certainly not for the post of CIGS. Somebody said to me at this time: 'Hore Belisha does not know it yet, but he has raised a regular

Frankenstein's monster in bringing back Ironside from the dead!' Most of us (at the War Office) felt that the combination of Ironside and Hore Belisha could not last. Some of us believed that Hore Belisha would find himself overshadowed by Ironside in the Cabinet Councils, and that he would soon find a way to get rid of him. Others felt the betting was the other way, and that Ironside would get rid of Hore Belisha. They were right.

And so, at the very early age of fifty-three, Gort had achieved his life's ambition of becoming Commander-in-Chief of the British Expeditionary Force at the start of World War II. And what an amazing career he had had—which would seem to have qualified him in every respect for this high appointment.

John Vereker was the elder son of the 5th Viscount Gort— an Irish title—who died when John was sixteen and he therefore inherited the title. Jack Gort, as he was generally known, was educated at Harrow and passed high into Sandhurst in 1904. From his early days at school he became dedicated to an Army career. He was squarely built and rotund in figure— though always hard and fanatically fit. At Sandhurst he was nicknamed 'Fatboy', a name which stuck to him, though he was later, during World War I, called 'Tiger' Gort. He won a VC, three DSOs and an MC and commanded his battalion of Grenadier Guards and finally a brigade. He gained a reputation for being an indomitable and fearless leader of troops in battle. He had been wounded three times, the last time severely. But he was no mere blood-and-guts battle fighter; he was recognised as being also a man of great intelligence and an earnest student of the art of war, although I would not class him as a strategist and military thinker in the mould of Dill or Brooke.

Quite soon after the war Gort met Captain Basil Liddell Hart, who was already making a reputation as a thoughtful and dynamic writer on military matters. Liddell Hart became an admirer of Gort and was to have a considerable influence on his future career.

Gort was nominated as a pupil in 1919 at the first postwar

course at the Camberley Staff College. He had then just been promoted to the substantive rank of major. Among his fellow pupils were Alan Brooke and 'Jumbo' Wilson. Among his instructors were John Dill, Philip Neame, VC, 'Boney' Fuller, of Tank Corps fame, and Harry Knox. In those days Gort's attitude to life was robust to the point of boisterousness but as always he was a dedicated student of his profession.

In 1921 Gort returned to Camberley for a three-year appointment as an Instructor, which put him on the road to high preferment in the Army and he received a brevet lieutenant-colonelcy. In these years he renewed his acquaintance with Dill, Alan Brooke and Philip Neame and got to know Archie Wavell, Henry Pownall and Ronald Adam. Major-General Ironside became Commandant of the Staff College in 1922 and I arrived as a student in the following year and first made Gort's acquaintance. His reputation at that time as an instructor was certainly very high.

In 1930 Gort returned to regimental soldiering and was given command of the 4th Guards Brigade. In 1932 he was posted to India as Director of Military Training. During the summer months he continued in Simla the 'Backward Boys' classes for officers aspiring to enter the Staff College which I had started under Brigadier Jack Collins in 1925. Like other officers who had distinguished themselves in World War I and then felt they were getting nowhere in the log-jam of peacetime soldiering, Gort found this period of his military life somewhat tedious. In his capacity as Director of Military Training, however, he had close connections with the Staff College at Quetta, where Bernard Montgomery was the Senior Instructor. They didn't get on well together and Montgomery was one of the chief critics of Gort's appointment to command the BEF.

In 1936, at the age of forty-nine, Gort was made Commandant of the Staff College Camberley, where he had already spent several happy years as pupil and instructor. Then came his meeting with Hore Belisha and his accelerated promotion to the topmost position in the Army. Accelerated promotion was regarded as 'a good thing' by those whom it benefited but

not by those who were accelerated over. I don't think Dill and
Brooke ever really forgave Gort for being promoted over their
heads—both in rank and as CIGS and Commander-in-Chief
of the BEF.

Gort was not allowed to take Adam with him to France as
his chief of staff as this would have removed both the Chief and
the Deputy Chief of the Imperial General Staff from the War
Office at one blow—though Adam was in France commanding
I Corps before the balloon went up in May 1940. Gort therefore took as his CGS, Major-General Henry Pownall, at that
time Director of Military Operations and Intelligence at the
War Office, who was promoted to Lieutenant-General—over
the head of Major-General Philip Neame, VC, who was
appointed Assistant to Pownall. Pownall was an ardent admirer
of Gort and never wavered in his loyal and whole-hearted
support of him. Neame, however, was not happy about Gort's
appointment. He had been one of his teachers at the Staff
College and later one of Pownall's.

Neame writes in his autobiography, *Playing with Strife* (p 245):

At the time of the Munich crisis in September 1938 I made
enquiries from the War Office as to whether I was earmarked
for any mobilisation appointment, for the 'Shop' [the Royal
Military Academy of which Neame was commandant] was
to close down in case of war and the cadets go to Officer
Cadet Training units. However, I was informed of no such
appointment until February 1939, when I heard that I was
to be appointed Chief of the General Staff (graded as Major-
General General Staff) of the Expeditionary Force to go to
France in the event of war with Germany. I heard some
details soon after from the nominated Commander-in-Chief,
Lieutenant-General (later Field-Marshal) Sir John Dill. He
told me, of course most secretly, that initially one Army
Corps of two divisions from Aldershot would go to France,
which was all we could then mobilise; that there would be a
skeleton GHQ behind the corps, to be organised under my
charge; and that when a second corps appeared he [Dill]

would hand over command of his corps and assume the sole task of Commander-in-Chief, with me as his CGS.

During the next seven months before war broke out, Neame on several occasions asked the War Office if they could tell him anything further and whether he could be allowed to study the plans for the move and employment of the BEF, but he was told that the plans were not yet sufficiently advanced.

Neame continues:

In July 1939 General Sir John Dill asked me to go to Alder-shot to take part in a four-days exercise with the First Army Corps, in order that I might get better acquainted with the troops who would go to France in the event of war. As he was directing the exercise he appointed me to command the corps utilising his staff and with the 1st and 2nd Divisions (commanded by Major-Generals Alexander and Lloyd) under my command. Dill had been over to France, and had some conversations with the French Generalissimo, Gamelin, but I was still in ignorance of the War Office plans.

On Monday September 4th I went to the War Office at 9 am, ready to fly over to France with the Quarter-Master General of the BEF, Major-General W. G. Lindsell. When I reached the War Office I was informed, on the day the BEF started to move, of a complete change of command of both the BEF and the War Office higher staff. In the BEF Dill was not to be Commander-in-Chief, I was not to be the CGS and the Adjutant-General was also changed. In the War Office the CIGS, the Director of Military Operations and the Director-General of the Territorial Army were all changed. Major-General H. Pownall became CGS of the BEF while I, though senior to him, was relegated as Deputy to him. Imagine my own surprise, and still more my consternation that Dill was not to be C-in-C.

After all the experience we had had, both in Government and in the Armed Forces in World War I, and then in the

Staff Colleges and at the Committee of Imperial Defence between the wars, we yet had a general post of the 'Top Brass' just as the war started—though it had been known for years that it was coming. People looked back with nostalgia to World War I where everything was so happily arranged. But was it? Douglas Haig considered that Sir John French was quite unfitted to be Commander-in-Chief of the BEF and thought he should be holding that post himself. Sir James Grierson, commanding 2 Corps, whom many people thought had got too soft and flabby, died of a heart attack in the train on his way to join his headquarters. Sir John French asked for Plumer to replace him; but Kitchener, without reference to French, sent him Smith-Dorrien, whom he didn't like. In fact the British are not too good about fixing their top battle commanders before the onset of a war. And when, at last, the commanders are appointed they are faced with unsurmountable initial situations—for which they generally have to take the blame.

However, in World War II, the British Army owed much to Munich, which gave them eight months' respite to put their house in order. Nevertheless, although the top generals were much too big and too loyal to show it (too frequently) whilst operations were taking place, there was quite a lot of veiled antagonism to Gort as commander-in-chief before the operations started and still more after they were over. Naturally Dill was bitterly disappointed at not getting the top appointment himself, and Brooke, who was Dill's greatest admirer, shared his feelings. Both these corps commanders were in strong disagreement with Gort over the decision that the BEF should, on the outbreak of hostilities, leave the fortified defence line they had been busy preparing all the winter and advance into Belgium if the Belgians called for their assistance—though this decision was made far above Gort's head.

General Georges, who was the Commander of the French Front of the North-East, under whose command the BEF was to operate, had allotted them the sector running from Maulde to Halluin, with a defensive flank along the river Lys as far as

Armentières. On 3 October Dill's 1 Corps took up its position on the right of the British line, next to the French 1st Army. It consisted of two divisions, the 1st commanded by Major-General Alexander, and the 2nd by Major-General Lloyd. On 12 October Brooke's 2 Corps took up its position on the left of 1 Corps. It consisted of the 3rd Division, commanded by Major-General Montgomery, and the 4th Division, commanded by Major-General Johnson, VC, the latter being held in reserve.

When the BEF arrived in their sector an almost continuous anti-tank obstacle already existed in the form of a ditch covered by concrete blockhouses built to mount anti-tank guns and machine guns. In accordance with plans prepared in peacetime, certain French technical troops continued to work on the sector. The whole scheme involved the immediate construction of field defences and the duplication of the anti-tank obstacle in the forward zone. It was consequently necessary to construct at an early stage reinforced concrete pillboxes to afford protection to those weapons which formed the backbone of the fire defence throughout the whole depth of the position.

Meanwhile the 5th Division (Major-General Franklyn) was formed in October and the 48th Division (Major-General Thorne) arrived in France in January 1940. At the end of March 1940 3 Corps (Lieutenant-General Sir Ronald Adam) arrived, consisting of the 42nd Division (Major-General Holmes), the 44th Division (Major-General Osborne) and the 51st Division (Major-General Fortune).

It was of course a tragic mistake on the part of the Belgians that they had insisted on remaining strictly neutral so that the Maginot Line could not be continued along their northern frontier—and then, on the day they were invaded, calling on the French and British urgently for help. Gamelin had foreseen that this was what would happen—as indeed had all the other Allied commanders. The question was, should they comply with the Belgian demand for help, or await the Germans in their prepared defence lines? If they did go forward, how far should they go? This of course was a decision of major strategy which had to be decided by General Gamelin. The British, with so small an army, and having already accepted French command, were not in a position to call any strategic tune. They did, however, have the right, and indeed the duty, to put forward their own point of view.

Having weighed up all the pros and cons General Gamelin proposed, at a top-level Allied conference held at Vincennes on 9 November, that if the Belgians called for help the Allied armies must move forward to meet the German onslaught. One of the chief reasons for his proposal was his desire to have the battle fought on the fields of Belgium rather than on the fields of France. That the British could appreciate—though it was not strictly a major strategical factor.

However, General Neame, DCGS to Gort, says, very rightly: 'I heard with my own ears Gamelin say in 1939: "The one thing I intend to avoid is an encounter battle with German armoured forces in the plains of Belgium." But this is exactly what he sent his armies into Belgium to do.'

This proposal of Gamelin's, which was known as Plan D, was for an advance to the river Dyle, with the object of halting the Germans on a front stretching from Antwerp through Louvain to Namur. The British sector would run from Wavre to Louvain and Gamelin proposed to locate a powerful 7th French Army between the BEF and the sea. This plan was accepted wholeheartedly by Gort and, with less enthusiasm, by Ironside. It was, however, strongly opposed by the two corps commanders, Dill and Brooke, and it was one of their chief criticisms of Gort's command that he had not resisted it more strongly. They based their criticism chiefly on the fact that, in the words of Field-Marshal Montgomery: 'In September 1939 the British Army was totally unfitted to fight a first-class war on the continent of Europe. . . . It must be said to our shame that we sent our Army into that most modern war with weapons and equipment that were quite inadequate and we had only ourselves to blame for the disasters which early overtook us in the field when fighting began in 1940.' (*The Memoirs of Field-Marshal Montgomery*).

Gort was perfectly well aware of the strength of the new model German Army, with its many armoured divisions and powerful supporting air force. He was also aware of the unpreparedness of the BEF to oppose such an army, chiefly owing to its almost total lack of tanks. What he and no one else could have foreseen was the weakness of the French Army and the appalling lack of leadership of their generals. Gort himself had serious misgivings at advancing into Belgium but he didn't express them as openly as Dill and Brooke did. Gort took the line that we had agreed to put our very small BEF under command of the much larger French military machine and it would therefore be wrong for us not to fall in wholeheartedly with their plan and do our best to make it work. The chain of command and the plan itself had been agreed at the highest military and political level in both France and Britain.

It is therefore to the eternal credit of Lord Gort that, feeling as he did and respecting as he did the orders of his superior French commanders and of his own British political masters, he should have taken on his own shoulders the very grave responsibility of going against both of them when he saw that the French plan had broken down and that the whole safety of the BEF was threatened.

Although I had originally agreed with Dill and Brooke that to leave our prepared defences and advance into Belgium was unwise, when I saw the state of the French Army I came to the conclusion that we had done the right thing—though for the wrong reason. I believe that had we not advanced into Belgium we would have been very hard to shift from those frontier defences and we would have been left holding them, whilst the French armies withdrew, leaving the BEF in a position from which we might have found a withdrawal impossible.

The other criticism of Gort's command before the operations started was that he became completely immersed in trivial details with regard to the men's equipment etc, instead of holding staff exercises and tactical discussions. Brooke, though he admired Gort's courage and his character, was severely critical of his handling of the BEF. He says: 'Nobody could have been more charming or considerate than he was, and in many respects he was the most delightful commander to serve under, but unfortunately his brain was geared to details the whole time. He wandered about scratching the barks of trees and you could never get him to come out and look at the wood as a whole!' (*The Turn of the Tide*)

Lieutenant-General Sir Philip Neame, who was Gort's Deputy Chief of Staff in France up to February 1940, when he was appointed to command the 4th Indian Division in the Middle East, said in a letter to me dated 2 February 1972: 'I gave Gort no marks at all as a C-in-C. He had the mentality of a Guards platoon commander!' Pownall, however, his chief of staff, who saw more of Gort than anyone else, both before and during the operations, had the highest opinion of him, which was enhanced by his handling of the British Field Force during the actual operations. Certainly, in the phoney-war period Gort's exuberant confidence, his energy and his close interest in everything that was going on were great morale-raisers to the troops. He knew he had two splendid corps commanders in Dill and Brooke and he left them to get on with the training and preparation of their own officers and men.

My own appearance on the historic battlefield as Commander of 127 Infantry Brigade in the 42nd Lancashire Division was achieved by a mixture of luck and a certain amount of (successful) guesswork—plus of course the all-important backing of Gort and Ronald Adam at the War Office. Gort had promised me a brigade in the BEF if I could manage to be in England on leave from India when the war started; and this I managed to achieve. We arrived in France on 23 April and took over a sector of the Field Defences on the Belgian frontier at Halluin.

On 2 May General Sir Ronald Adam, now my 3 Corps Commander, came to pay me a visit and on the next day the three brigade commanders of the 42nd Division were summoned to Divisional HQ to meet Lord Gort. We each had a private interview with him. I was much impressed that he should want to get our opinions on two subjects which were extremely important to us but which some people might have thought should have been settled without reference to us. The first was, would we like our Territorial battalion commanders replaced by regulars? I replied definitely 'No'. I told him that if he had asked me that question three months earlier I would have said 'Yes'. But now that the battalions were just about to go into action under the COs they knew and trusted it would not be a change for the better. Gort replied: 'None of the other Territorial brigadiers have agreed with you about this, but you know your battalions much better than I do so have it your own way!' And I never regretted my decision. The other point I agreed with at once—that I should change one of my Territorial battalions for a regular one. He gave me first choice of a number of battalions and I chose the 1st Battalion The Highland Light Infantry, with whom I had been brigaded when I had won my VC at Richebourg l'Avoué in 1915.

Gort and I didn't have much time for a private talk so we made a date for him to pay me a visit and walk round my defences in just over a week's time. But as he left he said: 'I somehow don't think we shall make that date, Jackie.' And how right he was. He looked cheerful, confident and in wonderfully good heart. I felt how lucky I was to be serving under people like Gort and Ronald Adam, to say nothing of George Holmes, my divisional commander, with whom I got on exceedingly well.

On 16 April Dill was recalled to the War Office to be Vice-Chief of the Imperial General Staff, and Lieutenant-General Michael Barker took his place as commander of 1 Corps. Again it seemed quite extraordinary to make a change of corps commander just as the battle was expected to start—particularly as Barker was not very highly regarded. He was certainly not Gort's choice and Montgomery thought that Gort should have resisted this appointment and insisted on having someone of his own choosing.

Brooke wrote:

Dill's departure left me in the depths of gloom. I had an absolute conviction that the German offensive was coming

soon. I now had no illusions as to the efficiency and fighting
value of the French Army. I had little confidence in Gort's
leadership in the event of attack and now Dill was gone there
was no one left in the BEF with whom I could discuss my
misgivings freely . . . Dill leaves a terrible blank behind him
and I have a horrid lonely feeling knowing that he is gone.
He is quite one of the finest men I have ever known. I know
of no other soldier in the whole of my career who inspired
me with greater respect and admiration. An exceptionally
clear, well-balanced brain, an infinite capacity for work,
unbounded charm of personality but, above all, an un-
flinching straightness of character; these were the chief
characteristics that made up one of the most remarkable
soldiers of our century. I owe him an infinite debt for all I
learned from him. (*The Turn of the Tide*, p 81)

The chief misgivings which Brooke had referred to were the
shortage of essential arms such as planes, tanks, anti-tank guns
and wireless. This was all too true but these shortages were the
result of years of inadequate financial provision for the armed
forces, which could not be made good in a short time.

Certainly the shortages of which all the top British generals
in the British Army were well aware could not be laid at
Gort's door.

On 10 May 1940 the so-called 'phoney war' ended with the
German invasion of Holland, Belgium and Luxembourg.

Gort summed up the campaign which followed in his
Despatch of March 1941 (published in the *London Gazette* of
17 October 1941) as follows:

So ended a campaign of twenty-two days which has proved
that the offensive has once more gained ascendancy in
modern war when undertaken by an army equipped with
greatly superior material power in the shape of air forces and
armoured fighting vehicles. The British Expeditionary Force
had advanced sixty-five miles from the frontier to the Dyle;
then the same distance back from the Dyle to the frontier;

finally a further fifty miles to the sea at Dunkirk. A frontal advance had become a flank defence; a flank defence the defence of a perimeter which at times exceeded one hundred miles, with my force of nine divisions (excluding 51st Division on the Saar front, and parts of three semi-trained and partially equipped divisions sent to France for labour duties). Finally had come the withdrawal to the sea and the shrinkage of this wide front to the twenty-four miles of the Dunkirk bridgehead.

The series of situations which the BEF had to face was not brought about by failure on their part to withstand enemy attacks when holding a position of their own choosing; it was caused by the enemy breaking through completely on a front many miles away from that held by the BEF. Nevertheless this breakthrough, once it began, was destined to involve in its ill-fated consequences both the French 1st Army and the BEF.

The brief but historic campaign, which ended with the re-embarkation of the British Field Force at Dunkirk, has filled volumes of books and has been described in every detail and from every angle by many writers. It is not for me in this book to describe the operations again but only to highlight certain important points which serve to illustrate the theme of my book—the generals and their leadership in battle. On 10 May Plan D was immediately put into effect and four armies of General Georges' North-Eastern Command swung forward into Belgium. Connecting them with the Maginot Line on the right was General Corap's 9th Army, consisting of second-line troops. They had only to carry out a short wheel to the defile of the Meuse, facing the thickly wooded Ardennes, which the French regarded as almost impenetrable. On their left was General Blanchard's 1st Army, containing some of France's finest troops, with a strong force of tanks; on their left again was the BEF, and between them and the sea was General Giraud's 7th Army, also considered to contain some of France's most highly trained troops. Marshal Foch would at once have

criticised the French plan of advance for the fact that there was
no strategic reserve. As the Germans had the initiative and
could strike when and where they liked this lack of a reserve
was a palpable error which became more apparent as such at a
very early stage of the operations. In fact the speed with which
the French Plan D was put into operation and its initial success
played into the German hands and made their own deadly and
unexpected thrust all the more effective.

On 13 May, only three days after the operations had started,
General von Kleist's Panzer group, the spearhead of the
German 12th Army, smashed its way through the Ardennes
and crossed the Meuse, making a breach of fifty miles in width.
Corap's 9th Army was shattered and the right of the 1st Army
was also pierced. Immediately Plan D had been completely
torpedoed and a most dangerous situation had been created for
the Allied forces, from which they never recovered.

The BEF, way out on the river Dyle, was at once in peril, and
on 16 May Gort began his withdrawal to the Scheldt. The
Dutch Army had already surrendered and the Belgian Army
had fallen back on the left of the British. The whole French
Command machinery became disrupted and the French
Government made no attempt to conceal its dismay. Prime
Minister Winston Churchill and General 'Pug' Ismay—now
appointed head of the office of the Minister of Defence, and
Churchill's personal trusted liaison officer with the Chiefs of
Staff—flew out to Paris to confer with M. Reynaud, the
French Premier.

Though enemy pressure had been severe on the French 1st
Army, and slightly less heavy on the BEF and the Belgians, it
was not this which was forcing the Allied armies to withdraw,
but the much more menacing situation which was developing
in their rear. The breakthrough on the Meuse had become a
widening and ever deepening spearhead which was tearing the
whole of the French Army's organisation and life lines apart.
By the 17th the vanguard of German armour was in St-Quentin
and by the 18th they had captured Peronne and were still
pressing forward.

In the absence of any coherent orders from above to deal with the situation Gort, on the 17th, had with commendable speed created a scratch force to protect the right flank of the BEF. This was known as 'Macforce' by reason of the fact that Major-General Mason Macfarlane, his own Director of Military Intelligence, was detailed to command it, with Lieutenant-Colonel Gerald Templer as his chief staff officer. Field-Marshal Sir Gerald Templer, as he afterwards became, quoted from J. R. Colville's *Man of Valour* (p 199) as follows:

Macforce, over the period of its existence, performed its task satisfactorily. It reconnoitred, it carried out considerable demolition programmes over canal and river lines. It was an organised force, it directed stragglers, it kept its finger to the best of its ability on the pulse of the French formations on its right, it did what it could to direct the terrible refugee traffic, it shot down a considerable number of German dive bombers, it fought some small actions, it fed itself without worrying superior authority, and it controlled looting.

In fact it proved a wise and invaluable decision on Gort's part. He of course was criticised by his detractors for off-loading from GHQ his two most important intelligence officers. But needs must when the devil drives, and what was the good of intelligence officers in this very unintelligent situation, where no one knew whether anything they were told was true or false? The very presence of 'Macforce' and the threat it imposed on the long, strung-out German flanking columns constituted a far greater deterrent than its actual fighting strength warranted. In fact, for the first vital week of its existence it consisted only of my 127th Infantry Brigade; and in that week I not only had some exciting experiences but got to know more about 'the generals', both French and British.

Noel Mason-Macfarlane, or 'Mason-Mac' as he was generally known, was a very old friend of mine. In India we had soldiered together, played cricket and polo together, and got to know one another well. He had married the younger sister of General Ronald Adam's wife and the two families were very close. Although Mason-Mac had had practically no experience of command and had been in semi-political intelligence appointments during the immediate prewar years, there was no one I would have served under with greater confidence in a situation such as this. For Mason-Mac was, as I knew very well, a born leader of men. With his powerful physique, cool temperament, dynamic energy, and above all his grand sense of humour, he had all the basic attributes of the modern commander. Also he spoke French fluently, and that seemed as if it might be one of the greatest assets in our current situation, as we would undoubtedly be mixed up with French formations of every sort. In addition, he spoke German and had been British Military Attaché in Berlin before the war. This qualification was to be useful to us too as we shot down several German aircraft from which some of the pilots baled out.

During those few days the Germans were trying by ground and air reconnaissance to find the exact position of my troops while Mason-Mac and I were visiting a lot of French formations to try to discover where their troops were. The fog of war was really quite dense but Mason-Mac, with that crooked grin on his face and the inevitable cigarette hanging from the corner of his mouth, was never ruffled, never dismayed and never lost his sense of humour. We all enjoyed being under his command and were very sorry when a minor disaster on our 42nd Division front forced Gort to replace us and send us back. (I have described these operations in detail in my book *Before the Dawn*.)

I did not see Mason-Mac again for several years and by then he was an embittered and desperately sick man. He was embittered because he was never given a fighting command after Dunkirk and he had also developed spinal trouble which eventually completely crippled him. He stood as a Labour candidate in the election of 1945 and became a Member of Parliament; but he was too ill ever to take his seat. In his last years, which were years of increasing pain, I visited him often and got him into Stoke Mandeville hospital where, despite all their attention, he failed to recover and died shortly after my last visit to him.

During the operations with Macforce I had been much impressed with Gerald Templer. When I next met him he was a lieutenant-general and he finished up as Field-Marshal Sir Gerald Templer KG, GCB, GCMG, KBE, DSO—one of the great soldiers of our time.

About midnight on 18/19 May General Bilotte, Co-ordinator of the Allied Armies, visited Gort's headquarters to give him an account of the situation as he saw it. He told Gort of the measures which were being taken to restore the situation on the front of the French 9th Army, though he made it clear that he had little hope that they would be effective. With the establishment of the Escaut position the situation of the armies of the north had for the first time become static. To the south, on the other hand, the German thrust towards the sea continued with unabated speed. In Paris Paul Reynaud had decided to dismiss Gamelin, and Weygand had been invited to accept the post of commander-in-chief.

On 19 May Gort took a long, cool look at the immediate position of the British Expeditionary Force. Already his lines of communication had been severed and he was cut off from his main supply dumps of food and ammunition. He also realised that no reinforcements from Britain could reach him and that his future air support was problematical (*vide* Gort's Despatch on the operations). He considered that there was an imminent danger of the north-eastern area—that is to say the French forces next to the sea, the Belgian Army, the BEF and the bulk of the French 1st Army immediately on their right—being irretrievably cut off from the main French forces in the south. He therefore considered that there were three alternative courses open to the northern armies under General Bilotte. First, in the event of the gap being closed by successful counter-attacks, made simultaneously from north and south, it would in theory be possible to maintain the line of the Escaut, or at any rate the frontier defences, and thence southwards on one or other of the canal lines. Second, there was the possibility of a withdrawal to the line of the Somme. This plan had the advantage that it meant falling back on existing lines of communication and, if successful, would not entail the abandonment of large quantities of equipment. But it would obviously be unwelcome to the Belgians and might also be so to the French High Command. Third, there was the possibility of the BEF withdrawing north-westwards, or northwards—preferably in concert with the French and the Belgians—towards the Channel ports.

Gort commented:

I realised that this course was in theory a last alternative as it would involve the departure of the BEF from the theatre of war at a time when the French might need all the support which Britain could give them. It involved the virtual certainty that even if the excellent port facilities at Dunkirk continued to be available it would be necessary to abandon all the heavier guns and much of the vehicles and equipment. Nevertheless I felt that in the circumstances there might be no other course open to me. It was therefore only prudent to consider what the adoption of such a plan might entail. On this day therefore (19 May) at about 1.30 pm the Chief of the General Staff telephoned to the Director of Military Operations and Plans at the War Office and discussed this situation with him.

At this time the War Cabinet in London was considering the urgent and incessant demands from Paris that they should have all the fighter aircraft that Britain possessed. Reynaud's claim was that if the battle in France was lost then the war was lost: Winston Churchill had at first been inclined towards the French view, but Air Marshal Dowding, Commander-in-Chief of Fighter Command, resisted this idea most strongly and his pressure, and Churchill's own shocked surprise at the hopeless defeatism of the French Government, combined to change the mind of the British Prime Minister. He therefore telephoned to Reynaud saying that Britain had already sent to France more fighter squadrons than she had agreed to do and that fighter strength in Britain had now been reduced to a minimum. The decision reached by Dowding and Churchill was one of the most momentous made during the whole of the war. Had it not been reached the odds would have been weighted fatally against Fighter Command when the Luftwaffe made its big air assault on Britain later in the year.

On receipt of the three alternatives conveyed by General Pownall to the War Office on the 19th, Churchill held a Cabinet meeting at which Ironside advocated strongly his preference for Gort's first suggested alternative—to close the gap. The Cabinet agreed and Ironside arrived at Gort's headquarters on the early morning of 20 May with orders for the BEF to march south to Amiens and take post on the left of the French Army.

Gort made it clear to the CIGS that, although the closing of the gap had been his first alternative, the impetus for closing the gap must come from the French Army in the south. The BEF was already fully engaged on the line of the Scheldt and there was grave uncertainty of the condition of the Belgians and the French on his flanks. The arrival of Weygand as Supreme Commander in place of the vacillating Gamelin was certainly a morale-raiser for everyone. However, it had now become obvious that neither the Belgians nor the French 1st Army was in a position to take any offensive action.

It was on 23 May that Brooke, commanding 2 Corps, wrote in his diary:

Nothing but a miracle can save the BEF now. We carried out our withdrawal successfully last night to the old frontier defences and by this morning we were established in the defences we had spent the winter preparing. But the danger lies on our right rear. The German armoured divisions have penetrated to the coast; Abbeville, Boulogne and Calais have been rendered useless. We are therefore cut off from our sea communications and beginning to be short of ammunition. Supplies still all right for three days but after that scarcity. This evening the Germans are reported to be pushing on to Bethune and on from St-Omer, namely in our right rear.

The position was not quite so bad as it appeared to Brooke. The BEF was put on half-rations but the troops managed to supplement them fairly well from the many deserted farms and other local sources; the provident General Montgomery drove along with him several herds of cattle. However, Brooke was right in saying that a miracle was required—and Gort produced it.

The BEF's breakthrough to the south, which Gort had been ordered to undertake, was due to start on the 26th, under the overall command of the French General Altmayer. Gort had given the British command to Adam, GOC 3 Corps, with two divisions, the 5th and 50th. The French General Blanchard, now commanding the French 1st Army, had promised three or four more divisions. On the 25th, however, Gort was faced with a rapidly worsening situation. Macforce was heavily engaged at Cassel and the 48th Division was sent to relieve them. Brooke was being hard pressed and was calling urgently for reinforcements. Gort sent him his last reserve, but it was only one brigade. The collapse of the Belgians appeared imminent. Adam had discovered that Blanchard's estimate of the strength he could command was moonshine. It turned out that he could supply only one division instead of four. Adam was on the line to Gort to ask whether his offensive next day should therefore go forward or not.

Just before 6 pm Gort had made up his mind; he cancelled the attack of the 5th and 50th Divisions and ordered the 5th to proceed with all speed to Brooke and the 50th to follow as well. He informed the French General Altmayer that he had done so. His Chief of Staff, Henry Pownall, though agreeing with Gort's decision, felt bound to remind him that his action was against the orders they had received and that, if he took these two British divisions away, the French 1st Army might not be able to attack at all. Gort merely replied that he realised this perfectly well—but it just had to be done. Gort's decision undoubtedly saved the whole of the BEF from destruction or captivity. And that would inevitably have meant the invasion of Britain—and very probably the loss of the war.

The same evening 'Operation Dynamo', the evacuation of the armies from Dunkirk, was set in motion and the BEF began its fighting withdrawal to the Dunkirk salient. Gort ordered Adam to hand over command of 3 Corps and proceed to Dunkirk to organise a perimeter defence there.

Brooke remarks in his diary on the 26th, when he had heard of Gort's decision: 'It is going to be a very hazardous enterprise and we shall be lucky if we save 25 per cent of the BEF.' Again, as it turned out, Brooke was a bit pessimistic; but Prime Minister Winston Churchill, when addressing the House of Commons on 4 June 1940, said: 'I feared it would be my hard lot to announce from this box the greatest military disaster in our long history.'

It was saved from being so only by the masterly handling of the withdrawal of the BEF to Dunkirk by Gort himself, his Chief of Staff, General Henry Pownall, and by his subordinate commanders. Brooke proved himself to be as able a commander in battle as he had been an outstanding staff officer. However, to get the British Field Force back to Dunkirk was one thing, the second part of 'the miracle of Dunkirk' was another. And that was the evacuation of over 336,000 troops—234,000 of them British and most of the remainder French—by the British Navy and 'the little ships' under the protection of the British RAF Fighter Command. Even so the BEF lost everything in the way of weapons and equipment except for some personal weapons. That wonderful ditch, the English Channel, gave the defeated British Army time to re-arm and live to fight another day.

We can now look at Gort's vital decision on 25 May from the point of view of the Prime Minister, Winston Churchill, who wrote:

In the evening of the 25th May Lord Gort took a vital

decision. His orders were still to pursue the Weygand plan of a southerly attack towards Cambrai in which the 5th and 50th Divisions, in conjunction with the French, were to be employed. The promised French attack northwards from the Somme showed no signs of reality.

The last defenders of Boulogne had been evacuated. Calais still held out. Gort now abandoned the Weygand plan. There was in his view no longer hope of a march to the south and to the Somme. Moreover, at the same time, the crumbling Belgian defence and the gap opening to the north created a new peril, dominating in itself. At 6 pm he ordered the 5th and 50th Divisions to join the 2 British Corps to fill the impending Belgian gap. He informed General Blanchard, who had succeeded Bilotte in command of the 1st Army Group of his action; and this officer, acknowledging the force of events, gave orders at 11.30 pm for a withdrawal on the 26th to a line behind the Lys canal west of Lille, with a view to forming a bridgehead round Dunkirk. Early on May 26 Gort and Blanchard drew up their plan for withdrawal to the coast. In all this Lord Gort had acted on his own responsibility. But by now we at home with a somewhat different angle of information had already reached the same conclusions. On the 26th a telegram from the War Office approved his conduct and authorised him to operate towards the coast forthwith in conjunction with the French and Belgian armies . . .

It was a severe experience for me, bearing so heavy an overall responsibility, to watch during these days in flickering glimpses this drama in which control was impossible and intervention more likely to do harm than good. There is no doubt that by pressing in all loyalty the Weygand plan of retirement to the Somme as long as we did, our dangers, already so grave, were increased. *But Gort's decision, in which we speedily concurred, to abandon the Weygand plan and march to the sea were executed by him and his staff with masterly skill and will ever be regarded as a brilliant episode in British military annals.* (*The Second World War*, Vol 2—my italics)

If Gort had made this decision—and failed—then he could not have expected anything but the most severe censure from his Allies and from his own government and people. But as he succeeded—and did so to a much greater extent than anyone had believed possible—he surely should have received very much more credit than was in fact accorded to him. He not only saved the BEF, but saved Britain from invasion and in all probability saved the war for the Allies. And yet there isn't even a statue to him in Whitehall. I feel more strongly about the ingratitude than about his not having been given another fighting command—though *he* felt this more bitterly than anything else as he was first and last a fighting soldier. But if you start at the top there are few other places to go.

Brooke remained coldly critical. Having repeatedly urged Gort to send him reinforcements and then being given the 5th and 50th divisions because of Gort's courageous decision to go it alone, all he says is: 'I can hardly believe I have succeeded in pulling the four divisions out of the mess we were in with the allies giving way on all flanks.' (*The Turn of the Tide*)

Montgomery had never been an admirer of Gort and he says in his *Memoirs*:

I have always held the opinion that Gort's appointment to command the BEF in September 1939 was a mistake; the job was above his ceiling . . . GHQ of the BEF had never conducted any exercises either with or without troops from the time we landed in France in 1939 to the day active operations began in May 1940. The result was a total lack of any common policy or tactical doctrine throughout the BEF; when differences arose these differences remained and there was no firm grip from the top.

I cannot see how any number of tactical exercises would have prevented the breakthrough of the Panzers on the Meuse and the supine attitude of the French High Command which followed. However many common policies or tactical doctrines Gort had evolved, he knew from the start that he would have to

conform to the orders of the French High Command. But
Monty did at least give credit where credit was due. He
continues:

> When the crisis burst on the French and British Armies, and
> developed in ever-increasing fury, Gort was quick to see that
> there was only one end to it: the French would crack and he
> must get as much of the British Army as he could back to
> England. Thereafter Gort never wavered; he remained steady
> as a rock. It was because he saw very clearly, if only for a
> limited distance, that we all got away at Dunkirk. A cleverer
> man might have done something different and perhaps tried
> to swing back to the Somme keeping in touch with the
> French. Gort saw clearly that he must, at the least, get the
> men of BEF back to England with their personal weapons.
> For this I give him full marks and I hope history will do the
> same. He saved the men of the BEF. And being saved they
> were able to fight again another day: which they did to some
> purpose as the Germans found out.

Alexander wrote in his *Memoirs:* 'I am of the opinion that
our C-in-C Lord Gort, who had the over-all responsibility, has
not received sufficient recognition for his conduct of the whole
withdrawal operation.'

On 30 May Churchill ordered Gort, as the evacuation from
Dunkirk was proceeding, to return to England as soon as his
command had been so reduced that it could be handed over to
a corps commander. And on the evening of the 31st Gort duly
handed over to Alexander and returned home. General Brooke
had returned home on the 30th. Brooke comments in his diary
on his first day in England: 'Time and again throughout the
years of the war I thanked God (but not Gort!) for the safe
return of the bulk of the personnel of the BEF.' Perhaps,
however, Gort was on God's side—or God on Gort's!

Winston Churchill said in his report to the House of Commons on 4 June: 'We have to constitute and build up the
British Expeditionary Force once again, under its gallant

Commander-in-Chief, Lord Gort'. But nothing further materialised as far as Gort was concerned. Brooke was sent across to France on 12 June to command the British formations that were still in France. Dill had become CIGS in place of Ironside on 27 May. The latter had then become Commander-in-Chief Home Forces, but on 19 July Ironside relinquished this command to Brooke. Gort was given the somewhat meaningless appointment (at this critical time) of Inspector of Training and the Home Guard. But with Dill and Brooke once more at the head of the Army—where they had hoped to be before the war started—Gort's chances of a command of any importance did not seem very bright. He naturally felt very bitter about it—though he made no complaint.

At last, in April 1941, Gort was offered the Governorship of Gibraltar, which was far removed from the active service appointment he wanted. However, he accepted with such grace as he could. In March 1942, when Churchill's confidence in Auchinleck had been shaken, he had thought of sending Gort to replace him in the North African Command. Brooke, who was then CIGS, strongly opposed this idea and managed to dissuade the Prime Minister. Alexander, however (*Man of Valour*, p 245), believed that Brooke was wrong and that Gort might well have defeated Rommel in the summer of 1942. I would think that Brooke was right and Alexander wrong over this. Gort's military experience had been rather far removed from the handling of mechanised forces in desert warfare—but of course it could be argued that Auchinleck's had been also.

Anyway, Gort knew nothing of this controversy. On 7 May 1942, a year after his arrival in Gibraltar, he was flown to Malta as Governor of that much embattled island in place of the gallant General Dobbie, who was worn out by his exertions. This was a do-or-die appointment more after Gort's own heart and he played a noble and important part in the historic resistance of the George Cross Island. In 1943 Gort was made a field-marshal and the King presented the baton to him when he visited Malta in June of that year. In 1944 the people of Malta presented him with a sword of honour in recognition of his courage and leadership and, in July of that year, he was appointed High Commissioner in Palestine. He was now, however, not only a very disappointed man but a very sick one. He was flown home in November 1945 and died of cancer on 31 March 1946 at the age of only fifty-nine.

Now to look back on some of the other generals who emerged from 'the miracle of Dunkirk'. Brooke became Chief of the Imperial General Staff, which appointment he took over from Dill in November 1941, to become one of the great military figures of the war—and possibly the greatest British general of them all. He was not of course tested in battle to the extent that some of the other field-marshals were, but he had proved, when in command of 2 Corps at Dunkirk, that he was a fine commander of troops in battle—as well as being a great staff officer.

Brooke was very tough in mind and body—as anyone who worked closely with Winston Churchill had to be. Brooke admired the Prime Minister enormously—his greatness, his tremendous energy, his foresight, his grasp of the big strategical picture, his determination, his courage, and above all his dynamic national leadership. At the same time he recognised his faults, his occasional wrong decisions and his mistaken ideas on personalities and military tactics—and no politician has ever interfered in these matters to the extent that Winston did. Brooke stood up to Churchill over things which he considered to be of vital military importance and Winston seldom over-ruled the Chiefs of Staff on such matters. But they had to make their points to him in probing arguments which sometimes went on until the small hours of the morning and were most exhausting for everyone but Winston, who slept in the afternoons and was as lively as a cricket in the small hours. Brooke said one day to his staff at the War Office:

Winston is extraordinarily obstinate. He is like a child that has set his mind on some forbidden toy. It is no good explain-

Page 49
(*above*) Field-Marshal Lord Gort, Governor of Malta, talking to Private Paul Green of Bryson City USA, on 7 September 1943. Private Green was a member of the only American unit in Malta during the siege; (*below*) General Sir Archibald Wavell, Commander-in-Chief Middle East with Lieutenant-General O'Connor, Commander of the Desert Forces, during their devastating defeat of the Italians in the Western Desert in 1940.

Page 50
(*above*) General Sir John Dill CIGS and Foreign Secretary Sir Anthony
Eden, on 19 February 1941 in Cairo, discuss the fateful question of sending
British troops to Greece; (*below*) the British Chiefs of Staff in conference,
December 1941. Left to right: General Sir Hastings Ismay, Admiral of the
Fleet Sir Andrew Cunningham, General Alan Brooke CIGS (chairman),
Air Chief Marshal Sir Charles Portal (back to camera), and General Dill
who had been appointed the Prime Minister's representative with the
American Chiefs of Staff

ing that it will cut his fingers and burn him. The more you explain, the more fixed he becomes in his idea. Very often he seems to be quite immoveable on some impossible project, but often that only means that he will not give way at that particular moment. Then suddenly, after some days, he will come round, and he will say something to show that it is all right, and that all the personal abuse has been forgotten.

(Sir John Kennedy, *The Business of War*, p 275)

Brooke was prepared to let some things go rather than oppose them. And, as well as having the trust and support of his lord and master, he also had the complete confidence of the generals in the field.

Alexander and Montgomery, commanding the 1st and 3rd Divisions respectively at Dunkirk, had enhanced their reputations, and Gort selected Alexander to take on the final evacuation when he was ordered home. General Curtis and I were ordered to select a final position for Alex's rearguard to hold between evacuation of the Dunkirk salient and actual embarkation. Brooke writes of these two up-and-coming commanders:

In taking over the 1st Division (in 2 Corps) I was for the first time having the experience of having Alexander working under me. It was a great opportunity . . . to see what he was made of, and what an admirable commander he was in a tight place. It was intensely interesting watching him and Monty during those trying days, both of them completely imperturbable and efficiency itself, and yet two totally different characters. Monty, with his quick brain for appreciating military situations, was well aware of the very critical situation he was in, and the very dangers and difficulties that faced us acted as a stimulus to him; they thrilled him and put the sharpest of edges on his military ability. Alex, on the other hand, gave me the impression of never fully realising all the very unpleasant potentialities of our predicament. He remained entirely unaffected by it, completely composed and appeared never to have the slightest doubt that all would come right in the end. It was in those critical days that the appreciation I made of those two commanders remained rooted in my mind and resulted in the future selection of these two men to work together in the triumphal advance from Alamein to Tunis. (*The Turn of the Tide*, p 107)

General Sir Ronald Adam, Commander 3 Corps, enhanced his already high reputation and did a wonderful job in organising the Dunkirk defences. After Dunkirk he became GOC Northern Command 1940–1 and Adjutant-General to the Forces from 1941 to 1946, when he retired from the Army.

Lieutenant-General Henry Pownall, who had been Gort's chief of staff in France, served afterwards as Vice-Chief of the Imperial General Staff, and then as chief of staff to Wavell in the Far Eastern war. I always felt Pownall might well have been made Army Commander in Burma. Like Gort he didn't get nearly enough credit for his part in saving the BEF— perhaps because he was such a warm supporter of Gort. Pownall was very helpful to me after the war in getting the official history of the 1942 Burma campaign presented in a more accurate and less biased manner.

Ironside was not really suited to be Chief of the Imperial General Staff—and he was never happy there. Built on very massive lines and always inclined to put on weight, he had previously kept fit by horse riding, golf and walking, and the sedentary life at the War Office did his health no good at all. He had had a fine career in the Army and Churchill made a wise decision to put Dill in his place.

There was one other very important military personage who had emerged at this period of the war. Colonel H. L. Ismay (later General Lord Ismay) had been for some years Deputy to Sir Maurice Hankey in the Chiefs of Staff Sub-Committee, the Cabinet, and the Committee of Imperial Defence. In 1938 Ismay had succeeded Hankey in all these offices and, on the advent of Winston Churchill as Prime Minister, had become his Chief of Staff as a major-general. Ismay was no stranger to Churchill and he quickly became the Prime Minister's trusted agent in all military affairs and his liaison officer with the Chiefs of Staff. Hankey mentions somewhat bitterly that Ismay had been a warm admirer of his 'until he fell under the very powerful and hypnotic influence of Winston Churchill'. (Roskill, *Hankey, Man of Secrets*, Vol 2, p 575)

Ismay was an Indian Army cavalry officer of great qualities of heart and mind, who had had the misfortune, in World War I, to be posted to an out-of-the-way theatre of operations, where he had, nevertheless, been awarded a DSO. In 1921, however, he passed into the Quetta Staff College and, having emerged with flying colours, was given a staff appointment at AHQ India, where I first made his acquaintance, and we remained friends all his life. But as the Indian climate did not suit his wife Ismay looked round for an appointment at home and secured the post of Assistant Secretary to the Committee of Imperial Defence under Sir Maurice Hankey. Then, in 1936, Hankey offered Ismay the post of Deputy Secretary of the Committee of Imperial Defence and he was in line for the top job when Hankey retired. Ismay had planned and worked hard to get there and managed to resist the endeavours of the Chiefs of Staff in India to get him back to regimental and brigade command. But he always knew where he wanted to go and had made some powerful friends at home who smoothed the way for him.

General Sir John Kennedy, the Director of Military Operations, says of him:

We were indeed fortunate to have Ismay to take so much of the initial shock of the Prime Minister's impact on the Staffs. He never claimed that he influenced Churchill to any extent, and probably he did not. No man with the inclination and capacity to deal seriously with Churchill could have retained Ismay's post for very long. He was always charmingly frank in admitting that his chief function was to act as a whipping boy, and as a person to whom Churchill could blow off steam at all hours of the night and day. We all felt we would not have his job for anything in the world. He was, in his own right, one of the most remarkable men of the war. (*The Business of War*)

Whilst the disaster, and yet the miracle, of Dunkirk had roused and united the whole British nation and the inspiring words of Winston Churchill had stimulated every man and woman in the country, the menace of German invasion weighed heavily on the minds of the Government and on the British military commanders. Although an almost incredible number of men from the BEF had been brought safely home, they were no longer a fighting force. Their guns, their equipment, their transport, their tanks (the few that we had) and much of their small-arms weapons too had been left behind in the Dunkirk salient. The BEF, which had been under-weaponed in comparison with the modern, highly mechanised German Army to start with, was now a mere skeleton of what it had been. And it was going to take some time to become reorganised and re-equipped. To anyone who, like myself, had an anti-invasion role, sometimes coast defence, then an anti-parachute landing role on the Yorkshire moors and then aerodrome protection, it seemed almost incredible that Hitler should not have chanced his arm and had a go. He would have found us full of fight but very thin on the ground. For some time there was only one fully trained and fully equipped division in the country.

By 15 July Hitler had completed the eclipse of France whilst the Luftwaffe had moved forward to airfields overlooking the Channel. It must by now have been apparent to him that Britain was utterly defiant and had no intention of coming to terms. The Germans had collected a large number of barges and boats and they had large numbers of paratroops and troop-carrying aircraft.

During the months of July, August, September and October 1940 I attended many conferences and discussions on what nearly all of us thought would be the coming German invasion.

Few people really believed that Hitler would not attempt it and I never came across anyone, who had inside information, who did not pray fervently that he would not try. At one big exercise that was held in Eastern Command it was considered that a German invasion plan on the following lines would be the most difficult to counter.

(1)   Feints by German naval forces against the north of England and Ireland with the object of drawing off part of our Home Fleet.

(2)   Three days' intensive night bombardment of fighter aerodromes using a high concentration of mustard gas as well as high explosive.

(3)   A large-scale dusk or dawn attack by parachute and glider troops on an area of eastern England, followed immediately by landings of troop-carrying aircraft on captured aerodromes. It was anticipated that the Germans would crash-land air transport planes on arterial roads and other suitable places all over southern or eastern England.

(4)   Sea landings on selected beaches covered by a heavy gas attack.

(5)   A swift advance on London from the sea and from the areas of the air landings.

The Germans would of course have to face heavy casualties and the invading troops would, to start with, have to live on the country, which they would no doubt do with the utmost brutality so far as the British civilian population were concerned.

It is true that such a plan did not ensure the preliminary destruction of the RAF, though the Germans would hope to ground them to a certain extent during the first critical period. But it would have left the Luftwaffe unweakened by its Battle of Britain losses and ready to operate from its forward aerodromes against Britain with all its strength intact.

We were desperately anxious about the defence of our

aerodromes. At one time I had to look after nine important ones in the Oxford area with one brigade, which had several other anti-invasion tasks as well. We were provided with buses —of a very derelict variety—and even if we had got the right information it was doubtful whether we could have got to the right place in time. I have always thought that the German Air Marshal Goering was our greatest ally at that critical time. He had assured Hitler that the Luftwaffe would shoot our British fighters out of the sky—and make everything simple for the invasion.

Accordingly, in August, the great German air offensive on Britain began and, in that month and the following month, was fought what has come to be known as the Battle of Britain— one of the most decisive battles in our history. It was entirely an air battle, waged between the bombers and fighters of the Luftwaffe and Britain's Fighter Command. It was a battle waged mostly in daylight, the German objective being, by persistent attacks against aerodromes and other vital targets, to force the British fighters into the air and then gradually to wear them down until such time as the Luftwaffe had gained complete air superiority over southern and eastern England. They had no difficulty about the first half of their objective. The grand young British fighter pilots took the air eagerly, whatever the odds against them, and fought like tigers. The battle worked up to a crescendo, until finally on Sunday, 15 September, fifty-six German aircraft were shot down over Britain. The Battle of Britain had been won, but by what a narrow margin will never really be known. And to our great relief Hitler never tried an invasion of Britain.

Sufficient credit for victory in this epic air engagement— perhaps the most decisive that Britain has ever fought—has never been given to Air Chief Marshal Dowding, who was the Air Officer Commanding-in-Chief of Fighter Command. A tremendous burden was placed on the shoulders of this shy and self-effacing man. Ever since the war started in September 1939 he had carried a responsibility greater than that of any other man—except Churchill himself.

Dowding was a man of remarkable foresight, great integrity and altogether a military leader of high stature.

General Brooke had been entrusted with the ground defence of Great Britain with his headquarters at St Paul's School in London. Adam had Northern Command, with Alexander and George Holmes (formerly commander of the 42nd Division in France) as his corps commanders. Montgomery was given command of 5 Corps in July 1940 and later was transferred to 12 Corps in Kent, which was the most likely invasion corner of England, and Auchinleck had Southern Command, which was the next most likely danger area. Later, in November 1940, when my brigade had been taken off coast defence and came temporarily into reserve, Auchinleck asked me to go down to Salisbury to spend a day with him looking round his defences and then spend the night at his HQ.

Following his successful campaign against the Mohmands on the North-West Frontier of India in 1935 Auchinleck had been appointed Deputy Chief of the General Staff at AHQ India in 1936. His main and all-important task was to make a comprehensive survey of India's armed forces and the measures which must be taken to prepare them to play their part in the world war which was pending.

In January 1940, however, Auchinleck was ordered to fly home to the United Kingdom to take command of 4 Corps, which was in the process of formation in England prior to joining the BEF in France.

However, on Sunday, 28 April 1940, Auchinleck was ordered by General Ironside, then CIGS, to take charge of the operations in Norway. This was a very unenviable assignment, as Norway had already been a theatre of war for three weeks. However, it was a great feather in Auchinleck's cap that he, as an Indian Army officer, should have been thought of so very highly by the Chiefs of Staff in London as to have been given a corps command and then this assignment in Norway. Both Ironside and Dill, who was then Vice Chief of Staff, had a great opinion of 'The Auk' and Dill remained his staunchest supporter when he relieved Ironside as CIGS. Auchinleck was officially appointed GOC-in-Chief of the Anglo-French Forces in Norway and the British Air Component in that area. He was on Norwegian soil for just under four weeks—from 11 May to 7 June. In an early letter to Dill, when he had studied the situation, he wrote —very wisely: 'If the Government think that the commitment involved in the preservation of Northern Norway is worth adding to their other commitments I trust that they will set aside definitely the forces required for the purpose. I feel very strongly that if they are not prepared to do this it would be better to come away now than to risk throwing good money after bad by failing to provide the necessary forces.' (John Connell, *Auchinleck*)

In truth, Norway was an unwise and unwarranted detachment for Britain to make at that particular time and we were fortunate to get out of it as well as we did. And on 20 May the new prime minister, Winston Churchill, suggested to the Chiefs of Staff that in view of the crisis developing in France the sooner we withdrew from Norway the better. A few days later Auchinleck was ordered to evacuate his force, which he did with the maximum of efficiency and the minimum of loss.

Auchinleck summed up his experiences in Norway as follows: 'To commit troops to a campaign in which they cannot be provided with adequate support is to court disaster. No useful purpose can be served by sending troops to operate in an undeveloped and wild country such as Norway unless they have been thoroughly trained for their task and their fighting equipment well thought out and methodically prepared in advance. Improvisation in either of these respects can lead only to failure.' (John Connell, *Auchinleck*)

Dill had become CIGS on 27 May and he saw to it that Auchinleck's reputation did not suffer from the débâcle in Norway, which the latter could not possibly have prevented. On his arrival in London on 13 June Auchinleck was informed that he was to form 5 Corps in Southern Command with an anti-invasion role. Alan Brooke was appointed the Army Commander. On 19 July, however, General Ironside at that time Commander-in-Chief Home Forces, was retired, made a field-marshal and given a peerage; and Brooke was appointed as C-in-C Home Forces to meet the invasion. Auchinleck succeeded Brooke as GOC-in-C Southern Command and Montgomery took over command of 5 Corps.

'Auk' and Monty were oil and water; Monty says in his *Memoirs:* 'I cannot recall that we ever agreed on anything!' They were both strong characters with decided views. Auchinleck says: 'However, we got on, though we had one row.' This arose when Auchinleck discovered that Montgomery was corresponding direct with the Adjutant-General at the War Office with a view to getting officers of BEF experience posted to 5 Corps. This was more than Auchinleck could stomach and he put his foot down firmly.

To return now to my visit to Southern Command. I arrived at Auchinleck's headquarters at Wilton House, a beautiful setting, almost before he had finished breakfast so that we could make the most of the day. It was a lovely autumn morning and we set off in his car, taking our lunch with us. We had had the same military upbringing, had both been teachers at the Staff College—he at Quetta and I at Camberley—and had both served on the Indian frontier together, so we spoke the same military language. We saw much of his defences, walked miles over beaches and up and down sand dunes, checked arcs of fire, talked to local commanders and thoroughly enjoyed ourselves. He fired questions at me all the time and I gave him frank answers. At the end he said: 'Well, what do you think?' I replied, 'I think that, with the men and equipment and the supporting arms you have at your disposal you have tackled the problem wonderfully well—but the distances are terrific, the troops very thin on the ground and communications stretched to the limit. I only hope it never happens.' And with an infectious grin he said: 'Well, between ourselves, so do I.'

The Auk, though he didn't insist on runs before breakfast as Monty did, nor was he by any means a teetotaller, was a man of splendid physique and always superlatively fit. His buoyancy and enthusiasm were infectious. He was doing what he liked most—commanding troops and training them for battle. And everywhere he went the troops reacted to what he said and the way he looked. He had the ability to see the wood, and the individual trees as well, whereas Gort was inclined to be so obsessed with the trees and the minor mistakes in dress etc, that he missed some of the woods altogether—though he didn't miss the vital one.

We dined in the Mess at Wilton House, in the happiest possible atmosphere, no 'shop' talked, and the Auk the life and soul of the party. But it was after dinner, in his own quarters, that we had the important talk. He told me that a week or two previously Anthony Eden had lunched at Wilton House and told him that the Government wanted him to return to India as Commander-in-Chief. He was sorry to leave Britain and the British Army, but the immediate danger of invasion seemed to have passed and of course to become Commander-in-Chief in India had always been his life's ambition—and it was with the Indian setting and the Indian Army that he was really familiar. He also told me that as soon as he took up his appointment he was going to insist that I went back to India to command a division.

Auchinleck was relieved in Southern Command by Lieutenant-General Alexander, who was obviously being groomed as our leading battle general. Auchinleck flew off to India after Christmas, congratulated on all sides at home and in India on having been given the appointment for which he was so ideally suited, and for which he had always longed.

But within six months he was ordered to relieve Wavell in command of the Middle East. This was a most unwelcome order—but it had to be obeyed. And in just over a year Auchinleck had been removed from his North African Command and was back in India—without a job.

CHAPTER TWO

The Campaign in North Africa
First Phase

On 10 August 1940, just as the Battle of Britain was commencing, General Wavell, Commander-in-Chief Middle East, arrived by air in London to ask for some tanks to halt the imminent Italian invasion of Egypt. The Prime Minister, Winston Churchill, though faced with a grave crisis at home, made the very brave and vital decision to send immediately to the Middle East one regiment of heavy tanks, one of light and one of cruiser tanks.

Prior to the receipt of these reinforcements the British plan for the defence of Egypt had been to await the Italian assault in their fortified lines at Mersa Matruh and fight a defensive battle as best they could. Wavell, however, having obtained these valuable reinforcements, had conceived and prepared, in consultation with General 'Jumbo' Wilson, his Commander in Cyrenaica, and in the greatest secrecy, an offensive plan to take the Italians by surprise and nip their offensive in the bud.

Wavell's friendship and his association with Jumbo Wilson* was one of the most important in Wavell's career. The affectionate nickname 'Jumbo', which had been given him by his

---

* Jumbo Wilson had been one of my teachers at the Staff College Camberley. After the war he became President of the Distinguished Conduct Medal League, in which office he asked me to replace him in 1958. I always had the greatest admiration and affection for him.

friends and admirers in the Army, fitted him from two points of
view. He was indeed elephantine in build but his bulk did not
denote any softness of body and certainly not of mind. Provided
he could get a good horse to carry him—and Army Remounts
saw to that—he rode well across country and he was always fit
and very much harder than he looked. His mind was as sharp
as a needle and, like the elephant, he never forgot. He was
tremendously shrewd and level-headed, massively calm in all
circumstances and always a rock of strength in an emergency.
Through two years of changing fortunes, great victories and
harsh defeats, he and Wavell remained the closest friends.

Marshal Graziani's Italian Army, about 80,000 strong, which
had already crossed the Egyptian frontier, was spread over a
fifty-mile front in a series of fortified camps, separated by wide
distances and not mutually supporting. Between the enemy's
right flank at Sofafi and his next camp at Nibeiwa there was a
gap of over twenty miles. Wavell's plan was to spring an
offensive through this gap and then turn in towards the sea and
attack a group of camps on either side. For this purpose
Lieutenant-General O'Connor was given command of the 7th
Armoured Division (by no means up to strength), the 4th
Indian Division and the 16th British Infantry Brigade—the
whole force being mechanised or motorised.

The plan was a daring one as it involved launching most of
the available troops in Egypt into the heart of the enemy
position by a move of seventy miles on two successive nights
(7 and 8 December) over the open desert, and with the risk of
being observed and attacked from the air during the inter-
vening day. Besides this there were obvious difficulties with
regard to supplies of food and petrol.

To quote from Arthur Bryant's *The Turn of the Tide*, based on
the war diaries of Field-Marshal Alanbrooke:

When Graziani, furiously prodded by an impatient Mussolini, started to move forward with his long, strung-out army
of nearly a quarter of a million men to occupy Alexandria
and deprive the British Navy of its base General Richard

O'Connor, directing the small Western Desert Force, backed by the skill and daring of a few hundred RAF pilots, fell on his advance-guard at Sidi-Barrani with a single Indian Infantry Division and one weak armoured division and completely destroyed it. O'Connor proceeded to encircle and storm one after another of the Italian coastal strongholds in Libya and Cyrenaica, and finally, after a hundred and fifty mile dash across unreconnoitred desert with his dwindling armour, rounded up the remnants of Graziani's host. Altogether, with never more than two divisions at his disposal, this astonishing soldier advanced five hundred miles and, at a cost of less than 2,000 casualties, destroyed ten Italian divisions and captured 130,000 prisoners, 400 tanks and 850 guns.

Field-Marshal Sir John Harding, who was then O'Connor's chief of staff, wrote of this campaign:

Although he had the wise advice of Field Marshals Wavell and Wilson to aid him, the plan of battle was hatched in General O'Connor's brain. The tactical decisions on which success or failure depended were his and the grim determination that inspired all our troops stemmed up from his heart. It was his skill in calculating the risks, and his daring in accepting them, that turned what might have been merely a limited success into a victorious campaign with far-reaching effects on the future course of the war.

Then, during the early months of 1941, two other Commonwealth armies under Wavell's orders, one attacking from the north under General Platt, and the other from the south, under General Alan Cunningham, closed in on Italian forces four or five times their size in Eritrea and Abyssinia and by early summer had liquidated them, taking another 185,000 prisoners and restoring the Ethiopian Emperor to his throne.

Wavell's subsequent campaigns in Greece, Crete and Cyrenaica ended in disaster; but here he was up against

German troops and not Italians—which was a very different proposition indeed. Not only were our troops driven out of Greece and Crete but the weakening of our forces in the Western Desert, which these diversions necessitated, resulted in the loss of all the territory and the airfields in western Cyrenaica which O'Connor had captured in his brilliant offensive against the Italians. Weakened by the withdrawal of almost all their tanks and most of their guns to aid Greece, and attacked by German armour under Rommel, which had reached Tripoli in February, the British in Africa were thrown back in considerable disarray for nearly 300 miles and once more Egypt was threatened by invasion.

Nevertheless, Wavell had become a national hero by his devastating defeat of the Italian Army, which came at a time when Britain stood alone and, following the Dunkirk disaster, was threatened imminently with invasion. There were three factors which buoyed up the morale of the British people at this critical time, and these were the leadership of Winston Churchill, the courage and daring of the young pilots of Fighter Command, and Wavell's great victory over the Italians in North Africa.

Wavell was born on 5 May 1883 and was thus fifty-eight in 1941. He had been a Winchester scholar and passed fourth into Sandhurst in 1900 at the age of seventeen. He was commissioned into the Black Watch, saw service in the Boer War and on the Indian Frontier; and in 1909 he passed into the Staff College Camberley before he was twenty-six. In 1911 he was selected to do an attachment in Russia and attended the Russian manoeuvres in 1912 and 1913. In World War I he held staff appointments in France in the latter part of 1914 and 1915. He was Brigade-Major of 9 Infantry Brigade in the Ypres Salient in June 1915, when it lost 73 officers out of 96 and 2,000 men out of 3,500. Wavell was hit by a shell splinter and had to have his left eye removed. He was awarded the MC, promoted brevet lieutenant-colonel in June 1916, and was later on Allenby's staff in Palestine. After the war he had further staff appointments and then, in 1930, he got command of 6 Infantry

Brigade in the 2nd Division. With the exception of the ten months he had spent with the Black Watch in Germany he had been a staff officer for twenty years. Up to 1930 he was comparatively unknown but he then started to gain a reputation as an imaginative trainer of troops and as a lecturer and writer on training matters. Just after his fiftieth birthday he was promoted major-general and was then on half-pay for fifteen months. By this time he had made a considerable reputation as a writer on military subjects generally. In 1935 he was appointed to command the 2nd Division and his concentration on training became intense. He put out his ideas in writing, in tactical exercises and in lectures. In 1936 he was given the Palestine Command, then Southern Command in England and, in August 1939, became General Officer Commanding Middle East, with his headquarters in Cairo.

Wavell was a remarkable man and an unusual general. He certainly looked the part with his square, sturdy figure, fine head and air of invincibility. Opinions may differ as to his place amongst the top British commanders of World War II, but I very much doubt whether any of them were superior to him in sheer toughness of body, mind and spirit. The loss of his eye never seemed to bother him. He was a daring and enthusiastic horse-rider, an intrepid air traveller and utterly courageous and unflappable under all conditions. He was at the same time a scholar, a lover of poetry and a writer of considerable ability. As a public speaker he was somewhat dull and uninspired, but in committee he would make his points emphatically and in the fewest possible words. One of his marked characteristics was a habit of silence which was often disconcerting. This characteristic became more pronounced as he grew older, to the point almost of embarrassment.

Unlike some famous soldiers, General Wavell was a great family man and liked taking his wife and family around with him whenever possible—even in his wartime campaigns. And what of his faults? He had a fixed and mistaken conviction that the Italians and the Germans were much of a muchness as battle fighters and he had a long-established contempt for the

Japanese as soldiers—an obsession from which he never really deviated even up to the fall of Singapore and Rangoon. These two convictions led him into some disastrous errors, both in North Africa and in the Far East. The Germans and the Japanese did not just throw in their hands when their flanks were turned, nor could commanders—with inferior numbers and untrained troops—'get away with things' against them as they could against the Italians. Wavell, however, had no use for commanders who were forced to withdraw whatever the odds against them.

General Dick O'Connor was an old friend of mine and a man of sterling character, utter integrity and surprising powers of leadership. I say surprising because in appearance he was small, quiet, self-effacing and not in any way a striking personality. Yet beneath the surface he had a steely character, great daring, enormous courage and drive and was in fact one of the outstanding battle leaders of the war, though it must be remembered that he was opposing Italians and not Germans. Born in 1889 he was therefore fifty-two in 1941. He was educated at Wellington College and Sandhurst and had a most distinguished World War I, being awarded the DSO and bar, the MC and the Italian Civil Medal for Valour—rather ironic this, in view of the trouncing he gave the Italians in 1941—and he was mentioned in despatches nine times. He and I first met and collaborated in 1932 when he was at the War Office and I was an instructor at the Staff College Camberley. He commanded the Peshawar Brigade on the Indian Frontier from 1936 to 1938, which coincided with my command of Chitral Force—and he came up on to 'the roof of the world' to pay me a visit. And what a stroke of luck he—and the Army—had just had! He had been smitten with such acute rheumatism that a medical board had decreed that he must be retired from the service. It was then that someone advised him to approach the well-known osteopath and nature cure advocate, Stanley Lief, who ran the Nature Cure Clinic at Champneys (Tring). Although this establishment, and Lief's teaching, were not recognised by the medical profession it was surprising how

Page 67
(*above*) Left to right: Lieut-General Sir Philip Neame GOC Palestine, General Sir Archibald Wavell and Secretary of State for Foreign Affairs Sir Anthony Eden; (*below*) Lieut-General Neil Ritchie GOC 8th Army, directing operations against Rommel from his advanced headquarters in Libya. With him are his two Corps Commanders, Lieut-General Willoughby Norrie (right) and Lieut-General 'Strafer' Gott

Page 68
(*left*) General Sir Claude Auchinleck who had suc-ceeded Wavell as Com-mander-in-Chief Middle East in June 1941

(*right*) General Alexander, Commander -in-Chief Middle East 1942

many doctors and famous men and women went to Champneys. O'Connor went there and did a ten-day fast, with all the other 'decarbonising' treatment provided; and, as a result, completely got rid of his rheumatism. He applied for another medical board which passed him A1 and he was restored to the active list of the Army.

Wavell and O'Connor were complementary to one another and certainly had a mutual admiration. Having approved the plan, Wavell left the conduct of the battle entirely to O'Connor. Even when Wavell withdrew the highly trained 4th Indian Division (one of the finest formations of the war) from O'Connor's all-conquering force after Sidi Barrani and replaced it by the new and inexperienced 6th Australian Division, without consulting him, O'Connor did not waver in his admiration for his chief. The changeover, however, did result in considerable delay to O'Connor's operations and certainly had an adverse effect on the outcome of the Desert Campaign, which would otherwise undoubtedly have resulted in the capture of Tripoli. On 7 February 1941 O'Connor had captured Benghazi and a major decision then had to be made at the highest level as to whether he should push on to Tripoli. This further advance would have involved naval and air commitments, and they were already stretched almost to the limit. The Defence Committee decided that assistance to Greece and/or Turkey must come first, and at last O'Connor's triumphant advance had to be halted.

At this particular period of the war in the Middle East so many somewhat incredible decisions were made—or not made —so many wrong appreciations of the situation were made and accepted, and so many people in high places came clattering from their pedestals, that even now it is difficult to put them all into perspective. No one knew more about the military situation than Major-General Sir John Kennedy, who was Director of Military Operations at the War Office. His accounts of these and other operations are written most clearly in his book, *The Business of War*. The soldier must always be the servant of the politician; all educated soldiers have realised that this must be so, and that, in certain circumstances, military plans have to be subservient to political demands. It is up to the politician to weigh up the pros and cons and to pay full regard to the opinions of the generals before deciding that they must perhaps be over-ruled. Similarly it is the duty of the military commander or chief of staff to put his views clearly and forcibly—and then accept the decisions of his political master and endeavour to put them into operation.

On page 80 of his book General Kennedy gives the views of the General Staff as recorded on 16 February 1941. These are some extracts:

We are regaining the initiative slowly. In fact we have regained it as far as the Italians are concerned. But not yet against the Germans . . .

With regard to the Mediterranean theatre we should push on to Tripoli before the opportunity to do so has disappeared. If we do not deprive the Italians of this last base in Africa it is certain that the Germans will build up forces there. [How right these opinions were, but already events had overtaken them. The requirements of the campaign in Greece had halted O'Connor's advance and Rommel and his Germans had thankfully accepted the gift of Tripoli and were landing there in force.]

Nothing we can do can make the Greek business a sound military proposition. If we put four divisions into Greece, a month's hard fighting there would suck the bulk of our reserves out of the Middle East. . .

The chances of our getting four divisions into Greece are in any case extremely small. It would take a hundred ships or more to put them in in one flight. And it takes time to organise bases. . .

Anything we put into Greece, on account of the very important political aspect, we must be prepared to lose. We must not lose so much that our power of offensive action in the Middle East is killed, nor so much that our power of defence in the vital Egyptian centre is impaired.

These, then, were the military appreciations of the situation by the Chiefs of Staff.

The British Prime Minister, the Chiefs of Staff and General Wavell were thus faced with a problem of priorities. They weighed it all up very carefully—and they got the wrong answer. Even Winston Churchill, who had urged the Greek venture most strongly from the start—and succeeded in getting it accepted eventually by the Chiefs of Staff—was not in the end entirely clear as to what extent the Greek campaign should be allowed to weaken our position in the Western Desert. Nor was Wavell clear as to how much he considered could be taken from the Desert Army without fatally weakening our strength there in face of a probable German intrusion into North Africa.

Churchill says at the start of Chapter XI, 'The Desert Flank, Rommel, Tobruk' of his *Second World War*, vol 3:

All our efforts to form a front in the Balkans were founded upon the sure maintenance of the Desert Flank in North Africa. It was common ground between all authorities in London and Cairo that this must be held at all costs and in priority over every other venture. The utter destruction of the Italian forces in Cyrenaica, and the long road distances to be traversed before the enemy could gather a fresh army, led Wavell to believe that for some time to come he could afford to hold this vital western flank with moderate forces and to relieve his tried troops with others less well trained.

Churchill's clear statement of the priority of the Desert Flank had certainly not percolated down to General Wavell, as the following pages will show. In actual fact, complete priority was given to Greece, and Cyrenaica got only the unequipped and untrained units that were unfit for mobile operations.

Churchill goes on to say:

It was only after some weeks, marked by serious decisions (with regard to the demands of troops for Greece from the

Desert Force) that I realised that the 7th Armoured Division (withdrawn to Egypt to rest and refit) did not exist as a factor in the protection of our vital Desert Flank. The place of the 7th Armoured Division was taken by an armoured brigade and part of the support group of the 2nd Armoured Division. The 6th Australian Division was also relieved by the 9th. Neither of these new formations was fully trained, and, to make matters worse, they were stripped of much equipment and transport to bring up to full scale the divisions soon to go to Greece. The shortage of transport was severely felt, and affected the dispositions of the troops and their mobility. Because of maintenance difficulties to keep them in action further forward one Australian brigade was held back in Tobruk, where also was a brigade of motorised Indian Cavalry recently formed and under training.

In fact the Prime Minister had begun to have doubts as to the effect of his Greek adventure on the all-important Desert Flank. General Kennedy remarks:

On 19th February Eden and Dill arrived in Cairo; on the 22nd they were in Athens; on the 23rd they were back in Cairo en route for Ankara. At this moment opinions began to shift in a very curious fashion. The Prime Minister, who had urged the Greek venture from the outset, sent a signal to Eden on the 21st February in the following terms: 'If in your hearts you feel Greek enterprise will be another Norwegian fiasco, do not consider yourselves obliged to it. If no good plan can be made please say so. But you know of course how valuable success [in Greece] would be.'

(*The Business of War*, p 85)

General Kennedy continues:

Now there happened also a thing that I had not expected. Dill changed his mind. So did Wavell. We began getting telegrams which showed that they both considered that there was a fair chance of success [for Greece]. The Chiefs of Staff, after a meeting which lasted from 4.45 pm on Sunday 23rd February till 2.30 am the next morning, produced a paper in which they advised that, on balance, the Greek enterprise should go forward. It seemed to me very wrong that the Cabinet had never asked for or received a purely military view from either the Chiefs of Staff or from Wavell. All the Service advice given on this problem had been coloured by political considerations—a very dangerous procedure.

When the Cabinet discussed it on 24th February, the Prime Minister said that, on the evidence before them, he was in favour of the plan. It was then approved unanimously, subject to shipping being available and subject to the agreement of the Governments of Australia and New Zealand. The Prime Minister had good reason to doubt the wisdom of his policy but its momentum was now considerable and no note of caution had been sounded by Eden and Dill or, latterly, by Wavell. (*Ibid*)

Indeed Churchill says with regard to the latter: 'In London we accepted Wavell's telegram of 2 March as the basis of our action.' (*Second World War*, Vol 3, p 177)

This telegram of 2 March from Wavell to the Prime Minister (*Wavell—Soldier, and Scholar* p 381) was in answer to a request from the latter for a short appreciation of the effect of the new development on the defence situation in Cyrenaica as a result of the landing of German troops in Tripoli. Wavell had replied that recent enemy reinforcements in Tripolitania were two Italian infantry divisions, two Italian motorised artillery regiments and one German armoured brigade group. He had no evidence of more mechanical transport having been landed and he considered that the enemy must still be short of transport. The distance from Tripoli to Agheila was 470 miles and to Benghazi 600 miles—with a single road and inadequate water for 400 miles of the route. Wavell therefore felt that the enemy could only possibly maintain one infantry division and one armoured brigade along the coast road in about three weeks' time. If they had a second armoured brigade they might send it across the desert to attack the British flank. He ended his cable with the words: 'I do not think that with this force he will attempt to recover Benghazi.'

Wavell, however, was 'thinking Italian' and didn't appreciate the new factor that he was now dealing with Germans under a dynamic commander, General Erwin Rommel—a very different kettle of fish. Brigadier Shearer, Wavell's Director of Intelligence, had put up to him on 6 March an appreciation of the situation from the German commander's point of view (though he did not know at the time that he was Rommel), which indicated that the German Armoured Corps was quite capable of winning back the whole of Cyrenaica unless the British substantially reinforced their present forces. Wavell, however, disregarded this warning.

Wavell later accused himself (*Wavell—Soldier and Scholar*, p 384) of having made two serious mistakes. First, he did not appreciate the weakness of the new Cyrenaica Command, which Lieutenant-General Philip Neame, VC, had taken over from General Maitland Wilson when the latter was appointed to command the British forces in Greece. Earlier in the month Wavell had set up a Cyrenaica Command with Maitland Wilson as military governor and commander-in-chief. O'Connor took over Wilson's appointment in Cairo and went off for a badly needed spell of leave in Palestine. Later, on 4 March, Wilson went to command in Greece and Neame was appointed to Cyrenaica in his place.

Neame's command consisted, in name, of two divisions, the 2nd Armoured and the 9th Australian. Two of the brigades of General Leslie Morshead's 9th Division had gone to Greece and been replaced by two less well-equipped brigades from the 7th Australian Division. 9th Division staff was incomplete and only partially trained and the division was short of transport, Bren guns, anti-tank weapons and signalling equipment. The other division, the 2nd Armoured, had been brought out from England to replace the battle-worn 7th Armoured. Its commander, Major-General Tilly, had died suddenly at Bardia in

January, before the division had completed its training. In his place Wavell had appointed Major-General Gambier-Parry* whom he had known from the days of the First Armoured Force on Salisbury Plain. But it was certainly a misnomer to refer to the 2nd Armoured as a division. It amounted to barely one weak armoured brigade, completely untrained for desert warfare, under-equipped and not fully mobile.

The disaster which overtook Neame's army was to a considerable extent also attributable to the transfer to Greece of RAF squadrons which would have given him something like air parity. Wavell says in his Official Despatch: 'The position in Cyrenaica was rendered more difficult by the German air attacks on Benghazi in the absence of any effective defence, since practically all available fighter aircraft and anti-aircraft guns were required for Greece. This made it hazardous to bring shipping into Benghazi.'

In addition to all these deficiencies, Neame's Cyrenaica Headquarters was almost incapable of movement and lacked the trained staff and signal equipment which were necessary to enable it to control mobile formations in desert warfare.

'And my next great error,' Wavell says, 'was that I made up my mind that the enemy could not put in any effective counter-stroke before May at the earliest. I also thought that the German could never build up a supply system over the distance between Tripoli and the frontier of Cyrenaica in the time he did.'

What a pity that Wavell realised these errors only after the event rather than before! Had he done so he could hardly have laid all the blame for what subsequently happened on to General Neame and thus tarnished the reputation of a distinguished soldier. There is no greater autocrat than a commander-in-chief in the field where individual appointments are concerned. He can fatally damage, or sack, any subordinate commander and the latter has no redress, nor will anyone speak up in his defence—except perhaps many years after when it is too late. A prime minister even has not quite the same

* Gambier-Parry had been at the Staff College with me.

power in this respect. He at least is subject to immediate questioning and criticism in Parliament—and Lloyd George, without sufficient parliamentary support, found it impossible to sack Haig and Robertson in World War I. Winston Churchill, however, had no such inhibitions.

Our troops began to disembark in Greece in the first week in April. Well before this the effect of the Greek commitment had begun to be felt in Libya. And soon the much weakened Desert Army was in full retreat from Benghazi to the Egyptian frontier. General Kennedy, the Director of Military Operations, sums the matter up as follows:

The period December 1940 to March 1941 had marked the height of Wavell's greatness as a commander in the field. The destruction of the Italian Army in the Desert in December and January had been a brilliant feat of arms. Scarcely less remarkable had been the campaign in Abyssinia, which reached its culminating point with the occupation of Addis Ababa on 5th April. But Greece can hardly be regarded otherwise than as an error of military judgement. It was the first of the series of major mistakes that finally led to Wavell's removal from his command. But had Wavell advised against the Greek venture on military grounds, and had his advice been accepted, no doubt he would have been blamed later for missing a great opportunity. A commander in the field is always open to this kind of criticism, but that can be no excuse for failing to judge aright or for failing to give his Government an opinion in which the military prospects are clearly distinguished from political considerations. The military opinion tendered by Wavell and by the Chiefs of Staff to the Cabinet was proved wrong in every respect.

(*The Business of War*, p 86)

The Chiefs of Staff, however, were naturally loath to disregard the opinion of a commander-in-chief in the field.

It was only natural that Hitler should have been extremely displeased at the way the Italians had conducted their campaign in North Africa, and he voiced his displeasure in no uncertain terms to Mussolini. He followed it up by immediate action, as a result of which General Erwin Rommel, commander-designate of the German 'Afrika Korps', arrived in Rome on 11 February and was in Africa the next day. Where Rommel was concerned, not a second was lost or wasted. The particular reason for his speed at this moment was the Italian fear that O'Connor's devastating advance would reach and engulf Tripoli and capture its important airfields, in which case Rommel's task would have been infinitely more difficult.

Rommel did not know at first that the British advance had been halted some 400 miles east of Tripoli, or that the Desert Army and Air Force had been drastically reduced to further the operations in Greece. He thankfully took with both hands all that was offered him. On the afternoon of his arrival he was in the air over Tripoli and the desert to the east, having a look at the country. On 14 February German troops began to disembark in Tripoli and Rommel insisted that the operation should continue throughout the night, risking the danger of air attack because of the necessary lights. But he needn't have worried because, owing to the British shortage of aircraft, no air attacks were made. Every day, whilst his troops were arriving, unloading their stores and equipment and getting their tropical kit, Rommel was in the air familiarising himself with the terrain. In a letter to his wife dated 5 March he said: 'Speed is the thing which matters here.' But how much he had to thank the British campaign in Greece for the fact that what might have been a most difficult and costly landing turned out to be a piece of cake! This gave an unexpectedly favourable start to his operations and it wasn't until 24 February that British patrols made contact with the advancing Germans.

Rommel had been born in 1891 and was thus fifty years old at this time. He had become an officer cadet in 1910, and in World War I, in his early twenties, he made a reputation as a courageous regimental officer. When the war ended he was one of the 4,000 officers whom the Germans were allowed to retain. They were, of course, picked men. Between the wars he made steady but not spectacular progress in the German Army and, at the outbreak of World War II, became a major-general on the staff of Hitler's headquarters. He was then offered command of a Panzer division in February 1940. Until the spring of 1940 he had had no experience of commanding tanks in action, although he had been an acute observer and student of their use. He had long been imbued with, and had expounded, the principles and the objects of armoured warfare. He had formulated his own ideas of leadership in battle and these were aggressive, dynamic and unpredictable.

When the Germans struck in France and Belgium in May of 1940 Rommel's Panzer division was part of the German armoured force which surged across the Meuse in the historic *Blitzkrieg* which marked the beginning of the Allied collapse. As the operations progressed, his division, and the way he managed it, came in for increasing commendation. He broke all the accepted rules of command. Always he led from the front and his staff had to bring along the headquarters and supply the troops as best they could. But somehow they managed it, his system worked, and he gained tremendous prestige and the devotion of the men he led. On his arrival in North Africa in February 1941 he was beset by difficulties—from his own side. The German General Staff were not in favour of making a large and decisive advance in North Africa. They did, however, give Rommel tentative permission that when the 15th Panzer Division had arrived to join the 21st Panzer he could attempt to capture Benghazi. However, he pushed forward his 5th Light Division to Agheila with remarkable speed and then, on 31 March, he started an offensive at Mersa el Brega which showed him the weakness of the enemy's defences and convinced him that he had the opportunity of inflicting a decisive reverse on the British. By 3 April the British forces were in headlong retreat.

Philip Neame was born in 1888 and was fifty-three at the time of these operations. He had been educated at Cheltenham and then the Royal Military Academy Woolwich, where he passed out sixth in 1908 and was commissioned in the Royal

Engineers at the age of nineteen and a half. Short, slim and wiry, and always superlatively fit, he was at the same time a fine athlete and a dedicated and brainy soldier—utterly fearless and a man of strong character, with tremendous drive and determination. He was an outstanding rifle and revolver shot, a fine cross-country rider, a keen polo player, a mountaineer of high standard and an accomplished skier and big game hunter. There was nothing to which he turned his hand that he did not do extremely well.

In World War I Neame had arrived in France with the 15th Field Company RE in October 1914 and was up in the trenches with his company for the first battle of Ypres. He really did bear a charmed life, and no one was a bit surprised when he won the VC on 19 December 1914. Everyone knew that if he could only remain alive he would emerge from the war with great distinction. During the course of the war he added to his VC a DSO, Chevalier of the Legion of Honour, and French Croix de Guerre, and was mentioned five times in despatches. He held various staff appointments in fighting formations and obtained a brevet-majority. Just before the end of the war, when he was Chief Staff Officer of the 30th Division, he was transferred to the Tank Corps and appointed GSO 1 No 2 Tank Group. He had already had considerable experience of handling tanks in battle conditions. Plans had been in preparation for a great offensive campaign in 1919, and the keystone of those plans was the formation of an enormous armoured force to be the spearhead of the attack against the German armies. Three tank groups—which later would have been called armoured divisions—were to be formed, and Neame had been selected as GSO 1 of one of these.

Neame made a particular study of the use of tanks and when he was made an instructor at the Staff College from 1919 to 1923 one of his particular subjects was tank warfare. Between the wars Neame continued his interest and study of tanks, although the British Army had precious few. But he insisted on introducing them into all his tactical exercises. When he went from France in February 1940 to take command of the 4th

Indian Division in Egypt he concentrated his attention on getting them fully mechanised and motor-borne and then in training them in desert warfare in co-operation with the armoured troops available. He specifically trained the division in long cross-country desert movements in open formation by day and by night, with and without armoured formations accompanying it. He also staged tactical exercises in which the division was attacked by armour. General 'Jumbo' Wilson then directed a forty-eight-hour exercise to test the 4th Division and reported on its efficiency in mobile desert warfare to AHQ India in glowing terms.

When Neame was promoted to temporary lieutenant-general in August 1940 and became GOC Palestine, Trans-Jordan and Cyprus, he handed over the division to Major-General Beresford-Pierse. The 4th Division then took part in O'Connor's triumphant offensive against the Italians. The fine performance the 4th Division put up was attributed by Beresford-Pierse to the intensive training Neame had given them. So when Neame became Commander of Cyrenaica Army in February 1941 he probably knew a good deal more about the tactical handling of armoured formations than Wavell, or indeed than the commander of the 2nd Armoured Division, who had been one of his pupils at the Staff College.

Between the wars Neame went steadily up the ladder, seeing quite a lot of service in India, which he loved. He maintained his usual high standard of physical fitness, but nearly met his death when walking up a tigress alone. Only his tremendously tough physique saved him from his wounds. The tigress died! When World War II started Neame was appointed Deputy CGS of the British Expeditionary Force in France.

In August 1940 Neame was promoted to lieutenant-general and appointed to the command of Palestine, Trans-Jordan and Cyprus. Towards the end of February 1941 he received sudden orders to proceed to GHQ Cairo where he was told by General Wavell to take over command in Cyrenaica, as GOC-in-Chief and Military Governor, from Lieutenant-General Sir Maitland Wilson. Neame records in his *Playing with Strife*:

I was told in Cairo by General Wavell that our troops in Cyrenaica were being reduced to a minimum in order to provide for this expedition to Greece. But he said that opportunity might occur later for our resuming the offensive against Tripoli. The situation as depicted to me by the Intelligence Staff at GHQ was that Cyrenaica had now become a passive battle-zone, with no possible enemy threats owing to the complete destruction of the Italian Tenth Army in General O'Connor's victorious campaign. It was known that some German troops had landed in Tripoli and it was presumed that their task was the protection of the German airfields there. It was also known that General Rommel was in charge of the German Forces and I was given his dossier by our Intelligence. I must say I thought it unlikely that neither Rommel nor the German troops would be sent to Africa for a merely passive role. Within a few days of my arrival at Barce, my headquarters in Cyrenaica, I had visited all my troops, the forward area south of Agedabia, the ports of Benghazi and Derna and the fortress of Port Tobruk.

From air reports and air photography it very soon became apparent to me that large enemy forces were assembling on my front near Agheila and more were moving up from Tripoli. Intelligence agents brought in news of German troops near the front, and large convoys crossing the Mediterranean from Italy to Tripoli. By the middle of March, a fortnight after I took over, it was quite clear to me that a great German–Italian offensive was being prepared against Cyrenaica, and that it was imminent. I put forward very clearly to GHQ the poor condition of my army in training, equipment and numbers, and repeatedly signalled my most grave deficiencies—namely, anti-tank and anti-aircraft guns, armour, air support, and mechanical transport—all those things in fact which make a modern army. I requested reinforcements and also naval and air action against the enemy convoys, streaming over to Tripoli. But no effective action was possible; everything was going to Greece. I was told that reinforcements would ultimately be sent, but that little would be available before the middle of May—in two months' time—and that these would come from Abyssinia. The fact was that the British Middle East Armies and Air Forces were endeavouring to conduct three campaigns simultaneously—in Greece, North Africa and Abyssinia— and had barely the requisite force for one campaign— not to mention defensive commitments in Palestine and Iraq!

Wavell seemed to resent Neame's frank summing up of the situation—and was beginning to realise that his own appreciation was mistaken. But Wavell did not yet understand how very different the opposition had now become with German troops, under a dynamic and offensive-minded general, replacing the defeatist Italians.

On 17 and 18 March Field-Marshal Sir John Dill, Chief of the Imperial General Staff, and an old friend and admirer of Neame's, came to visit the Cyrenaica front with General Wavell. After hearing Neame's appreciation of the situation Dill said to him: 'You are going to get a bloody nose here, Philip, and it is not the only place where we shall get bloody noses!' Neame, as a highly educated soldier, much preferred this sort of attitude to the complete silence with which General Wavell received his reports on the situation.

I have already stated the after-thoughts of Mr Churchill and General Wavell on the weakness of Neame's position in Cyrenaica. Neame had already reported to Wavell the inadequacies of training, equipment and transport from which his troops suffered. He records these defects in rather more detail:

Major-General Morshead's 9th Australian Division was quite unfit for any campaign as it had not completed its military training and had done no higher training whatever to fit it for operations in the field. Only one brigade had any second-line mechanical transport and therefore the division could not be supplied properly. There were grave shortages. Three of the battalions had no transport at all and had to be left behind in Tobruk and there were grave shortages of armoured carriers, anti-tank rifles and Bren guns . . .

The rest of my army was in an even more parlous condition. My armoured force, the 2nd Armoured Division, consisted of the elements of 7th and 2nd Armoured Divisions whose equipment was considered unfit for service in Greece. The Divisional HQ arrived only eight days before Rommel attacked; they were woefully deficient in signallers and wireless and had never been in action before. The Armoured Car Regiment (King's Dragoon Guards) had no anti-aircraft weapons and the German dive-bombers took continual toll of them, the wireless in their armoured cars failed in the crisis of the battle through lack of charging apparatus; and they had no anti-tank weapons and no guns to compete with the well-armed German armoured cars.

The 3rd Armoured Brigade comprised three regiments. The first was a light tank regiment (the 3rd Hussars) whose tanks were utterly worn out, and none of them had any anti-tank guns. They could therefore not even compete with an armoured car. The second was a cruiser tank regiment (the 5th Royal Tank Regiment), which had only twenty-five tanks, instead of fifty and these twenty-five were in the last stages of mechanical decay. The third regiment (the 6th Royal Tank Regiment) had no British tanks at all, and was in process of being equipped with tanks captured from the Italians. To sum up—the 3rd Armoured Brigade was not a fighting formation at that time when they had to face Rommel's Afrika Korps of two armoured divisions, which in armoured vehicles must have outnumbered them by six or seven to one, whilst in regard to actual armament and efficiency the odds cannot be stated. Rommel also had supporting him portions of an Italian armoured division and an Italian motorised division with three or four Italian infantry divisions. The 3rd Indian Motor Brigade came under my orders at Mersa Matruh in the middle of March. It comprised three newly mechanised Indian cavalry regiments carried in trucks, but with no artillery or anti-tank weapons. They had no second-line transport.

The air support I had available was meagre in the extreme. I could count the available aircraft on the fingers of my two hands, while we had to face about a hundred German fighters and a hundred German bombers, with the same number of Italians. All the Middle East air strength, which had given General O'Connor complete air superiority over the Italians two months before had been transferred to Greece. Three sorties daily (Hurricanes) and on one day only one, were available for reconnaissance. And after the first few days no photographic machine was in the air. There were only six medium bombers for all tasks, including distant reconnaissance. These figures are hardly credible in view of our air strength in thousands later in the war. All naval assistance of monitors, gunboats and destroyers had been withdrawn for Greece and the Navy were unable to use Benghazi port to supply my force owing to German air attacks. My most forward base was Tobruk, 450 miles from my front. The whole supply and motor transport situation was one of extreme anxiety. The exercise of command in my Army was terribly handicapped by lack of signal equipment and trained personnel. All had gone to Greece. I had to depend on Italian civil telephone lines and captured Italian and Libyan Arab linesmen. Even for static peace control the signals were inadequate. For active mobile operations the situation was desperate and resulted in terrible delays in the transmission of vital information and orders. Personal liaison was no substitute owing to the great distances. Another millstone round my neck was a mass of 25,000 Italian prisoners at Benghazi who had not been evacuated. (*Ibid*)

Facing Neame was Germany's most up-to-date armoured corps with 600 armoured fighting vehicles, supported by 200 of her best aircraft. They had in addition thousands of MT lorries and they were backed by several Italian divisions.

Rommel had 'never had it so good' nor in any subsequent campaign were the odds so much in his favour. The German–Italian Army began to close up to Agheila a few days before their definite advance began on 31 March. On 30 March Neame received a personal signal from Wavell saying that no reinforcements would be available for two months and that his task was to delay the enemy's advance over the 150 miles from Agheila to Benghazi until the end of May.

Neame was naturally concerned about the desert route from Agheila or Agedabia to Mechili and Tobruk. If the Germans went that way without opposition all his troops on the coastal Agedabia–Benghazi–Derna line would be cut off. In any case there was no possibility of holding Benghazi as a fortress like Tobruk. His plan of defence therefore was to hold the front south of Agedabia with the 2nd Armoured Division, comprising all the armour and motorised infantry he had available; to occupy the escarpment north-east and east of Benghazi with the 9th Australian Division, its task being to block the only two roads up the escarp, which was the only available anti-tank obstacle; to hold Mechili with two regiments of the 3rd Indian Motor Brigade (there was not sufficient transport to supply the third regiment which remained at Tobruk); and to patrol and watch the desert routes south-west and south of Mechili. Neame hoped to be able to delay the German advance by counter-attacking in the neighbourhood of Agedabia, and then withdrawing the 2nd Armoured Division to the desert about Msus, or farther north, to deny the desert routes to the enemy. For this purpose he had prepared a large dump of petrol and water at Msus.

Meanwhile Winston Churchill expressed to Wavell on 26 March his concern at the rapid German advance to Agheila. Churchill said (*The Second World War*, Vol 3, p 178): 'I presume you are only waiting for the tortoise to stick its head out far enough before chopping it off.' Anything less like a tortoise than Rommel's highly mobile armoured divisions would have been difficult to imagine.

Wavell replied next day, 27 March, at considerable length.

He 'had to admit that he had taken a considerable risk in Cyrenaica after capture of Benghazi in order to provide maximum support for Greece. . . . Result is I am weak in Cyrenaica at present and no reinforcements of armoured troops, which are my chief requirements, are at present available'. However, he finished his cable with a sop to the Prime Minister with the words: 'But enemy has extremely difficult problem and am sure his numbers have been much exaggerated.' This was quite incorrect and very misleading. The situation reports which Neame and his own Chief Intelligence Officer had given to him were entirely correct.

Rommel's attack, which started on 31 March, was much as Neame had anticipated. It was three-pronged. On the left Rommel pushed forward down the coast road to Benghazi; his centre thrust ran via Antelat toward Msus to Mechili; and on the right no less than 200 armoured fighting vehicles moved across the desert, also directed on to Mechili.

By the evening of 31 March Neame's troops protecting the coastal road withdrew after fierce fighting. The 2nd Armoured Division withdrew to a position some twenty miles south of Agedabia. 1 April passed quietly. The enemy made contact again on 2 April. Neame visited the forward troops and found that German pressure was increasing and that an armoured fight had developed on the northern outskirts of Agedabia in which five of his precious cruiser tanks had been knocked out.

Neame then notes:

The Commander-in-Chief, Wavell, arrived by air at my HQ on the afternoon of 2nd April. He did not agree with my plans for employing the 2nd Armoured Division, which were to withdraw them from the Agedabia–Benghazi road to a more easterly location about Antelat or Msus, where they could deny the use of the desert routes to Rommel and also cover the open southern flank of the 9th Australian Division on the Er Regima position. He wished me to continue to block the road to Benghazi. Benghazi was by this time of no military use to me whatever and I had already given orders to implement the very comprehensive demolition scheme which I had prepared there. This plan was in exact accordance with my defence scheme, which I had fully discussed with the Commander of the 2nd Armoured Division.

As a consequence Wavell decided to bring General O'Connor up from Cairo and he arrived accompanied by Brigadier J. Combe on 3rd April. Meanwhile the 2nd Armoured Division had been forced eastward towards Antelat by vastly superior German armour, which threatened their complete envelopment. After discussing the situation, first with O'Connor and then with both of us, Wavell departed for Egypt, leaving O'Connor at my HQ to assist me for the next two or three days. (*Playing with Strife*)

Wavell says (*Wavell—Soldier and Scholar*, p 392) that on his arrival at Neame's HQ 'I soon realised that Neame had lost control and was making no effort to regain it by the only possible means, going forward personally. I wanted to go forward myself but no suitable aircraft was available and no one seemed to have much idea where our own troops or the enemy were. I sent a message for Dick O'Connor to come out and take over from Neame.'

Wavell does not indicate where he would have flown to if there had been an aeroplane available. All the troops were on the move. Neame's troops were doing their best 'to delay the enemy's advance over the 150 miles from Agheila to Benghazi' as ordered by Wavell on 30 March. But Neame's appreciation of Rommel's intentions was much more far-sighted and accurate than Wavell's. Neame was convinced from the start that Rommel's objective was far beyond Benghazi and might be as deep as Tobruk itself. And how right he was!

O'Connor received Wavell's message when he was having dinner in his house in Cairo and he had to leave at once. He was naturally most unhappy at the thought of taking over from another general 'in the middle of a battle which was already lost'. Moreover he was a close friend and admirer of Neame. O'Connor records: 'I thought the Chief was misjudging

Neame. I had known him in the past and thought he was first class. I therefore decided I would ask the Chief to reconsider my replacing Neame and to consider as an alternative my remaining with him for a few days. The Chief agreed to this proposition provided I remained until the situation had stabilised.' (*Wavell —Soldier and Scholar*, p 392)

O'Connor also records that Neame's plan for the use of the 2nd Armoured Division 'seemed to me to be eminently sound' and 'It seemed to me that the situation was definitely more serious than the Chief believed. Wavell continued to hope that the enemy's ultimate objective was no further east than Benghazi but I think the wish was father to the thought.'

No army commander in the middle of a critical battle in which his troops were fighting as best they could, on a plan which all of them understood, even if superior enemy forces made it difficult for them to carry it out, could have been treated worse than Neame was. His superior commander had made it absolutely clear that he had no confidence in him and had actually altered his plan of defence in the middle of the battle. Moreover he had put another general of equal rank to watch over him—but not to assume command. Fortunately Neame and O'Connor were close friends and could only do the best they could—together. Neame merely says: 'My force escaped to Tobruk by the skin of its teeth by a withdrawal of 150 miles in one night. If Tobruk had not been occupied [on Neame's orders] the fate of Egypt and the Suez Canal might have been sealed.'

In the middle of March Neame had flown to Tobruk and after a careful inspection had issued orders for it to be put into a state of defence. This included the restoration of the old Italian defences, barbed-wire fences, anti-tank minefields and, most important of all, the installation of anti-tank guns. Neame records: 'It eased my mind in captivity to know that Tobruk held out unrelieved for many months and thereby checked Rommel's advance on Egypt. For, when we were captured, we heard from German officers that Rommel's aim was, in their own words, Egypt and far beyond.'

Ronald Lewin describes this very unfortunate muddle as follows:

> Wavell should have backed Neame or dismissed him. To leave O'Connor looking over Neame's shoulder was to prevent a desert-worthy general from exercising command, and at the same time to suggest to Neame that he must maintain responsibility for the battle without his C-in-C's full confidence. There is no error a supreme commander can make more grave than to delegate responsibility with obvious doubt. Wavell also interfered with Neame's tactical instructions. Neame wanted Gambier-Parry to use the remnant of 3 Armoured Brigade in a withdrawal eastwards, to block a German advance towards Mechili. Wavell felt that this plan exposed Benghazi to an attack from the south. O'Connor, sitting in the wings, thought Neame's plan 'eminently sound', but Wavell ordered 3 Armoured Brigade, which by now was out of wireless touch with HQ 2 Armoured Division, to draw back west and south of the escarp towards Benghazi. This muddle in command at the highest level was followed by confusion among the fighting units. This was a sad day for the British. (*Rommel as Military Commander*, p 36)

'Ordres, contre-ordres, desordres' are said to follow one another automatically and the disorder which cancelled plans at the highest level percolated downwards to the fighting formations. Rommel took full advantage of the confused situation which resulted.

On 6 April Neame and O'Connor, with some of their staff, had established a forward headquarters at Marana. They left there at 8 pm to join their rear HQ at Derna and most unfortunately were captured by a German reconnaissance unit *en route*. In the early hours of 8 April General Gambier-Parry was also captured, as was Brigadier J. Combe. They were joined in captivity by Air-Marshal Boyd, who had made a forced landing in Sicily a few months earlier; later, on 23 April, they were joined by the intrepid General Carton de Wiart, VC, who had crashed into the sea off the Libyan coast when flying to Yugoslavia. De Wiart was a legendary figure, many times wounded, having lost an eye and one arm.

Neame and O'Connor continued their close friendship in captivity and were both enthusiastic escape plotters. After four unsuccessful attempts the fifth, from the Castello Di Vincigliata, organised and commanded by Neame (whose outstanding powers of leadership had never been more clearly displayed than in the prison camps) was successful on 29 March 1943. This involved an immense amount of detailed planning and exhausting physical labour, which is vividly described in Neame's exciting autobiography, *Playing with Strife*. It ends with this epilogue:

> Teach us delight in simple things
> And mirth that has no bitter springs;
> Forgiveness free of evil done
> And love to all men 'neath the sun.

Neame was appointed Lieutenant-Governor and Commander-in-Chief of Guernsey and its Dependencies on his return from captivity, was made a KBE in 1946 and retired from the service in the rank of Lieutenant-General in 1947. O'Connor was given command of 8 Corps in Field-Marshal Montgomery's Army in France in 1944, was General Officer Commanding in Chief Eastern Command India in 1945 and then commanded the Western Army in India in 1945–6, having been promoted full general in 1945. His last active list appointment was as Adjutant-General to the Forces 1946–7, and he retired from the service in 1948.

To return now to 6 April in the Western Desert, when Generals Neame and O'Connor had set off together on their fateful journey across the desert which ended in their capture. The Brigadier General Staff John Harding, with the ADC, who were following in the second car, had a miraculous escape. They eventually arrived in Tobruk, where Harding got through on the telephone to Wavell and told him that the two generals had disappeared. Wavell at once flew to Tobruk, taking with him Major-General J. D. Lavarack, the commander of the 7th Australian Division. They were met by Major-General Morshead, commander of the 9th Australian Division, whom Wavell put in command of the Tobruk defences. He appointed Lavarack temporarily in command of all the troops in Cyrenaica and Libya. Harding remained with Morshead and played an invaluable part in organising the defence of Tobruk.

In the defence plan for this all-important defended locality all the guns were allotted to anti-tank defence, as it was realised that tanks would be Rommel's chief offensive weapon. And the role of the Australian infantry was to take on the non-armoured German units. Morshead had six brigades of infantry at his disposal, four regiments of field artillery and two anti-tank regiments.

Rommel realised that his dynamic offensive could not maintain its momentum without capturing Tobruk, upon which he launched his first attack on 12 April. He was surprised at the strength of the defences and made no headway. He renewed his attack next day and then on the night of the 13th/14th he made his fiercest attack of all; but it was repulsed with heavy German tank losses. The immediate crisis in the Western Desert was over. However, in his lightning campaign Rommel had won back everything that O'Connor had gained.

Wavell wrote quite frankly: 'I have been praised for my decision to hold Tobruk but I doubt whether I really had much option. There was not sufficient transport to mount the Australian division and marching troops would have been at the mercy of an armoured force.' That is why Neame had left three Australian battalions in Tobruk in the middle of March. And he again had really no option as, with no transport, they were useless in the Desert. So out of evil came good. Those three battalions had been hard at work on the Tobruk defences.

Brigadier John Harding, who had been Chief General Staff Officer to O'Connor and Neame, was to become a Field Marshal, GCB, CBE, DSO, MC, and a baron—and one of the most distinguished British generals of the century. Small and slight in build, he had immense courage and endurance and great powers of leadership. Born in 1896, he served in World War I and won the Military Cross. He passed through the Staff College in 1928 and was made a brevet-major and brevet-lieutenant-colonel between the wars. In World War II he became a major-general in 1942 and a lieutenant-general in 1943. He was awarded the CBE, the DSO, with two bars, and the KCB. Montgomery, who had been one of Harding's instructors at the Camberley Staff College, had the highest opinion of him and gave him command of the 7th Armoured Division as soon as he took over command of the 8th Army. But it was as Alexander's Chief of Staff in Italy that Harding made such an outstanding reputation, and finally as a corps commander in Italy. After the war Harding went on from strength to strength, becoming Chief of the Imperial General Staff in 1952 and a field-marshal, and after that Governor and Commander-in-Chief in Cyprus at a very critical time. He was not only a great soldier, but a fine character, modest and charming, and giving much of his spare time to such worthy objects as the Not Forgotten Association and the Gurkha Appeal, in which endeavours I was privileged to work with him.

The burden and strain on General Wavell all this time had been really immense. And generals are only human. Defeat in Cyrenaica and Greece was followed by disaster and withdrawal in Crete and then the worrying Iraq campaign.

It was refreshing that another VC, General Freyberg, commanding the New Zealand Division in Crete, should speak his mind in no uncertain terms about the weakness of his defences. And he was in a much stronger position to do so than Neame had been because he had no compunction in also reporting direct to the New Zealand Government. Freyberg's signal to Wavell on 1 May 1941 read as follows:

Forces at my disposal are totally inadequate to meet attack envisaged. Unless fighter aircraft are greatly increased and naval forces made available to deal with seaborne attack I cannot hope to hold out with land forces alone, which as result of campaign in Greece are now devoid of any artillery; have insufficient tools for digging, very little transport, and inadequate war reserves of equipment and ammunition. Force here can and will fight, but without full support from Navy and Air Force cannot hope to resist invasion. If for other reasons these cannot be made available at once, urge that question of holding Crete should be reconsidered. I feel that under terms of my charter it is my duty to inform New Zealand Government of situation in which greater part of my division is now placed. (*The Second World War*, Vol 3)

This really did put the cat among the pigeons. On receipt of Freyberg's signal Wavell at once sent a long cable to the CIGS in London. Churchill signalled at great length to the New Zealand Government and then signalled to Wavell asking him to pass a very eulogistic message to Freyberg ending with the words: 'Throughout the whole Empire and the English-speaking world the name of New Zealand is saluted!' If Neame, when he arrived in Cyrenaica and discovered the nakedness of the land and the mammoth task he was expected to carry out, had only been a New Zealander or an Australian and sent a copy of his complaint to Wavell to his own government, how different his treatment would have been. Not that his frank report saved Freyberg from defeat, but at least the whole world knew what he was up against.

On 22 April Churchill informed Wavell that he was sending him '307 of our best tanks through the Mediterranean, hoping they will reach you around 10th May. You should furnish us with your plan for bringing these vehicles into action at the very earliest. If this consignment gets through the hazards of the passage . . . no German should remain in Cyrenaica by the end of the month of June'. It was largely owing to Churchill's courageous leadership that the Defence Committee eventually agreed to risk sending these tanks by this dangerous route. This was known as Operation Tiger and the tanks as tiger cubs.

Wavell had known for some time that Rommel would shortly be reinforced by the 15th Panzer Division and he planned to catch him unawares by a surprise attack before these valuable reinforcements arrived. In anticipation of the tiger cubs' arrival, Wavell decided to start his offensive and placed all his available tanks at the disposal of General Gott for action in the Sollum area.* With a force of 7 Armoured Brigade, mustering about fifty-five tanks, and 22 Armoured Brigade, Gott advanced on 15 May and captured Sollum and Capuzzo, the Armoured Brigade moving on to Sidi Azeiz. The enemy were quick to counter-attack and retook Capuzzo the same afternoon, inflicting heavy casualties on the Durham Light Infantry who had taken it. This enforced the withdrawal of 7 Armoured Brigade from Sidi Azeiz. However, a footing was obtained in Sollum, 500 German prisoners had been taken and considerable casualties had been inflicted on the enemy.

Wavell cabled Churchill on 18 May: 'Enemy proved rather stronger than we thought and has forced us back on defensive till Tiger cubs come into action. This will not be before end of month, and it would be better if they could be given more time to settle down but this may depend on situation. Enemy is collecting strength in forward area and may try further advance.' (*Wavell—Soldier and Scholar*, p 460)

The Tiger convoy reached Alexandria on 11 May with 82 cruiser tanks, 135 I tanks and 11 light tanks. Operation Battle-Axe started on 15 June. The whole force, comprising about 25,000 men, was under command of General Beresford-Pierse. Wavell gave as its object to defeat the enemy and drive them west of Tobruk, with which land communications must be established as soon as possible. The operation was to be conducted in three stages, the first to defeat the Axis forward forces and advance to the area Bardia–Capuzzo–Sidi Omar–Sidi Azeiz, the second to advance to Tobruk and El Adem, and the third to exploit the success up to Derna and Mechili and if possible beyond.

The first day was one of varying fortune—but if anything to Rommel's advantage. The British armour had been reduced to less than half its initial strength, whereas Rommel's had not

* Gott was another of my distinguished pupils at the Staff College.

yet been seriously engaged and his losses were very light in comparison.

On the second day a fierce tank engagement took place which went in favour of Rommel and was really the turning-point in the battle.

On the third day everything went Rommel's way and after heavy fighting the British were forced to withdraw. Battle-Axe had failed and the Western Desert Force had lost 122 officers and men killed, 588 wounded and 259 missing. Of the 90 cruiser and 100 I tanks which began the battle, 27 cruisers and 64 I tanks were lost through enemy action or breakdown. The RAF lost 33 fighters and 3 bombers.

On the German side, 93 officers and men were killed, 350 wounded and 235 missing. They began the battle with 190 tanks, of which 107 were gun tanks; 12 in all were destroyed by British action and a number of others broke down. Ten German aircraft were destroyed. Rommel said in his memoirs: 'Wavell was put at a disadvantage by the slow speed of his heavy infantry tanks, which prevented him from re-acting quickly enough to the moves of our faster vehicles. Hence the slow speed of the bulk of his armour was his soft spot, which we could seek to exploit tactically.' Battle-Axe was a sharp set-back but it was not a calamitous defeat. Rommel was extended strongly and, though he exulted in his victory, he had no hope of exploiting it or of advancing towards the Delta.

Winston Churchill, however, felt the defeat bitterly—and particularly the destruction of his tiger cubs. He writes in his *Second World War* (Vol 3, pp 308, 309):

At home we had the feeling that Wavell was a tired man. It might well be said that we had ridden the willing horse to a standstill. The extraordinary convergence of five or six different theatres with their ups and downs—especially downs —upon a single Commander-in-Chief constituted a strain to which few soldiers had been subjected. General Ismay, who was so close to me every day, has recorded the following: 'All of us at the centre, including Wavell's particular friends

and advisers, got the impression that he had been tremendously affected by the breach of his Desert Flank. His
Intelligence had been at fault and the sudden pounce came
as a complete surprise. I seem to remember Eden saying that
"Wavell had aged ten years in the night".'

On the afternoon of 21 June the Prime Minister sent over to
the War Office copies of two telegrams he had decided to send.
One was to Wavell to say that 'the public interest will best be
served by appointment of General Auchinleck to relieve you in
command of armies of Middle East', and appointing him
Commander-in-Chief in India, where he was to proceed at his
earliest convenience after handing over to Auchinleck. The
second was to Lord Linlithgow, the Viceroy of India, asking
him to inform Auchinleck that he had been selected to relieve
Wavell in the Middle East. The Prime Minister had already
been in touch with Lord Linlithgow. The latter had been
strongly opposed to this exchange. Auchinleck was the ideal
commander-in-chief for India at this particular time, when the
certainty of a war with Japan was realised by many of those in
responsible positions; and it was obvious that India would be
deeply involved as most of the troops for Malaya and Burma
would come from that country. Moreover the Indian Army was
undergoing a great expansion. Wavell was essentially a
'Westerner' soldier without anything like Auchinleck's experience of the Eastern theatre.

However, the Viceroy, having expressed his great uneasiness
and regret, finally conceded that 'On the Prime Minister's
judgement of the necessities of the situation he must express
his readiness to make any sacrifice.' (*Wavell—Soldier and
Scholar*). Amery, the Secretary of State for India, also opposed
the transfer. He thought that 'everybody would feel that India
was being saddled with a cast-off, whether for reasons of failure
or mere fatigue.' (Connell, *Auchinleck*, p 239). Dill, the Chief of
the Imperial General Staff, was so firmly against the Prime
Minister's proposed exchange of commanders that he wrote an
immediate minute to him couched in the strongest terms and

took it over to him by hand (*Wavell—Soldier and Scholar*, p 504). Dill was a friend and admirer of both Wavell and Auchinleck, particularly the latter whose career he had watched over and done his best to advance during a period of fifteen years.

Dill was a far-sighted strategist and was convinced that a war against Japan was imminent. He considered that Auchinleck was pre-eminently the right man in the right job as C-in-C India and he doubted whether he would be so ideally suited to a mechanised war in the Western Desert. He also urged that Wavell should not be sent to India and recommended that he should be brought back to the United Kingdom and given a good long rest, which he urgently needed.

Churchill replied to Dill that his reasons for sending Wavell to India were that he 'Could not have him hanging around London living in a room at his club' and that in India he could 'enjoy sitting under the pagoda tree'. (Connell, *Auchinleck*, p 239).

Wavell, however, was very soon to be involved in the command of armies in one of the most critical phases of the war in a theatre with which he was not familiar—and he was still a very tired man. What Auchinleck and Wavell thought about it all was nobody's business. They just had to do what they were told. Auchinleck expressed in forthright and forcible terms his feeling about the Prime Minister's telegram (Connell, *Auchinleck*, p 241). He realised, however, that it was an order which he must accept—and of which he must make the best. Wavell had made repeated requests for leave in the United Kingdom, which had been strongly supported by Dill. John Connell, Wavell's biographer, comments: 'The greatest of statesmen can be cruel and the most illustrious of generals can be tired and homesick. Wavell made no complaint: like the men he commanded he soldiered on. Five days after he had handed over to Auchinleck he flew to Delhi.'

Winston Churchill did not often over-rule his Chiefs of Staff on important military matters, and when he did he was usually wrong. This interchange of Wavell and Auchinleck was to have serious repercussions. Although there were very few

British generals who could have done better than Auchinleck in North Africa at that particular stage of the war, there were some—and Alexander and Montgomery were two of them. But for the war against Japan, which Dill for one knew was imminent, Auchinleck was the quite outstanding candidate for supreme British command in the Far East. There was simply no one who could compare with him—least of all a (very naturally) completely exhausted General Wavell.

With the existing shortages of trained troops, aircraft and tanks, and no British Navy at all, there was not very much that Auchinleck could have done over Malaya, but there was a great deal he would have done over Burma and it was a tragedy that he was not out there to do it.

CHAPTER THREE

The Campaign in North Africa
Second Phase

Auchinleck replied to the Prime Minister's telegram as follows: 'Thank you for your confidence in me which I shall do my best to justify. Hope to leave Simla by first available plane Friday 27 June and arrive Cairo by air 30th.' And Dill, CIGS, cabled: 'I welcome you as C-in-C Middle East. No British commander has been asked to assume greater responsibilities. You can, as you know, count on my whole-hearted support and you have my full confidence.'

At Dill's request the Director of Military Operations, General Kennedy, wrote a strategic review of the situation in the Middle East as he saw it following Auchinleck's appointment and Germany's attack on Russia on 22 June. It included the following main points:

Whether we can now hold on to the Middle East depends on one thing and one thing alone—whether the Germans concentrate seriously against us there. We are now relatively far weaker in the Middle East than we were at the beginning of the campaign last October. In a retrospect over the last few months, even making allowance for the great difficulties with which Wavell had to contend, it is clear that grave errors have been committed both in London and in the Middle East—but far worse in the Middle East than in

London. There has been a constant flow of directives and suggestions regarding both major and minor policy. The gravest mistake consists in the acquiescence by the Commanders-in-Chief in practically every suggestion which was put to them. On occasion they have expressed disagreement, but their disagreement has never been insisted upon. Much of the blame for the present situation must be laid upon the shoulders of the Commanders-in-Chief and of Wavell in particular. (*The Business of War*, p 137)

The Prime Minister lost no time in sending Auchinleck a long directive (2 July 1941). It started by hoping that 'you will consider Wilson for the Western Desert, but of course the decision rests with you'. The PM notes: 'It is much to be regretted that this advice, subsequently repeated, was not taken'. The 'suggestions' made by the Prime Minister on appointments in the field and suchlike matters posed an unfair problem to the Commander. If he did not reply, Winston repeated the 'suggestion', as he did in this case, and was offended if it was not accepted. But the main gist of his directive of 2 July was to press Auchinleck to start his offensive in the Western Desert much earlier than the latter thought advisable. Churchill said: 'It is difficult to see how your situation is going to be better after the middle of September than it is now. I have no doubt you will maturely but swiftly consider the whole problem.' (*The Second World War*, Vol 3)

Auchinleck replied on 15 July that although by the end of July he would have about five hundred cruiser, infantry and American tanks, for a major operation he would need a 50 per cent reserve, thus permitting 25 per cent in the workshops and 25 per cent for immediate replacement of battle casualties. He also stressed the importance of time for individual and collective training.

Churchill records: 'This was an almost prohibitive condition. Generals only enjoy such comforts in Heaven. And those who demand them do not always get there. It is clear from the foregoing telegrams that there were serious divergencies of views and values between us. This causes me sharp disappointment.' And Churchill notes: 'A far more serious resolve by General Auchinleck was to delay all action against Rommel in the Western Desert at first for three and eventually for more than four and a half months.' (*The Second World War*, Vol 3)

Auchinleck was beginning to realise that his command was not going to be a bed of roses and that the home front was not to be the least of his difficulties. He had begun to realise the tremendous authority which Churchill exerted, not only in the British Parliament and world affairs, but most particularly in the realm of defence. No other prime minister in our history, or in the history of the world, has ever influenced military planning, military tactics and military appointments as Churchill did. And it was in the military sphere that he was most prone to error—despite his great military capacity and experience.

Auchinleck remained commendably calm under the PM's pressure and the latter suggested that he should come over to London for a talk with him and the Chiefs of Staff. This proved very helpful and Churchill was impressed with Auchinleck's character and ability. But he was unable to persuade 'The Auk' to stage his major offensive, which was to be called 'Crusader', before 1 November. Nor could Churchill persuade him to entrust the operation to General Maitland Wilson. Auchinleck preferred General Alan Cunningham. In retrospect Churchill's selection of Wilson might have been right.

In London Auchinleck's two greatest supporters were Dill and Ismay. But Auchinleck found the continual talking and letter-writing very trying. He liked and admired the Prime Minister but found it very difficult to accept the position the latter had assumed as complete generalissimo in the sphere of military operations: however, he realised that this was something he would have to learn to put up with—up to a point.

The forces under Rommel's command had not been augmented and his Afrika Korps consisted of two Panzer divisions (15 and 21), the 90th Light Division and six Italian divisions, the XX Motorised Corps, the XXI Infantry Corps, investing Tobruk, and the garrison of Bardia.

Churchill still could not contain his impatience at the delay in launching 'Crusader' and expressed his irritation in letters and telegrams. But Auchinleck refused to be rushed. His first consideration was his selection of commanders—and some of his choices became the subject of general criticism. He nominated as GOC-in-C Western Desert (later designated Commander of 8th Army) General Sir Alan Cunningham, who had greatly distinguished himself as GOC East African Force. He was at the time fifty-four years old, slightly younger than Auchinleck himself. As the Prime Minister had 'suggested' Jumbo Wilson for this all-important appointment, Auchinleck sent him a private wire telling him why he had made this choice. Auchinleck admitted to Dill that he was handicapped by his lack of knowledge of those concerned but felt that some new brooms were required. Cunningham had under his command for 'Crusader', 13 Corps under Lieutenant-General Godwin-Austen, which comprised the New Zealand Division (Major-General Freyberg, VC), the 4th Indian Division (Major-General Frank Messervy) and the 1st Army Tank Brigade; 30 Corps (Lieutenant-General Willoughby Norrie), comprising the 7th Armoured Division (Major-General 'Strafer' Gott); the 4th Armoured Brigade Group (Brigadier Gatehouse), two brigades of the 1st South African Division (Major-General Brink) and 201 Guards (Motor) Brigade Group (Brigadier Marriott). There was also the garrison of Tobruk (Major-General Scobie) and several other armoured car and infantry formations. In reserve was the 2nd South African Division, consisting of two brigades under command of Major-General de Villiers, and the 29th Indian Infantry Brigade Group.

There was not a great difference between the two sides in number of tanks, but Rommel had an important ballistical advantage in that his tank and anti-tank guns were of 50mm (4½-pdr) and 75mm calibre. Cunningham's were 2-pdrs, both for tank and anti-tank work, and the effective armour-piercing range of this gun was 800–1,000 yards less than that of Rommel's

50mm. Rommel also had a certain number of 88mm guns which could knock out any British tank at 2,000 yards. There is no doubt, too, that at this stage of the Desert War the Germans held a marked superiority in the training and tactical handling of armoured formations.

In August Auchinleck received a letter from General 'Pug' Ismay begging him to write to the Prime Minister 'long, personal, chatty letters'. And at the same time Auchinleck had a long personal letter from Churchill, once again pressing him strongly to accelerate his date for launching 'Crusader'. He said: 'You are I am sure aware of the dangers of delay, and the very high price which may have to be paid for it.' To which Auchinleck replied: 'My dear Prime Minister, I realise to the full the need for speed and for balancing risks and I think of little else. I would however be raising false hopes if I were to say to you that I can see any prospect of carrying out a real offensive before November.'

Meanwhile Rommel was putting his Afrika Korps through a rigorous course of training directed particularly to the drill of the closest co-operation between tanks and anti-tank guns in the assault. And it was the lack of this training on the British side, due to their over-hasty preparations, that was to tell against them in the crises of the coming battle.

Towards the end of September Cunningham submitted his plan of attack to Auchinleck for approval. His object was the destruction of the enemy armoured forces, then the relief of Tobruk, followed by a vigorous follow-up designed to clear the enemy out of Cyrenaica. On 3 October Auchinleck approved the plan and 'Crusader' was ready for launching. Needless to say, Churchill involved himself at every stage with every detail of the plan and a voluminous personal correspondence on the subject continued between Churchill and Auchinleck. Churchill considered that 'Tedder's [Commander of the Air Force in Egypt] estimate of the enemy's numbers and strength actual and relative, is so misleading and relatively untrue that I found it necessary at once to send Air Chief Marshal Freeman to Cairo . . . You will find Freeman an officer of altogether larger calibre and if you feel he would be a greater help to you and that you would have more confidence in the Air Command if he assumed it, you should not hesitate to tell me so . . . Do not let any thought of Tedder's personal feelings influence you. This is no time for such considerations.'

At the end of September Cunningham's force was formally entitled '8th Army'—and what a famous name that was to become. A big explosion, however, occurred when, on 18 October, Auchinleck had written to the Prime Minister that as the cruiser tanks of 22 Armoured Brigade had arrived without having been 'modified' for the desert and the brigade must then be given an opportunity of doing a short period of training with them, the earliest date on which they could be put into battle would be 15 November. The Prime Minister was very angry at the delay and said in his reply: 'It is impossible to explain to Parliament and the nation how it is that our Mideast Armies have had to stand for $4\frac{1}{2}$ months without engaging the enemy, whilst all the time Russia is being battered to pieces.'

Here we see again how political and strategic priorities are apt to clash, and on occasions the latter have to give way. But, in doing so, the general should put his point of view quite clearly to the politician—and the soldier should not then have to take the blame if things go wrong. General Kennedy, the DMO, remarks on this particular point (*The Business of War*, p 173): 'The Prime Minister's domination over the Chiefs of Staff seemed greater than ever; and Dill [CIGS], on whom fell the whole brunt of opposing him, now began to show signs of great exhaustion.' And indeed, on 18 November, Dill was removed from his high office and replaced by Brooke.

I have already written quite a lot about Dill in this book. Curiously enough, although he was really cut out for a staff officer, he always hankered for command of troops in the field. And, contrary to general opinion, I believe he would have been a very great commander of troops in battle—if only because he would have been able to regulate his working hours to suit himself, particularly in getting to bed at a reasonable hour. Marlborough, Wellington, Napoleon, Douglas Haig, Foch,

Alexander and Montgomery—to mention only a few—always insisted on getting a good night's sleep, whatever the situation might be. Naturally the more junior (and younger) commanders had to 'make do and mend' with such sleep as the situation, and their superior officers, allowed them. I was amazed that Montgomery, even as a divisional commander in the rapidly moving Dunkirk operations, should have insisted that he should be in bed by 10 pm (*vide* his own *Memoirs*).

Dill was a Winston Churchill casualty if ever there was one. He was highly strung and of a (physically) nervous disposition and he simply could not take the erratic hours in which Winston revelled and to which he insisted that those working for him should conform. Moreover, Dill very much resented the Prime Minister's interference over his head in such matters as the appointment of commanders and the detailed tactical handling of their troops. Dill did not see the Prime Minister, as Brooke did, as a naughty child 'which has set his mind on some forbidden toy'! He saw the Prime Minister as rather a nuisance, constantly throwing spanners into the works. Dill was Brooke's friend and hero but the latter recorded in his diary that 'Dill, for all his brilliant intelligence, was temperamentally unfitted to work with anyone as overwhelming and impulsive as Churchill. In some ways he was almost too straightforward, in others too sensitive and highly strung. He became involved in incessant argument, and the clash of it both angered the Prime Minister and wore Dill down.' (*The Turn of the Tide*, p 255)

In the following December, just after Japan struck in the Far East, when Churchill was on the point of departure to visit President Roosevelt, Brooke managed to persuade him, though with the greatest difficulty, to take Dill with him as 'Head of the British Military Mission in the United States'. Brooke writes:

I had to press for this appointment and point out to the Prime Minister that, with Dill's intimate knowledge of the working of the Chiefs of Staff Committee and of our strategy there could be no better man to serve our purpose in Washington at the head of our Mission. Thank heaven I succeeded in convincing Winston, as few men did more in furthering our cause to final victory than Dill. From the very start he built up a deep friendship with Marshall [the American Chief of Staff] and proved to be an invaluable link between the British and American Chiefs of Staff . . . I look upon that half hour's discussion with Winston at 10 Downing Street on 11th December as one of my most important accomplishments during the war or at any rate amongst those that bore most fruit. (*The Turn of the Tide*, p 284)

Dill won golden opinions from the American Chiefs of Staff, who could not possibly have thought more highly of him. He died in harness in Washington following an operation.

Brooke found his new job as CIGS to be absolutely thrilling, though it constituted an enormous strain on a man approaching his sixtieth year. He got through a tremendous amount of work and yet managed to avoid becoming rushed and harassed. He was abstemious and, so far as his job would permit, kept regular hours. He insisted on making time for relaxation, walking in the Park or bird-watching. He never made Wavell's mistake in trying to defy the years by running before breakfast and strenuous horse-riding. 'Brookie', as his friends and colleagues always called him, was, however, a strict disciplinarian and very much master in his own house—and suffered no fools gladly.

But perhaps Brooke's greatest achievement was the way he handled his lord and master, Winston Churchill, and at the same time retained the trust and confidence of the commanders in the field. Brooke had a deep admiration and affection for the Prime Minister—as had Pug Ismay—without which their work with him would have soon become impossible. Brooke says in his diary: 'When it came to the political direction of the war— to seeing and expressing its broad fundamental truths in terms that men and nations could understand and translate into action—the Prime Minister had no equal.' (*The Turn of the Tide*, p 297)

But of course others—particularly such great soldiers as Dill and Auchinleck—found him quite impossible, whereas Alexander and Monty were his blue-eyed boys and managed him perfectly. But then the general war situation and the supply of up-to-date equipment—particularly tanks—had improved and they were winning.

To return now to Auchinleck's 'Crusader' operation in the desert, which started on 18 November 1941. The operation was basically a battle of tanks and it produced armoured clashes unsurpassed in violence during the whole of the North African campaign. It was also a battle between commanders in which the dynamic and experienced generals, Rommel and Cruewell, were opposed to Auchinleck and Alan Cunningham. When Rommel's command was raised to the status of a Panzer Group, General Cruewell was appointed commander of the Afrika Korps, with Bayerlein as his chief of staff.

The battle started well for Auchinleck and Cunningham, as they achieved their first object of complete surprise. The Afrika Korps was in process of taking up fresh positions for an attack on Tobruk to take place on 23 November and Rommel was on a visit to Rome when Auchinleck launched his offensive. Heavy rain had turned the German airstrips into seas of muddy water and the Luftwaffe was grounded. It was not until the afternoon of 18 November that the Panzer Group realised that the British had launched an offensive. It was not until the following day, 19 November, that the armoured battle began in earnest and developed into the struggle for Sidi Rezegh.

Auchinleck describes the situation in his final despatch, published in 1948, as follows:

Since the Panzer divisions now seemed to be committed to battle and were reported to be losing a considerable number of tanks, General Cunningham allowed the signal to be given for the Tobruk sorties to begin and for the XIIIth Corps to start operations. On 21st November however our difficulties began. The enemy, as was to be expected, reacted at once to the threat to Sidi Rezegh and his armoured divisions evaded the 4th and 22nd Armoured Brigades. The whole of the enemy armour then combined to drive us from this vital area and to prevent help reaching the Support Group and the 7th Armoured Brigade which was isolated there. Neither of these formations was designed to carry out a prolonged defence, and it is greatly to their credit that they managed to do so, unaided, throughout the 21st. The 5th South African Infantry Brigade, which was expected to reach the scene before the development of the enemy attack, failed to do so, partly owing to the opposition of the Ariete Armoured Division and partly because of inexperience in handling the very large number of vehicles with which it took the field.

Next day all three armoured brigades joined in the defence of the area. But our tanks and anti-tank guns were no match for the German, although they were fought with great gallantry, and on the evening of November 22 XXX Corps was compelled to retire, having lost two-thirds of its tanks and leaving the garrison of Tobruk with a huge salient to defend.

The enemy rounded off his success in spectacular fashion. In a night attack he surprised and completely disorganised 4 Armoured Brigade, whose hundred tanks represented two-thirds of our remaining armoured strength. On the 23rd he practically annihilated 5 South African Infantry Brigade, one of the only two infantry brigades General Norrie had under command—there was no transport for any more— and then on the 24th with his armoured divisions he made a powerful counterstroke to the frontier. Before this it had become quite clear that the first reports had grossly exaggerated enemy tank losses and that he had at least as many tanks as we had and better ones and was in a position to recover more from the battlefield, which remained in his hands. The shifting of the balance of strength between the opposing armoured forces produced a most critical situation.

During the opening phases of 'Crusader', General Cunningham had been severely handicapped by his lack of information as to how the battle was going. At last, however, on 22 November, news began to come through to his advanced Headquarters at Maddalena. By nightfall on that day he was able to get a picture of the general situation—and he found it deeply disturbing. Next day, Sunday 23 November, he paid a visit to General Godwin-Austen, 13 Corps, and by the time he got back to his own Headquarters the news was even graver than the night before. He was told that 7th Armoured Brigade had no tanks in running order and that 22nd Armoured Brigade was down to thirty. Cunningham came to the conclusion that, in view of these heavy tank losses, the enemy armour might well attack and over-run his infantry. He considered that this might give rise to a situation of such gravity that he might be forced to discontinue his offensive and adopt a more defensive attitude. He therefore sent an urgent request to the Commander-in-Chief to fly up to his headquarters immediately. And Auchinleck did so, taking Air-Marshal Tedder with him.

Auchinleck, having heard Cunningham's very pessimistic appreciation of the situation, nevertheless considered that our only course was to continue the offensive with every means at our disposal and he ordered the Army Commander to act accordingly. This was a very brave decision on Auchinleck's part but by no means a reckless one. He considered that the enemy was making desperate efforts to throw us off balance, create chaos in our ranks and so regain the strategical initiative. He admitted that the enemy had seized the local initiative but refused to admit that he had won the battle. Churchill records: 'By his personal action Auchinleck thus saved the battle and proved his outstanding qualities as a leader in the field.' (*The Second World War*, Vol 3, p 505)

Auchinleck and Tedder remained at Maddalena overnight whilst Cunningham drafted orders to comply fully with Auchinleck's orders. Auchinleck also issued a personal order of the day to the troops of 8th Army:

During three days at your Advance HQ I have seen and

heard enough to convince me—though I did not need convincing—that the determination to beat the enemy of your commanders and troops could not be greater and I have no doubt whatever that he will be beaten. His position is desperate and he is trying by lashing out in all directions to distract us from our object, which is to destroy him utterly. We will not be distracted and he will be destroyed. You have got your teeth into him. Hang on and bite deeper and deeper. Give him no rest. The general situation in North Africa is excellent. There is only one order: attack and pursue. All out everyone.

Auchinleck, however, had lost confidence in Cunningham and, that being the case, quite rightly decided to remove him immediately. He replaced him by his Deputy Chief of Staff, General Neil Ritchie. This appointment was described by Auchinleck as 'temporary'. It was the subject of criticism as such—and of still more criticism when it became permanent.

Meanwhile, Rommel, sensing that the battle had reached a critical stage, decided with typical audacity to strike across the southern flanks and communications of the 8th Army. He collected the greater part of the Afrika Korps and thrust down the El Abu road to Bir Shaferzen, narrowly missing the headquarters of 30 Corps and two great dumps of supplies, the loss of which would have been serious indeed.

Rommel's tanks crossed the frontier wire at several points and caused a good deal of damage and disturbance. They might indeed have succeeded in having a much more serious effect had it not been for the determined resistance of the 4th Indian Division, under their tough fighting commander, General Frank Messervy. As it was, Rommel's audacious gamble failed in its main object of wresting the strategic initiative from the British, and when he withdrew towards Tobruk on 27 November he had not had any considerable effect on the battle and had lost several tanks and other vehicles which he could ill spare.

Auchinleck, however, makes a pertinent remark in his

Despatch with regard to this phase of the operations:

> In spite of the gallantry with which they fought, our armoured
> troops were worsted in almost every encounter with enemy
> tanks, not only because they were relatively inexperienced,
> but also because the enemy tanks mounted guns of greater
> range. Whenever our tanks attempted to take the enemy in
> the rear, they were confronted by formidable 88mm guns to
> which we possessed no counterpart.

Although the Prime Minister cordially approved Auchinleck's action of making a change in command of the 8th Army
he was not so happy at his choice of a successor. He therefore
cabled Auchinleck on 27 November: 'CIGS and I both wonder,
as you have saved the battle once, if you should not go up again
and win it now!'

Auchinleck replied that he had given careful consideration
to this suggestion but had decided against it as he thought he
was more useful at GHQ, where he could see the whole picture.
He would, however, go forward to visit Ritchie as required.
This question of command continued to be a matter of considerable controversy. Ritchie was of course much junior to the
corps commanders, over whom he had now been promoted—
in position, if not in rank. Moreover, he had not had anything
like their experience of command. It would have been a pity,
however, to take away either of the corps commanders at this
juncture and they had not shown any signs of being outstand-
ingly suitable for army command. Ritchie, at this time only
forty-four years old, was a splendid officer of vigorous personality, fine presence and considerable general experience;
moreover, as Auchinleck's Deputy Chief of Staff, he was
intimately conversant with the plan for 'Crusader' and very
closely in Auchinleck's confidence. It was in fact the greatest
pity that some arrangement was not made by the Chiefs of
Staff whereby another commander, say General 'Jumbo'
Wilson, could have been appointed to look after the back and
northern areas, leaving Auchinleck to do the job for which he

was pre-eminently suited—the command of the 8th Army in battle himself. This reorganisation was later put into effect by the Prime Minister.

On 12 January 1942 Auchinleck wrote to the Prime Minister reviewing the situation to date and giving his intentions for the future. He wrote: 'If we are to fight the Germans on the Northern Front in the coming summer under the same adverse conditions as far as equipment is concerned, the standard of leadership and tactical handling of our armoured forces must be improved' (*Auchinleck's Despatches*). Auchinleck urged that he should be allowed to go forward with his plan for the invasion of Tripolitania. He said that with the equivalent of two armoured and four infantry divisions General Ritchie had inflicted a heavy defeat on an enemy, not only nearly equal in numbers, but possessing undoubted advantages in tanks and artillery. The 8th Army had cleared Cyrenaica and relieved Tobruk—a notable achievement. Auchinleck estimated that the enemy losses since the opening of his offensive in November were 36,000 prisoners of war, of which some 10,000 were German, and 24,000 killed and wounded, including 11,000 Germans. Over 200 German and 120 Italian tanks and some 850 aircraft had been captured or destroyed. In addition the enemy had lost two-thirds of his artillery. Our own losses came to about 18,000 officers and men out of an army of 118,000; and although our tank losses had been much heavier than the enemy's, we were fortunate in having a fresh armoured brigade in training. Moreover, many of our tanks which were out of commission could be repaired, though our recovery and repair organisation would take some time to cope with the volume of work.

Ritchie must be given credit for having taken over the army command in a very critical situation and done so well. However, Auchinleck was always at his elbow and had actually stayed at Ritchie's headquarters for the first ten days of December.

On 8 December 1941 the war against Japan had started and very soon troops which were under Auchinleck's command, or on their way to join him, were diverted to the Far East. Amongst the latter were the 18th (British) Division, under command of Major-General Beckwith-Smith, and the 17th (Indian) Division, of which I had just taken over command. Auchinleck was to suffer still further withdrawals of troops and aircraft to meet the crisis in the Far East.

Early in the New Year (1942) there had been important changes of commanders within 8th Army, affecting two of the Indian Army's finest commanders. Major-General Frank Messervy, who had been commanding the 4th Indian Division, had relieved Major-General Herbert Lumsden as commander 1st Armoured Division. The latter had been wounded in an air attack. Frank Messervy (later General Sir Frank, KBE, CB, DSO) was educated at Eton and Sandhurst, had then been posted to the 9th Hodson's Horse and served throughout World War I. He had gained admission to the Camberley Staff College in 1925-6 and, in World War II, he had first commanded a brigade at Keren before gaining command of the 4th Indian Division in 1941. Later in the war he commanded, with great distinction, the 7th Indian Division and then 4 Corps in the Arakan and in Burma, against the Japanese. He made a reputation as a tough and competent battle commander.

Major-General Francis 'Gertie' Tuker (later Lieutenant-General Sir Francis, KCIE, CB, DSO, OBE) arrived in North Africa to command the 4th Indian Division in January 1942, after being Director of Military Training in India. Had Tuker not been smitten with rheumatoid arthritis at Cassino in Italy he would undoubtedly have gone right to the top. He had the character, the knowledge, the courage and the understanding. The ill-health which came upon him suddenly, and subsequently kept recurring until it killed him, was cruel bad luck. We corresponded regularly right up to his death in October 1967. He was literally worshipped by his regiment, the 2nd Goorkhas, and was a wonderful commander and trainer—particularly of Indian troops. He was also a brilliant strategic writer and thinker. He served throughout World War I with his regiment, was at the Staff College Camberley 1925-6 (two years after I was), and was all set for great things. Between the two world wars he made a great reputation as a trainer of troops with his original mind and far-seeing view. After his first bout of illness at Cassino he recovered sufficiently to command 4 Corps during the final period of the war against the Japanese in Burma. He finished up as Commander-in-Chief Eastern Command India in 1948.

It was a pity Tuker didn't arrive in the Western Desert rather earlier than January 1942. He would have been my outstanding selection for command of 8th Army, though he was only a major-general at the time—but so was Neil Ritchie. Tuker didn't get on with Monty, but of course not everybody did. Gertie Tuker was always fearlessly outspoken—that, perhaps, was one of his failings, if indeed it was a failing. I agreed with Bill Slim in classing Tuker as one of the finest commanders of his time.

Another important change of command in 8th Army at the beginning of 1942 was in 13 Corps, in command of which Major-General 'Strafer' Gott relieved Godwin-Austen. Gott was a splendid fighting commander, also well fitted for the army command.

On 21 January Rommel launched his counter-offensive and in doing so achieved the maximum of surprise, together with the maximum of Rommel punch. The events of the next few days were momentous and, from the British point of view, disastrous. By the end of the first day the Afrika Korps, attacking with the intention of splitting the British defences, had met with only weak resistance and captured a large number of guns and vehicles. The Luftwaffe gave them strong support as, under Rommel's forceful direction, they drove forward towards Antelat and Saunnu, causing the greatest confusion amongst British supply columns and rear services. The 1st Armoured Division had a narrow escape from being completely cut off, and lost 70 out of its initial strength of 150 tanks. The British tank units, with no previous battle experience, became completely demoralised by the speedy attack of the Panzers and the 1st Armoured Division really ceased to be a coherent fighting force. On the 25th Auchinleck, accompanied by Tedder, had flown up to Ritchie's headquarters, and he remained there until 1 February.

Once Benghazi had been lost—on 29 January—Derna could not be held and the whole of Cyrenaica was again in Rommel's hands. 13 Corps withdrew to a line running south from Gazala, and here 8th Army reformed and began to construct a defensive position. Auchinleck's winter campaign on the Western front had ended and he returned to his GHQ on 1 February. He says in his Despatch (my italics):

I returned to my General Headquarters disquieted by the failure of the 8th Army to check the enemy advance. The weakness of our armour was particularly disturbing. *Whatever happened I was determined not to allow Tobruk to be besieged a second time. The configuration of the coast invited investment and with my existing resources of infantry and armour I did not consider I could afford to lock up one and a quarter divisions in a fortress.* Admiral Cunningham agreed—particularly since the siege had proved very costly in ships—and so did Air Chief Marshal Tedder, who doubted whether we had sufficient aircraft to provide fighter cover. It was still my firm intention, however, to resume the offensive and for that Tobruk would be invaluable as an advanced base. Consequently I instructed General Ritchie to make every effort to hold Tobruk, short of allowing it to become invested.

This policy with regard to Tobruk was easier said than done, as events proved, and Tobruk was to fall between two stools, being something more than a base and not quite a fortress. Auchinleck's Despatch continues:

Having studied further the problem of destroying the enemy and occupying Tripolitania I reached two principal conclusions namely that, when we attacked again we must have complete superiority in armour and that our offensive must not lose momentum as a result of inability to maintain powerful forces beyond Benghazi. To achieve this superiority we needed at least half as many tanks again as the enemy, taking into account the relative efficiency of the German tanks and our own. Over and above this we needed a reserve equal to at least twenty-five per cent of the number deployed with units. Judging from past experience the reserves should have been double that figure, but I was prepared to take that risk.

Auchinleck hoped to be able to attain this position by 1 May. Later he revised this opinion and made it 1 June. By 26 February 8th Army had prepared a defensive position, well-mined and organised in depth over an area thirty-six miles square.

The position in Malta had now become serious and General Sir William Dobbie, the Governor, reported that, even on siege rations, supplies generally would last only until June, while stocks of diesel oil for submarines were sufficient for only two months. Yet it seemed useless to attempt to sail convoys to the island since out of three ships which left Alexandria on 12 February none arrived in Malta.

The Prime Minister and the Chiefs of Staff in London were deeply disturbed to receive Auchinleck's review of the situation. They were emphatic that Malta was vital to operations in Cyrenaica and were prepared to take the most drastic action to sustain the island. It was impossible to supply Malta from the west and the only chance of sailing convoys from the east was to secure aerodromes in Cyrenaica. Accordingly they asked Auchinleck to consider carrying out an offensive in time to enable adequate air support to be given to a substantial Malta convoy in mid-April. They also informed him that it had been decided to place the military garrison of Malta under his command—and this took effect from 11 April.

Auchinleck continues:

The divergence of views between London and Cairo as to the ability of 8th Army to mount an offensive appeared to be

Page 117

(above) General
Montgomery GOC 8th
Army in one of his
familiar talks to the
troops in the Western
Desert

(right) Lieut-General
Arthur Percival GOC
in Malaya when the
Japanese invaded in
December 1941

Page 118
(*above*) General Eisenhower decorates General Montgomery with the Legion of Merit; (*below*) Lieut-General John Harding, Chief of Staff to General Alexander in the Italian campaign

too great to be settled by correspondence, and the Prime Minister requested me (by cable on 8th March) to come to England for consultation. Reluctantly and after most anxious consideration I decided that at that time it was impossible for me to leave my command, even for ten days or a fortnight, and still remain responsible for it. To the Chief of the General Staff who pressed me to go, as there were many large questions of strategy to be discussed, I was compelled to make the same reply.

It is significant that Auchinleck was not in Cairo at the time but at 8th Army Headquarters. Whatever the rights and wrongs of his decision, there is no doubt that it started the chain of events which culminated in his removal from his command five months later.

The Prime Minister was furious and wished to replace Auchinleck immediately by Lord Gort, VC, from which Brooke managed to dissuade him. The existing situation, however, between Auchinleck and the Prime Minister had become quite farcical. The Prime Minister would ask Auchinleck for his review of the situation in the greatest detail. Auchinleck would reply at enormous length. The Prime Minister would then reply at greater length, disagreeing with a lot of Auchinleck's figures. Auchinleck would then write to the CIGS—and so on, and so on, and so on. In fact the paper war had assumed more importance than the actual operation.

Pug Ismay never did a worse thing than advise Auchinleck to write to Winston 'long and cosy letters'. It started a chain of interminable correspondence. To Winston no letter from a commander in the field was 'cosy' unless it told him that our side was winning—or was going to win very shortly. Wavell's success against the Italians was kept a secret—even from the Prime Minister—and the latter never forgave him for it. Auchinleck, of course, had immense responsibilities, beyond those of 8th Army, as C-in-C Mediterranean Command and felt he had to cover them all in his reviews. Winston always focused his attention on just one thing at a time—and at that time it was Malta. So in their long paper battles Churchill and Auchinleck never really met because they were not on the same wavelength—and therefore a personal meeting was quite essential. Auchinleck had appointed in Neil Ritchie an army commander in whom Churchill and the Chiefs of Staff had no confidence: and nor had Auchinleck really, as he rushed to Ritchie's help in any emergency. Churchill was continually suggesting that Auchinleck should take charge of 8th Army himself. And it would have been much better if he had done so; but Churchill and the Chiefs of Staff should have taken steps to relieve him of all his other responsibilities. Monty would never have beaten Rommel in the desert if he had had his GHQ in Cairo and all Auchinleck's responsibilities—in addition to 8th Army. But all those were taken off Monty's shoulders by Alexander—just as Mountbatten did for Slim in Burma, allowing the latter to concentrate his attention on 14th Army.

Auchinleck was of course right in principle in maintaining that the superior commander at the back should always come forward to confer with the battle commander, not the other way round. He hated the idea of endless discussions and arguments on matters in which he considered himself to be the authority. But Winston was a law unto himself and that just had to be accepted. In World War I Douglas Haig would never have remained in the saddle as C-in-C of the British Forces in France if he had not made frequent visits to London. Rommel had nothing like Auchinleck's strategic ability and brain-power; but Rommel and Winston had one thing in common— they saw the immediate problem as a horse with blinkers sees the next fence, with eyes fixed on that and that alone; and Rommel had no greater admirer than the British Prime Minister. Winston Churchill, the greatest man of his time and a splendid national leader, was an emotional thinker—as was Alexander; they thought from their stomachs and, over the big things, they were generally right. Auchinleck and Monty thought with their heads, and they reached the right conclusions in a different way—but it took longer.

During April and the first half of May Auchinleck issued

revised instructions to 9th and 10th Armies with regard to the action they should take in the event of enemy attack through the Caucasus and the improvement of defence and communication in Iraq and Syria. He was also much concerned with the Japanese threat to India following the loss of Burma. In his very detailed review of the situation, dated 3 May, Auchinleck said: 'The matter most in my mind at the moment is the threat to India. . . . If I have to choose now between losing India and giving up the Middle East, I would not hesitate. I believe we can still hold India without the Middle East, but we cannot for long hold the Middle East without India.' This so infuriated the Prime Minister that it was only with the utmost difficulty that Brooke was able to persuade him not to demand Auchinleck's immediate recall and supercession by Alexander.

The Prime Minister, in his reply to Auchinleck dated 5 May, said: 'While we are grateful to you for your offer to denude the Middle East further for the sake of the Indian danger, we feel that the greatest help you could give to the whole war at this juncture would be to engage and defeat the enemy on your Western Front.' (*The Business of War*, p 225) The Prime Minister informed Auchinleck that, despite the risk involved, his offensive must be launched in May to save Malta and to provide a distraction to help the passage of a convoy to Malta in the dark period in June. On 7 May Auchinleck said definitely that he did not want to attack on the date arranged. He backed this decision with a detailed statement of the comparative strength of his own and Rommel's forces—particularly in tanks. General Kennedy writes:

On 8th May Brooke asked me what I thought of it all. I said we were approaching the same sort of situation with Auchinleck as we had had with Wavell towards the end of his regime, when Dill [who was then CIGS] had said repeatedly to Churchill: 'You must either back your Commander-in-Chief or sack him'. I said it would be wrong for the Cabinet to order the offensive against Auchinleck's judgement—that would put everybody in a false position. If there was reasonable doubt about the soundness of Auchinleck's appreciation, then he should be removed. Brooke said he had come to precisely the same conclusion.

On 10th May Auchinleck cabled his reply [to Churchill's cable of the 5th]. He argued that the loss of Malta would not greatly affect our position in the Middle East. This was an incredible misconception. Apart from any question of prestige, the military value of Malta was very great, not only as a check on traffic from Italy to North Africa but as a staging-point for aircraft in transit to the Middle East and India; moreover we had some 30,000 soldiers and airmen in the Island and they could not be sacrificed. He went on to say that, in any case, it would take a long time, even if he were able to advance, to get himself sufficiently established in Cyrenaica to provide air cover for convoys. Rommel, he continued, would place himself at a disadvantage if he were left to attack first, whereas if we attacked prematurely and had our armour destroyed, it would be impossible to defend Egypt. Auchinleck had stated his case badly. The manner in which he had conducted the long discussions had lost him the confidence of both the Cabinet and the Chiefs of Staff.

(*The Business of War*, p 226)

On receipt of Auchinleck's telegram of the 10th Churchill called an immediate Cabinet meeting on that (Sunday) evening. As a result the Prime Minister gave a direct order to Auchinleck to engage Rommel at latest in time for the convoy due to be run into Malta in mid-June. However, the vexed question as to when Auchinleck should start his offensive was settled—by Rommel, who decided to anticipate it himself. He moved into the attack on 26 May.

Auchinleck was now in the classic dilemma in which other commanders had found themselves when their strategical appreciation of the situation conflicted with the demands of their political masters. Knowing the strength and state of readiness of his own forces, Auchinleck was convinced that he should not launch a major offensive against Rommel until the end of June. Before that he would have much preferred that Rommel should be persuaded to attack him and give him the opportunity of making a crushing counter-stroke when Rommel had disclosed his plan of attack and was in a somewhat disorganised and strung-out situation.

Churchill, however, as has been explained, gave first priority to saving Malta, a sea-and-air operation which would be greatly assisted if 8th Army was a good deal further to the west along the shores of North Africa than it was at that time. This was an operation which could not wait until the end of June and preparations had to be made accordingly. 8th Army therefore built up large forward dumps of supplies. Thousands of tons of stores were accumulated at Tobruk and at several other forward locations. When Rommel attacked these large supply dumps, which had to be protected, they hampered 8th Army's freedom of movement and tended to disorganise the flow of supplies and munitions to the fighting troops. In fact, Auchinleck had to be prepared for two different and conflicting eventualities—first and foremost to obey 'His Master's Voice' and dispose his troops for an early offensive, and second, to keep in mind the possibility—which, in his own view and from the information he received, became more of a probability every day—that Rommel would attack him first.

As a forward protective outpost position, for an army preparing an assault, the line Gazala–Bir Hacheim was fairly adequate, with its sequence of infantry localities or 'boxes', wired and mined, though with considerable distances between them. But as a forward position for a defensive battle it was most inadequate. However, that was not Auchinleck's fault, nor Ritchie's—they had been ordered to prepare for an advance.

But Auchinleck's letter to Ritchie of 20 May, which he sent by hand of his chief of staff, General Tom Corbett, dealt entirely with the coming attack by Rommel, which Auchinleck felt was imminent. He told Ritchie that the all-important point was that he should keep his armour concentrated and '*be most careful not to commit your armoured striking force until you know beyond reasonable doubt where the main body of his armour is thrusting*' (my italics). Perhaps Auchinleck would have done better to have taken over command of 8th Army himself then rather than on 25 June—as he did—when all he could do was to stabilise the front and prevent defeat from becoming disaster.

Ritchie, however, felt that the risks involved in leaving isolated infantry formations in the desert unprotected by armour were too great. He therefore separated his two armoured divisions and thereby lost his one chance of defeating the Afrika Korps' assault.

Rommel's plan, a complete copy of which fell into British hands quite early in the battle, was, as usual, simple and precise —and entirely optimistic. On the evening of 26 May the Afrika Korps and the 90th Light Division Battle Group were to concentrate at Segnali, about opposite the centre of the British defensive position. Rommel himself proposed to move with this main striking force. On 27 May, after a night advance, the Ariete Armoured Division was to capture Bir Hacheim, on the extreme south of the British defensive position, while the Trieste Motorised Division was to make a gap in the British minefield further to the north. Simultaneously the Afrika Korps was to move by night to a forming-up position south of Bir Hacheim and then advance northward and make for Acroma, destroying Ritchie's armoured force *en route*. On 28 May the Afrika Korps was to attack the northern British position from the east, whilst four Italian divisions attacked them from the west. Rommel aimed to capture Tobruk on 30 May. Actually he didn't do so until 21 June, and in the interim much hard fighting had taken place.

Although Rommel realised at the end of the first day of the battle on 27 May that 'our plan to overrun the British forces behind the Gazala line has not succeeded' (Lewin, *Rommel*, p 115), he nevertheless stuck to his objective and continued his drive to the north on 28 May. He said, however: 'I looked forward that evening [27th] full of hope to what the battle might bring. For Ritchie had thrown his armour into the battle piecemeal and had thus given us a chance of engaging them on each separate occasion with just about enough of our own tanks. This dispersal of the British armoured brigades was incomprehensible.'

The subsequent course of the operations is written in the history books and is put particularly well in Auchinleck's admirably clear and concise despatch. He is of the opinion, as also is Rommel, that the failure of 8th Army's counter-attack on 5 June was the turning-point of the battle. On 13 June, following a final disastrous battle round the Knightsbridge box and faced by a situation of the gravest peril, Auchinleck and Ritchie ordered an immediate retreat to the Egyptian frontier. All Churchill's and Brooke's hopes for the offensive were dashed. Simultaneously the two convoys intended to revictual Malta met with disaster. On 14 June the western convoy, escorted by a battleship, two carriers, three cruisers and seventeen destroyers, was attacked from the air off Sardinia, where the heavier units of the escort, after suffering severe loss, were forced to turn back. Next day Italian cruisers and destroyers joined in the attack on the merchant ships, only two of which got through to the island. The rest were sunk. The eastern convoy never arrived at all; attacked by Italian battleships as well as by swarms of German aircraft and U-boats, it was driven back to Alexandria, after losing a cruiser and three destroyers and two of its eleven merchant ships. Thus only two out of the seventeen supply-ships sent reached Malta. The island's survival, the implementation of Brooke's plans for the re-opening of the Mediterranean and the maintenance of the British base in Egypt were all in jeopardy.

The defence, and capture, of Tobruk by the Germans on 21 June was the subject of considerable controversy. General Kennedy, the Director of Military Operations, comments:

As the battle developed Churchill sent a succession of telegrams of advice and exhortation to Auchinleck. It is such a pity that Winston's fine courage and drive cannot be harnessed to the war effort in a more rational way. A more dangerous matter at the moment [16 June] is his pressure on

Auchinleck to hold Tobruk . . . the risk Wavell had run in holding Tobruk had been justified in the end, only because of the unexpected withdrawal of the Germans from the Mediterranean for the Russian war. [This applied particularly to the withdrawal of the Luftwaffe.] The limelight had been on the place so much that its political and prestige value had now become very great; that was bound to be a real difficulty for the Prime Minister.

(The Business of War, p 224)

Auchinleck had made it quite clear as far back as January 1942 that he was not going to hold Tobruk as a fortress with a lot of men locked up inside it and air force committed to its defence, as had been done by Wavell in 1941. This had been accepted by the Chiefs of Staff. But Kennedy expresses a doubt *(op cit,* p 577n) as to whether the CIGS had ever brought this firm decision by Auchinleck, and the Chiefs of Staff agreement to it, to the notice of the Prime Minister, knowing how much against it he would have been. And General Kennedy had said in a minute to Brooke on 6 February, in support of Auchinleck's decision: 'Tobruk last year might have proved another Kut had it not been for the outbreak of the Russian war. It was moreover a great strain on the naval and air resources in the Middle East. In my opinion it would be right to avoid such detachments in future' *(op cit,* p 243). The Prime Minister, however, had strong emotional feelings about Tobruk. On 14 June he cabled Auchinleck saying he 'presumed there was no question of giving up Tobruk; as long as Tobruk was held no serious enemy advance into Egypt was possible; we went through all this in April 1941'.

On 15 June Auchinleck replied that, although he did not intend that 8th Army should be besieged in Tobruk, he had no intention of giving it up. On receipt of this cable the PM cabled (from Washington, USA) to the War Cabinet asking them to confirm that this meant that if the need arose Ritchie would leave as many troops in Tobruk as were necessary to hold the place for certain. On 16 June Auchinleck replied to the Prime Minister: 'War Cabinet's interpretation is correct. General Ritchie is putting into Tobruk what he considers an adequate force to hold it even should it become temporarily isolated by the enemy.' But on 14 June Auchinleck had ordered Ritchie 'to deny the general line Acromu–El Adem–El Gubi to the enemy. The defence of Tobruk and other strong places will be used as pivots of manoeuvre but on no account will any part of the 8th Army be allowed to be surrounded in Tobruk and invested there.'

John Connell, Auchinleck's biographer, remarks, however (p 567): 'Ritchie conferred with Gott, whose influence over him was by no means small. Their discussion was lengthy. Gott impressed on Ritchie his own view, that if Tobruk were to be held at all, it was bound to be invested; he said that there was no need to lose all Tobruk's installations and supplies and asserted that the fortress could hold out without any difficulty for two months. He persuaded Ritchie to accept these opinions and set about preparing for the siege.' It will be noted that the word fortress is used by Churchill, Auchinleck, Ritchie and Gott.

As Auchinleck notes in his despatch: 'General Ritchie put four infantry brigade groups into Tobruk with their proper complement of artillery and some infantry tanks, and kept the rest of 8th Army as a mobile force outside it. Major-General Klopper, the commander of the 2nd South African Division, was put in command of the fortress.'

However, time—and Rommel—would not wait for any man. By the 19th he had virtually surrounded Tobruk and completed his plans for its assault and capture the next day. There were three factors which led Rommel to believe that this operation would be a great deal easier and more successful than his attack on it with the Afrika Korps alone in April 1941, which had failed. First, the defences of Tobruk had been much stronger then because it was really a fortress made ready for protracted defence. Now it was not. Only fragments of the old defences remained and many of the mines had been lifted. Second, the South African commander, General Klopper, had too few fighting troops and too many base units and raw reinforcements. He had not really been organised and prepared for an assault from all sides. Third—and much the most important—was the tremendous air blitz which Rommel laid on and which had not been available in 1941 because the Luftwaffe had been withdrawn from the Mediterranean and transferred to the Russian front. In 1941 the attack on the fortress—and it really was a fortress then—had to be made primarily by the tanks of the Afrika Korps, which were foiled by the accurate and well co-ordinated artillery fire of the defence. This time the Afrika Korps was merely used for mopping up and taking the surrender of the garrison. The defences and the defenders were crushed and pulverised by a massive air and artillery bombardment. It was the German *Blitzkrieg* at its most powerful because it was concentrated so heavily and accurately on such a comparatively small area, with so little reply possible from the RAF, which was moving its aerodromes back.

All the German bombers in North Africa and some from Greece and Crete were employed. For close support the captured landing grounds at Gazala and El Adem were invaluable. The withdrawn Desert Air Force could not hope to counter so massive a concentration. And the entire German and Italian artillery joined in the cannonade, which started at 5.20 am on 20 June.

Rommel's tanks entered the town of Tobruk during the evening of the 20th and next morning he accepted General Klopper's surrender with over 25,000 prisoners and a great mass of stores and equipment. No blame can be attached to General Klopper. He had wanted to try and break out on the early morning of the 21st; but his transport had all been destroyed or captured. The swiftness and completeness of the fall of Tobruk came as a very great shock to the Prime Minister, who was given the first information of it by the President of the United States in Washington on the morning of 21 June. It also came as a great shock to Auchinleck who reacted with his usual complete coolness and courage. He at once made plans to withdraw to Matruh. Rommel was determined to press the British hard and prevent them from reforming. By the 23rd Rommel's forward troops were in touch with the British in front of Sollum.

The enemy began his advance into Egypt on the 24th and by the 25th had come within forty miles of Matruh. The depleted British infantry divisions, under 10 Corps HQ (General Holmes), which had recently come from Syria, were taking up positions round Matruh and hastily extending the minefields. 13 Corps (General Gott), which had the 1st Armoured Division and was being reinforced by the New Zealand Division, was watching the southern flank. General Norrie, with 30 Corps HQ, was organising the defence of the El Alamein position and had under his command the 1st South African Division and such other troops as could be collected.

On 25 June Auchinleck decided that the position of 8th Army was so critical that he must assume command himself. He says:

I took this step with great reluctance as I knew well that one man could not carry out the duties of Commander-in-Chief and Commander of 8th Army with full efficiency. Moreover I had grave doubts as to the wisdom of changing commanders at so critical a time. I appointed my Chief of the General Staff, Lieutenant-General Corbett, to be my deputy at GHQ in Cairo and instructed him to deal with all matters except those of the highest strategical or political import. I then flew to the advanced headquarters of 8th Army and took over direct command from General Ritchie the same evening.

The Prime Minister gave his unqualified approval and support to this decision.

Brooke has this to say with regard to Ritchie:

I am devoted to Neil and hate to think of the disappointment this will mean to him. He had been my Chief of Staff in France in 1940 through all the Dunkirk days and on my return to France through Cherbourg. I had the very highest opinion of him; but to my mind he should never have been given command of the 8th Army at the time he was appointed to it. He had never yet commanded even a division, let alone a Corps. To be given an Army command in an emergency at that stage of his career was testing him too highly. When he returned to England I posted him back to a division to regain confidence in himself and he very shortly afterwards qualified for a Corps which he commanded admirably. It was a great pity he was ever placed in such a position. . . . A very fine man who did a wonderful 'come-back' after suffering a serious blow. (*The Turn of the Tide*, p 410)

He finished up as General Sir Neil Ritchie, GBE, KCB, DSO, MC, full of honours and universal esteem. I personally always thought highly of him and liked him immensely.

So Auchinleck was back where he really belonged, in command of an army in battle, faced with critical situations and critical decisions. To his everlasting credit during the next few weeks he produced order out of chaos and by the end of July he had wrested the initiative from Rommel, brought the latter's offensive to a complete standstill and created a breathing space for the Allied forces. And he had done it not by plugging holes in leaky defences but by punching holes in the Afrika Korps and knocking them back on their heels. Rommel himself admitted that the man who blunted his spearhead in the early days of July, and made this the beginning of the end for him in North Africa, was Auchinleck (Lewin, *Rommel as Military Commander*). It is a measure of Rommel that he could recognise with generosity the achievement of a worthy opponent and of some flaw in Montgomery's humanity that he could not allow the glow of his own achievement to be shadowed by his predecessor's success.

Auchinleck says in his despatch:

By mid-September 8th Army might be expected to be reinforced by two armoured and two infantry divisions and might then be able to make a frontal attack against what was likely to be a highly organised defensive position. Our immediate task was to re-organise and re-arrange our forces so as to provide an adequate reserve in the hands of the Army Commander, and to train the new divisions intensively for the offensive which I hoped might begin at the end of September. During July 8th Army took 7,000 prisoners; and although it had lost in battle some 700 officers and 1,200 men during that period, by supreme efforts it has stopped the enemy's drive on Egypt and laid firm foundations on which to build our future counter-stroke.

In the first week in August Churchill went out to Cairo full of plans for changes of commanders and of their responsibilities. He had with him Brooke, the CIGS, and he also asked General Smuts, in whose judgement he had great confidence, to join him from South Africa. Churchill had been informed that Auchinleck was anxious to lay down command of 8th Army and return to his wider sphere in Cairo (*The Second World War*, Vol 4). So the first task was to choose a new commander for 8th Army. The Prime Minister suggested Gott. Brooke had the highest opinion of this brilliant desert battle commander but considered he really needed a rest and thought that it should be Montgomery. However, the PM had the last word and it was Gott.

The Prime Minister had now come to the very wise decision that the Middle East Command should be reorganised into two separate commands:

1   The Near East Command, comprising Egypt, Palestine and Syria, with its centre in Cairo.

2   The Middle East Command, comprising Persia and Iraq, with its centre in Basra or Baghdad.

The 8th and 9th Armies fell within the first and 10th Army within the second. The Prime Minister remarked: 'Our proposal to divide the Middle East Command is made entirely on merits. I doubt if the disaster would have occurred in the

Western Desert if General Auchinleck had not been distracted by the divergent considerations of a too widely diverged front.' (*The Second World War*, Vol 4)

What a pity this quite obvious change was not thought of earlier! It would have been of enormous assistance to both Wavell and to Auchinleck in limiting their responsibilities to manageable proportions.

The Prime Minister informed Brooke that he had decided to remove Auchinleck from his command and would like Brooke to take over the new Near East Command. Brooke was very tempted to accept and he would have done it very well but he considered he would be of greater service by continuing as CIGS. Brooke records: 'The PM was not pleased with my reply but accepted it well.' Brooke had managed to get on with the Prime Minister as others might not have been able to do. Also he would have been only human if he had not given a passing thought to the graveyard of reputations of British army commanders since the beginning of the war—Gort, Neame, Wavell, Percival, Hutton, Cunningham, Ritchie, Auchinleck. It was a short life at the top for the battle commanders, and there was much more continuity amongst the Chiefs of Staff in Whitehall.

The Prime Minister then offered the Near East Command to Alexander, who was at that time serving under Eisenhower as GOC the British 1st Army in 'Torch'.* Alexander was succeeded in 'Torch' by General Anderson. It was decided that the Middle East Command should be offered to Auchinleck. It was also decided that General Corbett (CGS Near East), General Ramsden (30 Corps) and General Dorman-Smith (Deputy CGS Near East) should all three be relieved of their appointments. General McCreery was appointed Chief of Staff to General Alexander and General Lumsden to the Command of 30 Corps. All these decisions received the approval of the Cabinet.

On 7 August, however, General Gott was shot down and

* Torch was the Anglo-American invasion of French North Africa under Eisenhower.

killed whilst flying to Cairo. The unanimous choice as to his successor to command 8th Army was General Montgomery. He was ordered to fly out to Cairo immediately. Brooke had at last got the two men he wanted—Alexander and Montgomery—in the two top fighting commands. The Prime Minister now had the unpleasant task of informing General Auchinleck that he was to be relieved of his command and, on 8 August, he sent Colonel Ian Jacob (later Lieutenant-General Sir Ian Jacob, GBE) to him with a personal letter, which also offered him the new Middle East Command. Jacob returned the same evening, reporting to Churchill that Auchinleck had received this stroke with soldierly dignity but was unwilling to accept the new command. (*The Second World War*, Vol 4)

Brooke's diary states: 'The removal of Auchinleck from his command was, for all concerned, a most distasteful decision. Everyone admired him as a man of the highest character and splendid talents' (*The Turn of the Tide*, p 450). Sir Ian Jacob records: 'When I delivered to Auchinleck the Prime Minister's letter of dismissal I felt as if I were just going to murder an unsuspecting friend. He opened the letter and read it through two or three times in silence. He did not move a muscle and remained outwardly calm and in complete control of himself. I could not have admired more the way General Auchinleck received me and his attitude throughout. A great man and a great fighter.'

This was the most bitter moment of Auchinleck's life. Truly, the higher they rise the harder they fall. He had previously achieved his life's ambition—the appointment of Commander-in-Chief in India. Although he resented very much being so swiftly uprooted from this appointment he was very naturally flattered, as an Indian Army soldier, at being offered the highest fighting command then existing in the Allied cause. It was a great challenge which, after the first disappointment at leaving his Indian command had passed off, he accepted with the greatest enthusiasm. He threw himself into the assignment with everything that his character, his fine intelligence, and his military dedication could offer. And then, to find at the end of a very hard road, when he felt confident that he had mastered Rommel, that he was returned to India as a distinguished failure, was almost more than he could bear. And the last deadly blow at much the same time was the break-up of his marriage.

This disaster was not all Jessie Auchinleck's fault. Marriage was meant for being together. Archie Wavell had had one great advantage over 'The Auk'. Wherever he went, come wind or fair weather, in peace or in war, Lady Wavell went too. Claude Auchinleck abided by the 'Queensbury rules'—and suffered a knockout.

On 18 June 1943, an official statement from 10 Downing Street announced that Field-Marshal Wavell was to succeed the Marquess of Linlithgow as Viceroy of India and that General Sir Claude Auchinleck would assume the appointment of Commander-in-Chief in India. There was tremendous rejoicing at this appointment from all 'The Auk's' friends and admirers—and most particularly from the Indian Army. He was to become not only the last—but probably the finest—commander-in-chief in India. I can only repeat what Sir Ian Jacob said of him when he received his dismissal as GOC Middle East Command: 'He was a great man and a great fighter', to which I would add—and one of the finest organisers and administrators of his time.

Page 135
(*left*) Major-General 'Taffy' Davies, Chief General Staff Officer to General Hutton and General Slim in Burma in 1942 and then Commander 25th Indian Division

(*right*) Major-General 'Punch' Cowan, Chief of Staff to Major-General Smyth in Burma in 1942 and then Commander 17th Indian Division

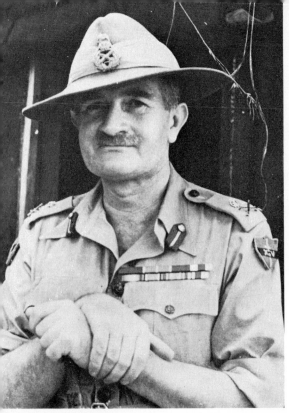

Page 136
(*left*) General Bill Slim GOC 14th Army, which conquered the Japanese in Burma

(*below*) Admiral Mountbatten Supreme Commander South-East Asia talking to the American General Stilwell in Burma

CHAPTER FOUR

Disaster in the Far East

The period from December 1941 to May 1942 was the most disastrous six months in World War II for the Allied cause—and particularly for the British. When the Japanese launched their aggression in the Far East it was quite obvious to the Chiefs of Staff in Washington and London that, with the resources they had available, as compared to those the Japanese could put into the field, there would have to be a period of 'make do and mend'; some stern rearguard actions would have to be fought and almost certainly some setbacks would be suffered before the tide in the Far East could be turned. The field commanders in the Philippines, in Malaya and in Burma were just very unlucky that they were faced with these situations.

The chief reasons for this state of affairs as far as the British were concerned were the losses they had sustained in men and material at Dunkirk; the losses in aircraft they had suffered in supporting the BEF and the French Army in France in 1940; and the losses in aircraft in the Battle of Britain. The British Fleet, which was supposed to steam at full speed for Singapore in the event of a Japanese threat of invasion, was non-existent so far as the Far East was concerned. They were more than fully occupied in Western waters. The two battleships—*Prince of Wales* and *Repulse*—which were sent to Singapore at the last moment, with no air cover, in a vain attempt to intimidate the Japanese, were just hostages to fortune. And their sinking on

137

10 December by Japanese torpedo bombers in a little over an hour, for the loss of only three aircraft, was the greatest morale-booster the Japanese could possibly have had—and it was presented to them on a plate. It was of course quite inevitable by all the rules of modern warfare, which does not allow battleships with no air cover to operate against an enemy in possession of complete air superiority.

The reason why General Percival in Malaya was so short of trained troops, and had no tanks at all—whilst the Japanese invaders had 300—was the low priority given to the Eastern Theatre by the British War Cabinet. Malaya came only fourth, behind Britain herself, the Middle East and Russia. The cream of the Indian Infantry reinforcements went to the 4th and 5th Indian Divisions in the Middle East: Malaya had to make do with the second-line infantry, some brigades of which had been reported as unfit for operations against a first-class enemy without considerably more training. The official history, *The War against Japan*, has this to say: 'Before the war spread to the Far East, the defence of Britain and the Middle East had been given precedence over those areas where war, though growing ever more probable, was not yet certain. As a result, in December 1941, the garrisons in Malaya and Hong Kong fell far short of the strength necessary for their security.'

Years before the war started the British Chiefs of Staff had realised that a Japanese attack on the important naval base of Singapore would not come directly on to the island under the noses of the formidable-looking naval guns which had been established there, but from the northern shores of Malaya. It became apparent therefore to the Army and Air Force commanders in the Far East that the defence of the naval base at Singapore did in fact involve the whole of the Malayan peninsula. Moreover, in the review of imperial defence made by the British Chiefs of Staff in 1937, they urged that no consideration for the security of British interests in the Mediterranean should be allowed to interfere with the despatch of a fleet to the Far East in the event of a Japanese threat against Singapore.

However, in August 1940 the Chiefs of Staff officially recognised that it would be impossible to send a fleet to the Far East and they also recognised that the Japanese advance southward, giving increased range to their aircraft, had all contributed to the development of the overland threat to Malaya. They realised therefore that the whole of Malaya would have to be held, with reliance primarily on air power, in order to defend the naval base at Singapore.

The role of the British land forces was defined as, firstly, the close defence of the naval and air bases; secondly, internal security; and thirdly, the defeat of any enemy land forces which might gain a footing on the mainland despite the action of the Air Force. It is important that this order of priorities should be kept in mind because it was on them that the plan of defence was made. It was estimated that 336 first-line aircraft would be required for this task. Two hundred Hurricane aircraft had been lost in the operations leading up to Dunkirk, and the Battle of Britain was then at its height, so it was obvious that no aircraft would be available for Malaya in the near future. It was laid down therefore that the air defence programme for Singapore should be completed by 1941.

In September 1940, Japanese troops occupied the northern portion of French Indo-China, which gave them a base within close striking distance of Malaya. This altered the whole conception of the defence problem because a Japanese invading force could no longer be attacked at sea on the voyage from Japan. On 16 October 1940 the commanders of the three services in Singapore recommended therefore that the figure of 336 first-line aircraft should be increased to 556. The fact that Japan had also, in September 1940, signed a tripartite pact with Germany and Italy and despatched naval and military missions to Berlin should have alerted the British War Cabinet to the fact that the Japs meant business. Yet when the balloon went up on 8 December 1941 Percival had only 140 second-class aircraft at his disposal. Moreover, it soon became impossible to reinforce him by air because the Japanese had captured the southern Burma aerodromes and cut the air route to Singapore. The Defence Plan therefore never got off the ground.

However, up to the last moment air reinforcements had been expected, so Percival had to dispose a considerable part of his strength with a view to protecting the aerodromes. But it would in any case have been necessary for him to hold most of Malaya if only to prevent the enemy from landing and establishing aerodromes. If he could have been told in good time that the Air Defence Plan could not be implemented he would have taken up more suitable ground dispositions.

Since August 1941 Percival had anticipated that the Japanese would make their main landings at Singora and Patani and had urged that he should be permitted to move into southern Thailand beforehand so as to oppose the Japanese on the beaches when they would be most vulnerable. The British and American governments were both most anxious that they should not be charged with being aggressors. And the Thai government, being much more frightened of the Japanese than anxious to help the British, declared its strict neutrality and its determination to oppose any troops entering its country—though it did not oppose the Japanese.

The Commander-in-Chief Far East, Air Chief Marshal Brooke-Popham, under whose command Percival operated, was therefore given very strict orders that there was to be no move into Thailand without the permission of the War Cabinet in London. A plan was evolved under the code name of 'Matador' whereby a mobile force was held in readiness to move into Thailand at the appropriate moment. If Matador could not be launched in time, a covering position further south would be held to oppose the Japanese advance. This, of course, was all most unsatisfactory both for Percival, with his paucity of troops, and for the divisional commander whose task it was to operate the two alternative plans.

Sir Robert backed Percival strongly with the Chiefs of Staff in his urgent requests for seventeen more infantry battalions and two tank regiments. These were his minimum requirements for the defence of Malaya—in addition of course to the large air reinforcements he had been promised. It must be made quite clear, however, that the big decision as to whether 'Matador' could be implemented or not was to be taken at the highest level between the Commander-in-Chief Far East and the British Chiefs of Staff.

In November 1941 Japanese aircraft began to fly over British territory, both in Malaya and Burma. It was obvious that they were on photographic reconnaissances which would not have been undertaken unless an invasion was imminent.

On 3 December the battleship *Prince of Wales* and the battle-cruiser *Repulse*, escorted by four destroyers but with no aircraft carrier, arrived at Singapore. This was a great morale-raiser for the British but didn't worry the Japanese in the slightest. They knew much too much about their own superior air strength and that battleships could not live in narrow waters against modern bombers and torpedo bombers. And the gallant and highly efficient Admiral Sir Tom Phillips, who commanded the battleships, was well aware of this also. It had now become obvious to the Chiefs of Staff in London, as well as to the British commanders in Malaya, that a Japanese invasion was imminent. They therefore, on 5 December, authorised Sir Robert to launch 'Matador' without reference to London if he had information that a Japanese expedition was approaching with the apparent intention of landing in south Thailand or if the Japanese had already violated any other part of Thailand.

But the Chiefs of Staff had so worded their instruction that the chances of its success were greatly reduced, for it would be too late to take action by the time Brooke-Popham could be absolutely sure that a Japanese expedition was making for the Isthmus of Kra.

Perhaps if Nelson had been the C-in-C at that critical moment he would have read the instruction with his blind eye and given 'Matador' the 'Go' signal immediately. What a difference it would have made to the start of the operations—and even then they would only just have been in time. Large Japanese convoys were sighted on the 7th, but they might possibly have been making for the anchorage at Koh Rong on the west coast of Indo-China, so Brooke-Popham felt that, within the terms of his instruction, he would not be justified in launching 'Matador'.

General Heath commanding 3 Corps was, however, ordered at 10.30 pm to stand by for 'Matador'. And then soon after midnight Brigadier Key commanding 8 Indian Brigade at Kota Bahru in north-east Malaya reported that the Japanese were landing on the beaches. The Japanese Imperial General Headquarters had detailed the 25th Army (Lieutenant-General Yamashita) to undertake the invasion and occupation of Malaya. This Army was composed initially of the 5th and 18th Divisions, the Imperial Guards Division and the 56th Division. They were experienced and highly trained formations which had, over a period of four years, taken part in operations in China and were fully practised in making landings and in jungle warfare. The 5th Division was to act as the spearhead of the invasion and effect the main landings at Singora and Patani and the 56th Infantry Regiment of the 18th Division was to make a subsidiary landing at Kota Bahru. These landings were to take place simultaneously in the night of 7/8 December 1941.

Major-General Murray-Lyon commanding the 11th Division was kept in a state of suspense and uncertainty for two days about 'Matador' and then ordered to carry out the alternative plan too late for it to succeed.

The Japanese landings in the main beaches had been unopposed. Percival's forces had got off to a bad start, through no fault of his, from which they never really recovered. Within forty-eight hours the Japanese had obtained complete air and sea control over Malaya and two days later the great British battleships *Prince of Wales* and *Repulse* were attacked and sunk by Japanese torpedo bombers.

From then on the general pattern of the Japanese advance was simple and most effective. They concentrated all their effort on the western coast line where road communications were best and they could use their command of sea and air to turn the flanks of every defensive position. They used their tanks boldly to spearhead their attacks.

Although the British, Australian and Indian troops of Percival's command were mostly only semi-trained and inexperienced, he had some fine divisional, brigade and battalion commanders. But the dice were loaded heavily against them. No commander could have handled an almost hopeless situation better than Percival.

It is not the purpose of this book to describe the operations in Malaya. I have done that in a separate book (*Percival and the Tragedy of Singapore*). Suffice it to say that the British Chiefs of Staff never considered that Malaya could be held with the forces available (*The Turn of the Tide*). And General Sir John Kennedy, the Director of Military Operations at the War Office, wrote as follows: 'Our view was that the "Last ditch" in the defence of Singapore would have to be on the mainland of Johore and not in Singapore Island. The Island had never been considered defensible from close attack—the channel was narrow, mangrove swamps impeded the fire of the defences; and the aerodromes, water supply and other vital installations were within artillery range from the mainland.' (*The Business of War*).

Could anything have been done to save Malaya? Not really, 'with that wind blowing and that tide'. Higher priority could of course have been given to it much earlier, but it would have had to be at the expense of the Mediterranean theatre and Russia. Certainly the loss of Singapore came as a very great shock to Churchill, and he said afterwards that he had never been warned of its weakness. That may have been true. But he was a difficult man to warn about something he didn't want to hear. Alanbrooke thought that Winston's priorities were probably right. But it was not possible to have it both ways—and Singapore had to be sacrificed, as did Burma also.

The Chiefs of Staff could not be accused of lack of foresight over Malaya. Well before the war started General Sir John Dill (then Director of Military Operations) had realised how vitally important Singapore was going to be and he wanted the officer of whom he thought most highly, Colonel Arthur Percival, to study the problem at first hand and give him an expert opinion (*The Turn of the Tide*, p 264). He therefore sent

Percival out as General Officer First Grade Malayan Command
in 1936.

The plan which Percival put forward then for the defence
of Singapore was, in the main, the one finally adopted and it
was accepted by the Chiefs of Staff. The only trouble was that
the troops and the air forces required to make it practicable
were just not available.

In 1937 Dill brought Percival back to England as Brigadier
General Staff of his own Aldershot Command, took him across
to France with 1 Corps when war was declared, then gave him
command of a division and, in March 1941, promoted him to
lieutenant-general above the heads of all his contemporaries
and sent him out as General Officer Commanding Malaya. At
that time Dill considered Percival to be one of the finest
soldiers in the British Army and he was grooming him to
succeed him one day as CIGS.

However, as the commander of what Winston Churchill
considered the greatest disaster in our history, Percival was
given all the blame. How much of this was just? He was in no
way a striking personality; he lacked the panache of Montgomery, the immaculate perfection of Alexander, or the
bulldog dourness of Bill Slim. He was in appearance thin and
rather insignificant. But beneath his quiet exterior was a core
of steel and he was a man of immense courage. In World War I
he commanded every unit from a platoon to a brigade, won
two DSOs and an MC and gained the reputation of an intrepid
leader of troops in battle. After the war he was an outstanding
battalion commander and gained golden opinions as a student
and instructor at the Staff College Camberley from Generals
Ironside and Dill.

There can have been few campaigns in our history in which
the general on the losing side had so few opportunities of turning
the tide as in Malaya. The complete command of air and sea
which the Japanese achieved within the first forty-eight hours
of the campaign put generalship at a discount. Montgomery
has so rightly said that there is no greater morale-raiser than
unbroken victory. And he himself proved that this was true.

But what about unbroken defeat? Where does that get you? Communications by road, rail, air and radio were bad. The troops were spread over a wide area and command had to be decentralised. Those who were in close touch with Percival spoke highly of him. All he could do in the circumstances was to try to gain as much time as he could for reinforcements to arrive. And he managed to get several important convoys into Singapore under the noses of the Japanese bombers, almost entirely without loss. But all these last-minute reinforcements were much too late. If the 18th British Division and the two brigades of the 17th, with a number of other miscellaneous formations, could be made available in January and February 1942 they could have been made available in 1941, when they might have been of some use.

The most serious misconception was made with regard to air reinforcements. By capturing the British aerodromes in Lower Burma as a first priority, early in the operations, the Japanese effectively cut the air route to Singapore and thenceforward aircraft could get there only by sea in crates, and even then under difficult and hazardous conditions. In fact it was not until the middle of January 1942 that fifty-one crated Hurricane aircraft, with twenty-four pilots, arrived in Singapore by sea, with one infantry brigade of the 18th Division.

The final withdrawal of the Malayan Command troops from the mainland into Singapore island took place on the night of 30/31 January 1942. The Japanese, with their complete command of the sea and air, could have made their attack on Singapore island anywhere. Percival was convinced that they would make their main assault down the west coast of Malaya— ie, against the north-west side of the island—and it was this area he gave to General Gordon-Bennett and his Australians to defend. And it was there that the main threat came.

The outcome is a matter of history. The Japanese assault, preceded by a very heavy artillery bombardment, started on the night of 8 February—and was devastatingly successful— and on Sunday the 15th, with the Japanese Air Force in complete command of the skies and with his water, petrol, food and ammunition practically finished, Percival was forced to surrender.

Wavell had flown out to India at Churchill's request in July 1941 to take up the post of Commander-in-Chief. He had, however, no operational responsibility of any kind at that time —except that India was the source of the supply of troops in the Middle East and Malaya. He had last served in India thirty years earlier and was unfamiliar with the Eastern scene. He had never been east of Calcutta. He did not know Burma, Malaya, Thailand or the Dutch East Indies and knew nothing of Japan or China. His knowledge of Indian troops was confined to the 4th and 5th Indian Divisions which had served under him in the Middle East. These fine divisions were the elite of the Indian Army and they had the first priority for everything in the way of reinforcements of officers and men and equipment which India could supply. Wavell had a deep affection and great admiration for these two divisions—particularly the 4th, which he knew best. He was apt thenceforward to regard all Indian troops as being up to this standard and did not realise that many of those troops which were sent to garrison Malaya and Burma were perforce of a much lower standard of fighting efficiency.

To meet all these requirements the Indian Army had, by 1941, already expanded to at least four times its peacetime strength. This expansion had led inevitably to an extensive withdrawal of regular and experienced officers and men from existing units so as to provide a nucleus for newly formed units— a process known as 'milking'. Not only were Indian Army units destined for Malaya milked heavily before leaving India, but the milking process continued after their arrival in Malaya. This fact alone shows the very low priority given to the defence of Malaya. And in addition there was a great shortage of weapons and equipment.

Perhaps the two most serious weaknesses in most of the Indian battalions were the shortage of junior British officers who knew their men and could talk their language, and the inexperience of many of the Indian officers. But these failings and shortages did not apply to the senior commanders and staff officers, who were prewar regulars of a high standard. 3 Corps Commander, Lieutenant-General Sir Lewis Heath, although not Staff College trained, was an officer of great experience and high repute. He had distinguished himself earlier in the war at the battle of Keren and been awarded the KBE. Major-General Barstow, who commanded the 9th Division, was an Indian Army officer of wide experience who had been at the Camberley Staff College with Percival and myself. He was unfortunately killed in an ambush on 20 January 1942. Murray-Lyon, the first commander of the 11th Division, was a gallant officer who some years before the war had transferred from the British to the Indian Army. Major-General B. W. Key—who, like Barstow, was in my own battalion of the 15th (later 2/11th) Ludhiana Sikhs—commanded both 8 Infantry Brigade and the 11th Division with great distinction. And Major-General H. Gordon-Bennett, who commanded the 8th Australian Division, had gained a high reputation for courageous and forceful leadership in World War I. After that war he had returned to civilian life and then, still only fifty-two years of age, attained command of the 8th Division.

Wavell was always an intrepid air traveller and, on arrival in India, lost no time in paying visits to Burma and Malaya; but he never managed to appreciate the urgency or the potential danger of the Japanese threat. As a result of his second visit to Malaya in early November 1941 he wrote a brief note to Auchinleck on the 8th of that month (only a month before Pearl Harbour and the invasion of Malaya), in which he said: 'I should think the Jap has a very poor chance of successfully attacking Malaya and I don't think myself there is much prospect of his trying' (John Connell *Wavell—Supreme Commander*, p 41). Yet all informed opinion had considered for months previously that a Japanese attack on Singapore was inevitable and imminent.

General Percival could have told Wavell that there was every indication that a Japanese invasion was imminent.

Japanese aircraft were beginning to fly over British territory, both in Malaya and Sarawak. They flew high and it was impossible to intercept them but it appeared obvious that they were engaged in photographic reconnaissance and no nation would risk creating a diplomatic crisis in this way, and at this particular time, unless it was prepared for war. But the low opinion that General Wavell had formed of the Japanese characterised all his thinking; it continued right up to the fall of Rangoon and led him into serious misappreciations of vital situations. Nigel Nicolson, author of the excellent book *Alex— The Life of Field-Marshal Earl Alexander of Tunis* (1973), wrote that 'Wavell despised the Japanese Army'.

On 12 December Burma was put under General Wavell's command and on 30 December he became Supreme Commander of the Allied Forces in the South-West Pacific, the so-called ABDA Command (American, British, Dutch and Australian). This was indeed a thankless task in the existing circumstances, with the Japanese sweeping across South-East Asia; but Wavell took it on with his usual complete imperturbability, merely remarking: 'I have heard of having to hold the baby but this is twins.'

Wavell was the last person to question any assignment he was given, however unwelcome and unwise he may have considered it to be. This applied to his appointment by Churchill to the India Command and now to this vast and complicated ABDA Command, which lasted only six weeks and did not further the Allied cause in any way. During these six weeks India was left without a commander-in-chief and a chief of staff, as Hutton had (most unwisely) been sent to Burma. General Sir Henry Pownall, who had only just relieved Air Marshal Sir Robert Brooke-Popham as Commander-in-Chief Far East in Singapore, was taken away by Wavell to be his own Chief of ABDA Staff. Pownall was a very capable officer and it would have been much more logical to make him Army Commander in Burma and to leave Hutton in India.

Field-Marshal Alan Brooke recorded on 17 December: 'Personally I feel there is not much hope of saving Singapore but feel that we ought to try and make certain of Burma' (*The Turn of the Tide*, p 295). Brooke obviously considered that the British 18th Division would be more useful in trying to make certain of Burma than in being thrown into a rapidly deteriorating situation in Malaya. However, this was a matter left for Wavell's own decision.

Wavell made his first visit to Malaya as Supreme Commander on 7 January 1942. After a succession of grim withdrawals, and with no British aircraft in the sky over the area of operations, the situation was serious and most of the troops were fought to a standstill.

Major-General Key, who commanded first 8 Indian Infantry Brigade, and then the 11th Indian Division, extremely well through the campaign, wrote:

Wavell had been a wonderful soldier and I had the greatest regard for him but in Malaya he hardly uttered and was not inspiring. He was inclined to adopt the attitude that the Japs were a rabble—and why couldn't we stop them? But you and I knew that they were fine soldiers and fanatics. When the Japs had landed in Singapore Island and were approaching the Ford Works Wavell issued an 'Order of the Day' saying it was time for the commanders to get out in front of their troops and lead them etc. etc. In 11 Div I refused to send it out to my commanders as they were first class. (Letter to the author, 29 December 1969)

Most of the other commanders took the same line with regard to Wavell's wounding last message. They tore it up and got on with the job.

Wavell was very critical of Percival, his main criticism being that the Japanese were second-rate soldiers and why couldn't he defeat them? Wavell's biographer John Connell posed two questions: should Wavell have replaced Percival on his first visit to Malaya as Supreme Commander in January 1942? Working on the principle of 'sack him or back him' he probably should have done so, but as the Malayan situation was at the time far the most important issue in his ABDA Command he might well have done as Auchinleck did on several occasions in North Africa—taken over command of the Army himself for a week or so. If he had decided to replace Percival he would probably have selected the Australian Gordon-Bennett whose colourful personality appealed to him more than any of the British generals.

The other question Connell posed was: should Wavell have taken personal command on his last visit on 10 February and have fought on to the end in Singapore? It would have been very wrong for him to do so at that juncture and spend the rest of the war in a Japanese prison camp.

But none of these things would have made any difference to the outcome of the operations in Malaya.

On the night of 10 February Wavell had decided to sleep in his flying-boat in Singapore and take off at dawn. Most unfortunately, he had a heavy fall just as he was about to embark and broke two small bones in his back. He was in great pain and became unconscious. His flying-boat arrived safely in Batavia, where he was taken first to a Dutch hospital and then to a British military hospital. With his usual courage he absolutely refused to be put on the sick list, but there is no doubt that the very severe shock and the injuries he had received considerably impaired his judgement in the next vitally important few weeks, in which both Singapore and Rangoon were lost. And it must be remembered that Wavell had undergone an incredible strain in the Middle East and was a very tired man—mentally rather than physically—when he went out to India. And this poses another interesting question. Who can insist that a Supreme Commander be hospitalised if he refuses to take the doctor's advice? We were shocked by Wavell's appearance on his next visit to Burma, but he was determined to carry on and he did so. From such decisions disasters are made.

With regard to Burma the Official History says:

The importance of Burma to the Allied cause in general and

to the defence of India in particular in a war against Japan is obvious from a glance at the map.

From the viewpoint of Allied strategy it was essential that China should be enabled to continue her struggle with Japan and thus contain large enemy forces. Through Burma lay the only route by which the Chinese armies could be kept supplied and the American air bases in China maintained. From India's point of view, so long as Burma was held, Calcutta and the great industrial centres of north-east India were practically immune from air attack, and her eastern land frontiers were secure from the threat of invasion.

(*The War against Japan*, Vol 2, Chap 1, p 1)

The War Office and the Chiefs of Staff in London must bear a considerable part of the responsibility for the complete absence of any defence plan for Burma, as they had been in charge of it from 1935, when that country was separated from India. Then, in December 1941, when Japan struck, they transferred the responsibility back to India with almost indecent haste. The least they could have done, when it had become obvious some time earlier that the Japanese were most likely to come into the war, was to have sent an army commander to Burma when they sent Percival to Singapore in May 1941. The person who was more aware of the danger to Burma than anyone else was Generalissimo Chiang Kai-shek, who at once offered Wavell two Chinese divisions for the defence of Burma, to be followed by more. Wavell refused them. Two months later Wavell was screaming for Chinese support and General Hutton was sent by air in a vain attempt to obtain it. The Americans were highly critical of Wavell's decision and maintained that it was the chief reason for the loss of Burma. Chiang Kai-shek realised that Burma would very soon become a vital theatre of operations and that the retention of the port of Rangoon, and the line of communication with China via the Burma Road, would be an outstanding object of Allied strategy.

Field-Marshal Bill Slim says in his book *Defeat into Victory* (p 116):

A most obvious instance of the lack of preparation was the smallness and unsuitability of the forces provided to defend Burma. Two ill-found, hurriedly collected and inexperienced divisions, of which one (17 Div) had been trained and equipped for desert warfare and the other (1 Burma Div) contained a large number of raw and unreliable Burmese troops, were tragically insufficient to meet superior Japanese forces in a country of the size and topography of Burma. The eventual arrival of the Chinese adjusted the numerical balance in favour of the Allies, and if they could have been got up to the front in strength before Rangoon fell, they might, in spite of their lack of almost all the necessities of a modern army, have changed the result. It is perhaps doubtful if, with the transport and supply resources available, their forward concentration could have been achieved; the pity is it was not tried.

As regards these Chinese divisions, Wavell said in his Burma campaign despatch, written in 1942 and published in the *London Gazette* of 11 March 1948 (my italics): 'I had every reason to suppose that I should have ample British, Indian and African troops available to defend Burma *which did not seem immediately threatened*. Obviously it was desirable that a country of the British Empire should be defended by Imperial troops rather than by foreign.' But surely we should have been glad of the help of Australians, Americans, Africans and Chinese, and any or all of our Allies—as we were on other fronts. There is no doubt that a much more determined effort should have been made to avoid the loss of Burma.

The other important decision was the appointment of a Burma army commander. Wavell quite rightly realised as soon as Burma became his responsibility that such an appointment must be made; but he did not realise how soon Burma was going to become a battleground of vital importance, and not just an administrative area. So he sent his own chief of staff in Delhi, General Hutton. This was a mistake from two points of view. Hutton was a brilliant staff officer whom India could ill

spare at this time, but he was not the dynamic fighting commander which coming events in Burma really demanded.
Hutton's Brigadier General Staff, Taffy Davies, who became
Slim's chief of staff later, wrote to me after the war: 'To do him
justice, Tom Hutton had begged Wavell not to give him an
executive command.'

When Singapore fell and the Japanese turned their full
attention to Burma the Chiefs of Staff soon began to put
pressure on Wavell to accept a replacement for Hutton; and
early in March General Alexander flew out to assume the
Burma army command. Churchill wrote in *Hinge of Fate* (Vol 4
of *The Second World War*), p 146: 'No troops in our control could
reach Rangoon in time to save it. But if we could not send an
army we could at any rate send a man.' However, it was then
much too late to save Burma.

It is no part of this book to describe in detail this first Burma
campaign. The operations are described in my two books,
Before the Dawn (1957) and *The Only Enemy* (1959). However, as
the loss of Burma was attributed (quite rightly) by Hutton,
Wavell, Churchill and all the historians to the Sittang disaster
in which my 17th Division was the only formation concerned,
and as this incident became a matter of historic importance
and considerable controversy, I will describe it as we—my
brigade commanders and I, who had to fight the battle—saw
it. And in the end—sixteen years later—it was this point of
view which the official historian accepted. But the 17th
Division had to live with all the obloquy in the meantime.

On Sunday, 28 December 1941, I was summoned by Wavell
to an interview at his residence, Flagstaff House, New Delhi.
Having been called back by Auchinleck earlier in the year
from the Western war theatre, where I had commanded a
British brigade at Dunkirk, I had been promoted acting
major-general in October and ordered to form the 19th Indian
Division. Very soon after I arrived in India, however, Auchinleck and Wavell changed places, the former becoming GOC-in-
C Mediterranean Command and the latter C-in-C India.*

*As Auchinleck had been instrumental in getting me back from England to

Early in December 1941, the General Officer commanding the 17th Indian Division having gone sick, Wavell sent a signal to me in Secunderabad asking me to transfer to command that division, which was on the point of embarking for the Middle East. The men had been fitted out with thick battledress and half-track mechanised vehicles, but their training, which was solely for desert warfare, had been much impeded and they were to undergo six weeks' intensive training in Baghdad before being given any operational assignments. I had already despatched 45 and 44 Brigades and was proposing to follow with my Divisional HQ and 46 Brigade when I received Wavell's summons.

I was then informed by the General Staff in Delhi that both 45 and 44 Brigades had been diverted at sea to Singapore.* They also informed me that General Hutton, whom I had never met, had been sent out to Burma as army commander. 'He will see to the administrative side,' they said, 'and you will do the fighting.' This suited me entirely.

Despite the fact that the news from Malaya could hardly have been worse, General Wavell was his usual solid and imperturbable self. He welcomed me most cordially and led me into his study, where he gave me a strategical review of the war situation. I had always had a great admiration for this remarkable soldier, though I had met him on only one or two occasions, between the wars, when I had been an instructor at the Camberley Staff College and he had been commanding an infantry brigade in the Aldershot Command. The fact that we were comparative strangers to one another was to be an important factor in the battle for Burma—and certainly one of

* 45 Brigade had at once to be thrown into a desperate battle in Malaya in which it was practically annihilated and its Brigadier (Duncan) killed whilst leading a bayonet charge. 44 Brigade, under Brigadier Ballantyne, went into the bag on Singapore island.

command an Indian division and I had served under his command before, he may well have been behind my change of command and I would gladly have served under him again.

the chief reasons for the disaster which ensued, though I doubt whether anyone of my rank could have really moved him, at that time, from his fixed idea that the Japanese were no good and that my very second-line troops were on a par with the 4th and 5th Indian Divisions he had had under his command in the Middle East. I was flattered at being the sole audience at his expert review of the war situation, though puzzled as to why the threat to Burma—which to me was very serious and very real—should form such an unimportant part of it. However, a call to tea interrupted us—and a most delightful tea it was with the charming Lady Wavell and her family. Belying his usual reputation for taciturnity, the general was enthusiastic about pigsticking, into which sport he was throwing himself whole-heartedly, at an age when most people would have been content to watch from the howdah of an elephant. After tea he saw me off himself, saying 'The General Staff will brief you.' And then, with a smile and a warm handshake, he said: 'Look after Burma for me.'

These 'famous last words' were indeed almost the last he ever spoke to me as, by the time he paid the first of his few visits to me in Burma with General Hutton, I had already had to make several withdrawals, all of which he thought quite unnecessary against such a second-class enemy as he considered the Japanese to be.

The main resistance to the Japanese advance on Rangoon was the task of my so-called 17th Division, two brigades of which had been detached and sent to Singapore. To the remaining 46 Brigade was added 16 Indian Brigade, the battalions of which consisted largely of hastily trained recruits, and a brigade of Burma Rifle battalions. The latter would have been very useful indeed if I had been allowed to use them in a guerrilla role, which I strongly recommended. But this was considered by the Army Commander to be derogatory to their status. The result was that they were a danger to the other troops and to themselves and a great chance was lost of partially overcoming the immobility of our own forces, as compared with the Japanese, by throwing into the jungle lightly equipped

Burma riflemen who could have lived on the country and harassed the flanks and rear of the advancing Japanese. I also received later the valuable reinforcement of 48 Gurkha Brigade which had been part of my 19th Division in Secunderabad and for which I had asked as soon as I had arrived in Burma.

The whole so-called 17th Division was entirely untrained and unequipped for jungle warfare. They had no pack transport, no pack rations and no pack wireless. There wasn't even any mepacrine, the anti-malaria drug which, in the later Burma campaign, was considered almost more essential than ammunition. They were entirely road-bound and lorry-supplied and therefore suckers for the favourite Japanese tactic of 'the hook', which Bill Slim so vividly describes in *Defeat into Victory*. Nevertheless, despite all these disadvantages the much-criticised 17th Division fought remarkably well against the best-trained jungle fighters in the world. And I had some really splendid brigadiers and commanding officers and a loyal, devoted and efficient Headquarters Staff.

Although the Chiefs of Staff in London must bear the blame for the unpreparedness of Burma for defence up to the start of the Japanese war, the lack of any sort of urgency on the part of India Command, Burma Command and ABDA when it did start was most reprehensible. The Japanese were in top gear and overdrive, the British in second gear with no one co-ordinating or controlling the machine at all.

To take just a few examples. More troops and equipment could have been made available for Burma. There were no troops in the Indian Army trained or equipped for jungle warfare, but the division most capable of taking on the Japs in December 1941 was the 19th (Dagger) Division which I had raised in Secunderabad in October of that year. I did manage to get the Gurkha Brigade of that division sent out to join me in Burma later on, but the other two brigades just sat in Secunderabad. The battalions of this division were hard and fit as they had all come from the Indian frontier, where they had left their trained mules and drivers. There was a crying need for the latter in Burma—surely a couple of trains could have brought them down to Calcutta and they could then have been shipped to Rangoon? We had no pack wireless or pack rations. But most battalions in Britain and many in India had these things. And why did we have to be so outnumbered in the air in Burma? The air communications line to Singapore had been cut by the end of December 1941, but the air lines to Rangoon were open until March—and should have been buzzing with aircraft if the defence of Burma had then been given the first priority.

Half-way through the operations General Wavell cabled the War Office for a light tank brigade. They arrived too late to save Rangoon but were very useful in assisting Bill Slim in his withdrawal back to India. They should have been sent for in December 1941—or even earlier.

Years later, in the supplement to the *London Gazette* of 11 March 1948, Wavell wrote, speaking of his appreciation of the situation in Burma as he saw it in January 1942:

I admit that I did not at this time consider the threat to Burma serious. I over-estimated the natural difficulties of the wooded hills on the Burmese frontier. Nor did I realise the unreliable quality of the Burmese units, nor the lack of training of the British and Indian troops. I was certainly guilty of an error of judgement in minimising the danger to Burma, but it is doubtful whether, even if I had appreciated it thoroughly, I could have done much to help Burma. India had been sucked dry of trained troops by the requirements of the Middle East, Iraq and Iran, and those most nearly approaching completion of their training had been sent to support Singapore. The same applied to administrative units. India was deficient of equipment for her own needs and could not meet those of Burma as well. Finally, and most important of all, India had no modern air force with which to support the Burma Army.

This is, of course, a handsome apology on Wavell's part for

all the strictures made on the commanders and troops of the 17th Division. But supplements to the *London Gazette* issued six years after the event do little to correct criticism made at the time. I certainly never saw this supplement until 1969 and I don't suppose many of my 17th Division, those who were still alive, ever saw it at all.

The operations on the Burma front in early 1942 can best be described by quoting Brigadier Taffy Davies, General Hutton's most experienced and efficient Chief General Staff Officer, in the foreword he wrote to my book *Before the Dawn*.

Moving and fighting in the jungle needs special techniques, special equipment and pack transport. To put a mechanised division into the jungle means that you tie it irrevocably to a road because only by means of that road can you supply it. But in the absence of anything else the 17th Division had to serve and it was, therefore, with the dice heavily loaded against it that this untried formation was despatched hurriedly to re-inforce the tenuous defences of Burma. At this time there was no real appreciation of the formidable character of the foe we were facing. General Wavell himself regarded the Japanese as a second-class enemy. This illusion persisted after we had lost Malaya and Burma and after the experiences of the Americans in the Philippines and elsewhere. In fact, the Japanese Imperial Army, with its savage, hardy and completely fanatical infantry element, constituted as formidable an enemy as has ever been faced by any British Army. In addition the Japanese armies had been specially trained for years, in ideal training areas for the type of campaign on which they were setting out.

General Smyth, commanding the 17th Division, was unfortunate enough to find himself in the position which so often confronts senior British commanders at the beginning of most of our campaigns. He was fighting on a shoe string with inadequate, ill-equipped and semi-trained troops against a formidable enemy. He was ordered to gain time at all costs and to attempt to retain control of huge areas of territory. These orders compelled him to disperse his forces in widely separated forward localities without mutual support. Moreover, on some occasions he was not permitted to withdraw from an untenable position without orders from higher authority. While all his military instincts urged him to concentrate well back and to fight on ground of his own choosing, the political pressure being exercised on his Army Commander enforced a forward policy with which, in loyalty, General Smyth had to conform. How hardly this bore on the troops during the nerve-shattering withdrawal from the Siamese frontier to the Bilin River is graphically brought out in General Smyth's narrative, while his clear analysis of the events leading to the disaster on the Sittang stresses once again the unwisdom of limiting the freedom of action of the executive commander.

Throughout the nightmare campaign, which started on the Burma–Thailand border in the Dawna Hills, east of Moulmein and ended over 500 miles further north on the Assam frontier, I was Brigadier General Staff with General Hutton, the original Army Commander, and then, after the evacuation of Rangoon, with General Slim* commanding the makeshift Burma Corps. In this capacity I was in close touch with the formation commanders in the field. Our great anxiety was always lest the continuous series of reverses and rearguard actions, fought in generally unsatisfactory tactical conditions, allied to the absence of supporting arms, of air support and many of the essentials of life, should sap the morale of the fighting troops to such an extent that they became unreliable. That this never happened must go to the everlasting credit of the divisional, brigade and unit com-

---

* Field-Marshal Slim writes in *Defeat into Victory* (p 25): 'I was fortunate in my BGS. Taffy Davies was something more than a brilliant staff officer; he was a character in his own right. His tall bony figure grew more and more emaciated as the retreat dragged on while he gave himself no rest, either physical or mental. But he got—and kept—that scratch headquarters working. From nothing, and almost with nothing, he formed, organised and infused it with his own spirit.' Brigadier Davies later became a major general and a divisional commander.

manders who led and encouraged their men with unfailing resource and courage. It is, I suggest, comparatively easy to be a good leader when one's troops are on the offensive and things are going well. It is a very different kettle of fish when everything is going badly, when the troops are strained and discouraged and when one's own mind is full of foreboding and anxiety. If, in such circumstances, a commander can sustain his own and his troops' spirits and by his personal will-power and determination inject renewed confidence into his command, then he must be a real leader. We had such leaders in Burma and Jackie Smyth was one of them. I never saw him other than composed, cheerful and radiating confidence, whatever his real feelings may have been. I know it always did me good to visit him.

It is my personal opinion that the army in Burma, by its grim defensive tactics and by its refusal to surrender its freedom of action saved India from invasion in 1942, when all the dice were loaded in favour of the Japanese.

As soon as it became obvious to the British War Cabinet in London and to General Wavell in Java, early in 1942, that the very scratch and inadequate troops available in Burma were not going to be able to hold the Japanese invaders, frantic efforts were made to obtain substantial reinforcements. In the first appreciation of the situation I sent to General Hutton soon after I had arrived in Burma in early January 1942, I urged that two more divisions at least would be required immediately to have any chance of saving Burma—and that the 48th Gurkha Brigade of my former 19th (Dagger) Division should be sent out to me immediately. The latter arrived on 8 February, under command of Brigadier Hugh-Jones. The partially trained 63 Indian Brigade arrived early in March—too late to have any bearing on the battle for Rangoon. Only when the situation had become almost irretrievable were any real efforts made to get some of the Chinese troops which Chiang Kai-shek had offered originally—but there wasn't a hope at that late hour.

Winston Churchill also made strenuous efforts to persuade Mr Curtin, the Australian Prime Minister, to allow one of the Australian divisions, which were on their way back to Australia from the Middle East, to land in Burma. In his letter to Mr Curtin of 20 February 1942, Churchill said: 'It can begin to disembark at Rangoon about the 26th and 27th February. There is nothing else in the world that can fill the gap—and save Burma.' General Wavell had also made a similar request a few days earlier. He had asked for a whole Australian army corps. And Winston cabled President Roosevelt to the same effect and asked him to bring his own pressure to bear on the Australian Government.

President Roosevelt telegraphed to Mr Curtin saying:

If Burma goes it seems to me our whole position, including that of Australia, will be in extreme peril. Your Australian division is the only force that is available for immediate reinforcement. It could get into the fight at once and would, I believe, have the strength to save what now seems to be a very dangerous situation. (*The Second World War*, Vol 4)

The extent to which all these high-ups were out of the picture as to the true situation on the battle front (ie the 17th Division) became clear from the following statement of the facts. From the start of the Burma Campaign General Wavell had made it quite clear to General Hutton, commanding Burma Army, that the task of the 17th Division was to oppose the Japanese as far forward as possible and on as wide a front as possible, so as to block all possible approaches. The area of responsibility allotted to the 17th Division therefore extended over several hundred miles of country. General Bruce Scott's weak 1st Burma Division, which was bled white to supply me with what reinforcements he could spare (one or two battalions), had been located in the Shan States—and did not take part in the fighting in January and February 1942, when the fate of Rangoon was decided. I quite understood General Wavell's reasoning with regard to this forward defence. It was comforting for Winston Churchill and the Chiefs of Staff in London, for Generalissimo Chiang Kai-shek, for the Viceroy of India and for the Governor and Government of Burma, to see each morning the red line on the map depicting the position of the 17th Division as far in front of Rangoon as possible; but this was a political defence plan, not a military one. It soon became obvious to me and to my brigadiers and staff that my troops, untrained and unequipped for jungle fighting and without any mobility, owing to their dependence on lorry transport, could give a good account of themselves—and indeed provide the resistance and delay which General Wavell required—only if they could fight concentrated and on ground of my own choosing. The present policy had resulted in the occupation of some very militarily unsuitable places like Moulmein, in which I was ordered to put a whole brigade, in withdrawals which were much too late—in fact, in increasing the advantage which the Japanese already held by reason of their higher training in jungle warfare and their mobility, instead of bringing them to battle and inflicting losses upon them.

I have always felt certain that had General Wavell not been a very exhausted man he would have come up to my battle headquarters, as Auchinleck had done to Neil Ritchie's in North Africa, and either stayed for two or three days or, if he was still dissatisfied, have taken charge of the battle himself.

Everything depended at that moment of time on the 17th Division; there were no other fighting formations in Burma. There was absolutely nothing in the whole of the ABDA command that mattered as much as this.

Crisis day, when the fate of Burma was really decided, came on Thursday 12 February. My original brigades, 16 and 46, had become considerably weakened by the widely dispersed positions they had been ordered to hold, and the Japanese divisions were everywhere infiltrating between our defences. The Burma Rifle battalions continued to show that they were not capable of standing up to the Japanese in a regular role. However, on 8 February I had received a very welcome reinforcement in the shape of 48 Gurkha Brigade. On 10th and

11th February I held conferences with my brigade commanders to review the situation. We agreed that unless the division could be concentrated immediately and give battle on ground of our own choosing, we faced total defeat. The only position which offered a really good opportunity for protracted defence was Sittang, where the broad, swiftly flowing river provided a formidable obstacle and the open ground on the far bank was favourable for the operations of my troops—particularly the brigade of light tanks which was on its way from the Middle East to join me.

It had been my intention (of which all my staff were aware), had I been allowed to adopt my own plan, that we should get across the broad Sittang in good time, with at least a week in hand, so that we could prepare a strong defensive position on the far bank. The river lay some forty miles behind us and the metalled road for the last seven miles or so petered out into a dusty track—passable by our lorry transport, but with difficulty. It must be remembered that the supply of food and ammunition to the troops and the evacuation of the wounded depended entirely on motor transport—and one could reduce the supply only if one reduced the demand. We also had to allow for the fact that our movement would be made more difficult by the attentions of the Japanese Air Force. We had not anticipated that we would also be bombed by our own air forces.

The narrow iron railway bridge over the broad Sittang river had been planked to take wheels and marching troops. The bridge had been prepared for demolition by the Army Sappers. It could of course have been destroyed at any time by the Japanese, with their superior air force, but it was obviously of prime importance to them as it gave them quick and direct access to Rangoon, which, equally obviously, was their main objective. Their aircraft therefore gave the bridge a very wide berth. I had laid back such odd units, and parts of units, as I could spare to form a small bridgehead defence force. It was of course imperative that the bridge should not fall into the hands of the Japanese. That would result in the immediate loss of

Rangoon and a very early end to Burma's resistance. At all costs we must not delay our withdrawal to the Sittang so long as to be caught by the rapidly advancing Japanese and attacked when we were in the act of crossing the river. That would be military suicide—which indeed it turned out to be.

So on that fateful 12 February I sent my Brigadier General Staff, 'Punch' Cowan, down to Rangoon to make one more urgent appeal to General Hutton to allow me to concentrate my widely dispersed troops behind the Bilin river immediately, and then without delay to withdraw behind the Sittang. The Bilin was a useful concentration line as it was marked on the map and was visible on the ground as a river, though at this time of year it was just a wet ditch in thick jungle which anyone could jump across. As a defensive position on which to fight a battle it could not have been more unsuitable for our troops.

I quite realised the pressure put upon Hutton by Wavell to fight always as far forward as possible, but I was convinced that a crisis point had been reached where the extreme implementation of Wavell's policy would result in complete disaster and that in fact he would kill the goose (the 17th Division) which laid all the eggs he had in his very rickety Burma basket. I also sent a personal telegram to General Hutton to the same effect. But to no purpose. His orders were that we were to stay exactly where we were and make no movement without his personal permission. Despite this order, however, as all my brigadiers were emphatic that we must concentrate or perish, on 14 February I ordered a withdrawal from our scattered localities to a more concentrated position behind the Bilin. There was immense relief on the part of all units. 16 and 46 Brigades marched all through the night of 14/15 February to take up their new positions, where they were joined by 48 Gurkha Brigade. My GSO 1, Colonel F. C. Simpson, in a letter to me after the war said: 'This was certainly the best decision you ever made. As I said at the time, we would have lost the whole division then if you had not done it.'

But I received a severe letter of censure from General Hutton for making a move without his permission. The Official

History (p 46) records this letter and says: 'It is easy to understand how, to Hutton, this withdrawal appeared at the time to
be unnecessary, though afterwards he agreed it was justified
and carried out only in the nick of time.'

With regard to my own plan to cross the Sittang in good
time so that I could prepare a really strong position on the far
side. When this matter was under discussion during the writing
of the Official History in 1956, General Davies wrote to the
War Historian, Major-General S. W. Kirby, on 4 February
1956 as follows (though his letter did not find a place in the
Official History):

Wavell's misjudgement of the Japanese and his insistence on
holding them up on fronts hundreds of miles wide, undoubtedly influenced General Hutton. It was in the light of
Wavell's constantly expressed views that Hutton turned
down Smyth's very much sounder proposal to concentrate
and fight a divisional battle on ground of his own choosing.
I think I must mention that in discussing Smyth's appreciation with General Hutton I made it quite clear that I
agreed with Smyth's conclusion. The deductions I make are:
  1 General Wavell's false ideas about the Japanese led
  him to force Hutton into unsound decisions.
  2 Smyth, whose appreciation was absolutely sound, was
  placed in a series of impossible tactical positions.
  3 The decisive battle for Rangoon, which had to be
  fought at the Sittang River, found 17 Div placed at the
  maximum disadvantage.

On 16 February General Hutton visited my HQ and
repeated his order that there was to be no withdrawal from
the Bilin without his personal permission. From 15 to 19
February the 17th Division was held in close conflict in thick
jungle country by two Japanese divisions, who were at the same
time employing their usual tactics of the 'hook' round both
flanks which they had employed so successfully in Malaya—
and which was their basic tactical manoeuvre. If the Japanese

had been asked to choose what plan they would most like us to adopt, this was undoubtedly it. And every day that we stayed on the Bilin was a good day for them. The Official History (p 34) makes it clear that the 33rd and 55th Japanese Divisions, which were opposing me, intended to 'turn the flank of any British position on the Bilin and drive forward across the Sittang River to Pegu'—which would place Rangoon at their mercy. As we had no idea how long we would be kept on the Bilin we could make no concrete plans for withdrawal. Every day our situation reports to Army HQ showed more units pushed into the front line to hold our position, including the newly arrived Gurkha Brigade. The Official History records (Vol 2, p 61) that on the 18th I had reported to Army HQ that the troops were fought to a standstill and that I had been forced to throw in my last reserve battalion, the 4/12th Frontier Force Regiment. This was exactly the situation the Japanese required.

On Thursday 19 February General Hutton came up from Rangoon to visit my HQ and gave me permission to withdraw behind the Sittang—seven days after I had requested so urgently that I should do so. John Connell records (*Wavell—Supreme Commander*, p 186) that Hutton found the troops 'very weak and exhausted', which was hardly surprising. Prime Minister Harold Wilson once said that 'in politics a week can be a very long time'. In war twenty-four hours may be vital to success or defeat. We had given the Japanese a much longer start than this. All we could do now was to get the brigades disengaged and move back to the Sittang with all possible speed.

The Official History says: 'In view of the great importance of getting 17 Div safely across the Sittang, Hutton might have been wiser, once action had been joined on the Bilin, to leave Smyth a free hand' (*The War against Japan*, Vol 2, p 76).

The Official History continues:

Smyth sent Brigadier Cowan back to Rangoon on 12th February with a request to this effect. He told him to impress on Hutton the grave danger in which 17th Division stood of being cut off from the Sittang Bridge, and to urge that he might be allowed to withdraw the division behind the Bilin immediately and that there should be no delay in the next stage of the withdrawal, which should be behind the Sittang River.

John Connell writes:

In Delhi and in London the rapid crumbling of the defences in Burma was watched with dismay. The Viceroy of India sent Churchill a signal setting out with sharp candour his own view, which he said was shared by many officers in India. He declared: 'Our troops in Burma are not fighting with proper spirit. I have not the least doubt that this is in great part due to a lack of drive and inspiration from the top.' He went on to a severe criticism of Hutton as a commander, giving him credit however for having been an excellent C.G.S. Churchill sent the full text of this chilling telegram to Wavell, adding that the Chief of the Imperial General Staff wanted Wavell's opinion; if Wavell concurred with Linlithgow, he would at once send General Sir Harold Alexander, who was then G.O.C.-in-Chief Southern Command in England to replace Hutton. Churchill concluded: 'I do hope you are getting over your accident.'

(*Wavell—Supreme Commander*, pp 181–2)

With regard to this last sentence, Sandy Reid Scott, Wavell's ADC, recorded on 18 February: 'The Chief looks tired, worried and tucked up, though considering the severity of the fall he had at Singapore he has made a rapid recovery and astonished his Dutch doctors.' Nevertheless, there is little doubt that the spate of ill-judged and ill-informed signals Wavell sent from Java to Hutton in Rangoon and the CIGS in London, which are recorded in John Connell's biography, were due to the state of his health. Wavell replied to Churchill's signal on 18 February, saying he was reluctant to change

Hutton but asked how soon Alexander would be able to reach Rangoon.

Considering how tired the troops of the 17th Division were, and how closely engaged, the breaking of contact on the Bilin on the night of the 19th and the subsequent withdrawal on the 20th and 21st reflected the greatest credit on the brigade and battalion commanders. There was also quite a lot of lorry transport to get back, and wounded to evacuate from advanced dressing stations—all on the one road. The brigades leapfrogged back through one another and by the morning of the 20th were clear of the Japanese division which had been opposing us on the Bilin; but our real worry was with regard to the other division which had been turning our flanks steadily ever since we had been on the Bilin. It was a race against time with the odds heavily on the Japanese.

The brigadiers had orders to keep the men on the move, however tired they might be. That fine soldier, Lieutenant-Colonel (later Major-General) Joe Lentaigne, commanding the 1/4th Gurkhas, describes the ordeal of his battalion in vivid terms in his Regimental History—and Gurkhas are very tough. Not even at Dunkirk have I seen troops so tired.

My BGS, Brigadier Punch Cowan, summed it up in a few words: 'As a result of the Bilin delay we were doomed. We withdrew much too late, over a ghastly dirt track. We were bombed to hell by our own aircraft. We were already surrounded by Japs.' We had expected to be heavily bombed by the Japs during our withdrawal to the Sittang—and we certainly were; but the bombing by our own Air Force was the last straw. Air support had to be arranged from Rangoon as we had no wireless set which could reach that distance.

The Official History describes the bombing as follows:

The 21st was very dry and hot, and dense clouds of thick red dust and a shortage of water added to the trials of men and beasts alike. During the day the column on the main track (which was flanked by dense jungle on either side), and the troops in the Bayagi Rubber Estate, were repeatedly bombed and machine-gunned, first by Japanese aircraft and later by aircraft carrying Allied markings. As a result vehicles, including ambulances full of wounded, were ditched or destroyed; mules, carrying weapons and wireless sets, broke loose and vanished with their loads into the jungle; casualties were numerous; the march was delayed; considerable disorganisation was caused and morale suffered . . . [There were also many cases where the Burmese drivers, frightened by the bombing, disappeared into the jungle, leaving their ambulances full of wounded on the track.]

Most of the persistent attacks which caused havoc were, owing to a grievous error, made by British and American Volunteer Group aircraft. Air reconnaissance in the morning had falsely reported an enemy column of three hundred vehicles moving through Kyaikto to Kinmun. All available aircraft at Rangoon were ordered to attack and were given the Kyaikto–Mokpalin road instead of the Kyaikto–Kinmun road as the western limit for the bombing operations.

Although the 17th Division could by no possible stretch of the imagination be blamed for this grievous and damaging error, it was at the time and for many years to come charged against us as part of the whole Sittang disaster bill.

All through the night of the 20th and the day of the 21st the troops ploughed steadily on; but the dusty state of the track, the weariness of the men, short of food and water, the heat and the dust and the constant bombing, all contributed to slowing down the pace. By the evening of the 21st the transport, which had arrived back first, was starting to cross the bridge. The approaches were deep in dust and we could show no lights but we had to take a chance. A staff officer arrived from AHQ with important news. First they had received information that the Japanese might make parachute landings early next morning on the open ground to the west of the river to try and take the bridge from that side. I had realised all along that the capture of the bridge was their main objective, so did not take this warning lightly. At 3 am I stopped the transport and moved

1/4th Gurkhas, the leading battalion of 48 Brigade, across the river for the anti-parachute task. The staff officer also informed me that 7 Armoured Brigade had arrived in Rangoon, but as all the dock labour had fled the men were having to unload all their tanks, stores and petrol themselves and could not get up to me for at least another twenty-four hours. If only we had been in a prepared position across the river, what a strength they would have been and what a knock we could have given to the Japs!

On the evening of the 21st I had a good look round the Sittang bridgehead defences, which consisted of detachments from three or four battalions, including a company of the Duke of Wellington's Regiment, which had just arrived to join us. All through the night of the 21st/22nd the transport continued to cross the bridge, the approaches to which became increasingly cut up and difficult, particularly in the pitch darkness. Several lorries overturned, one in the middle of the bridge, which caused two hours' delay. However, my brigadiers had reported that the troops were absolutely all-in and must have a few hours' rest and time to cook some food.

At first light on the 22nd I crossed the river to have a look at the 1/4th anti-parachute positions and select positions for the brigades when they arrived. I put Brigadier Hugh-Jones, commanding 48 Brigade, in charge of the bridgehead defences. My staff established an operational HQ within a few hundred yards of him at a small railway station, from which we could get in touch with AHQ in Rangoon, who naturally were in urgent need of information. Up to this moment I thought that I might be going to experience another 'Dunkirk Miracle'. Then suddenly there was a great burst of firing from the east side of the bridge and the Japanese, who had been lying up in the jungle ready to pounce when the time was ripe, interposed the best part of a division between our bridgehead defence troops and the greater part of the 17th Division.

The first Japanese attack cut clean through the portion of the perimeter held by a battalion of the Burma Rifles, and the medical part of my Divisional HQ, including my ADMS, were all taken prisoner. I now had to take a chance on the parachute landings and put the 1/4th Gurkhas in to counter-attack, which they did magnificently, restoring the situation. From this time onward, however, one Japanese division was bringing increasingly heavy pressure on the bridge, whilst the other was attacking the troops of the 17th Division strung out along miles of road east of the river. The only wireless communication I had with the brigades was by the one lorry-born wireless set which each brigade had. As the brigades were immediately forced off the road all communications with them ceased. The fog of war was complete and the noise of battle from across the river continuous.

As so many different accounts have been given about this engagement and the decision to blow the Sittang bridge, and no one except myself and my staff were there, I will make clear what I knew at the time, and what I didn't know—and what the immediate object of my thinking was. First, I did not know what was happening on the far side of the river but, realising the disadvantageous position in which my brigades had been put, caught as they were on the march in the act of crossing a broad river, and submerged in what was obviously a dog-fight in the jungle, I feared the worst. This was exactly the situation I had always tried to avoid. What I did know was that the increasing Japanese pressure on my comparatively weak bridgehead defences might result in their capturing the bridge, in which case the fate of Rangoon—and Burma—would be sealed immediately. What I also knew from Brigadier Hugh-Jones was that there had been no sign of any formed bodies of the 17th Division being able to break through the strong Japanese forces attacking the bridgehead.

Throughout the 22nd anxious enquiries had been coming from the Army Commander in Rangoon and my presence was requested at a conference with him next morning at a point half-way between Rangoon and Sittang. No time could have been more inconvenient for me to leave my HQ, but I would have to see what the night brought forth. As darkness fell and the fighting from across the river died down, I left my GSO 1 with Noel Hugh-Jones at the bridgehead and moved back to my Ops HQ to get some food and a few hours' sleep. There was absolutely no sign of any of our troops on the far side of the river being able to break through, but every indication that the bridgehead defence troops might be unable to hold the increasing Japanese pressure. My orders to the brigadier were that at all costs the Japanese must not be allowed to capture the Sittang bridge.

At 4.30 am Punch Cowan woke me up. Brigadier Hugh-Jones was on the phone. During the night pressure on the bridgehead troops had increased. After a consultation with his COs he had decided that he could not guarantee to hold the bridgehead against a dawn attack and if the bridge was not blown under cover of darkness he couldn't be sure he would be able to blow it at all. He therefore wanted my permission to withdraw the bridgehead troops and blow the bridge immediately. I just wanted to make certain that amongst the COs he had consulted were Lieutenant-Colonel Joe Lentaigne of the 1/4th Gurkhas and the CO of the 4/12th Frontier Force Regiment, both of whose opinions I valued. When this was confirmed I had a short discussion with Punch Cowan. It was not a pleasant decision for any commander to have to make, but I had all the pros and cons clearly in my head. If we blew, it was in the knowledge that two-thirds of the division was left on the far bank of the broad Sittang. If we did not blow, a complete Japanese division could march straight on to Rangoon. The decision was one that had to be mine alone, and having made it, I should of course take complete responsibility for it. It took me less than four minutes to make up my mind. I gave the order that the bridge should be blown immediately. It was very gallantly destroyed under heavy fire by our Indian Sappers at 5.30 am, after the remnants of the bridgehead defence troops had been withdrawn.

General Joe Lentaigne, who was commanding 1/4th Gurkhas at the time, as part of Brigadier Hugh-Jones's bridgehead defences, wrote in his Regimental History as follows:

All day of the 22nd and throughout the night of 22nd/23rd very heavy firing could be heard from beyond the river. A bitter and desperate battle was being fought to break the Japanese block. It was a soldier's battle, with great confusion and no control possible. At 03.30 on the morning of the 23rd the enemy brought machine-gun fire to bear along the whole length of the Sittang Bridge. Pressure was increasing. A dreadful decision had to be taken—whether or not to blow the bridge. The prime factor was that it must not fall into Japanese hands intact. It was becoming more and more clear that it could not be destroyed by daylight; when it would be under observed fire. It was doubtful even whether it could be held until daylight. To destroy it meant to sacrifice the division but all the indications were that in any case the division could never now reach the bridge. The matter grew more urgent, the decision was taken and the bridge was blown.

Joe Lentaigne had of course no more idea than I had that the result of the blowing would be the withdrawal of both Japanese divisions, thus enabling over 3,000 of our troops to cross the river. Neither Punch Cowan nor I, nor Bill Slim, with whom I discussed the matter later, had any doubt whatsoever that there was any other course open to me. Brigadier Hugh-Jones had behaved entirely correctly.

If the Japanese had been allowed to capture the bridge they would have been hot on my heels as I went to keep my rendez-vous with the Army Commander and, even if he and his staff had reached Rangoon, they would have been 'in the bag' very shortly afterwards. The Armoured Brigade would have been caught on the march up from Rangoon; 63 Infantry Brigade could not have landed in Rangoon; there would have been no Alexander–Slim fighting withdrawal towards the frontiers of India; and, what is more, all our troops on the east of the Sittang would have been killed or captured. As it was, the Japanese, frustrated in their main object of a quick advance on Rangoon, at once broke contact and moved ten miles up-river to build a temporary bridge, giving us nearly ten days' respite. Some 3,000 officers and men were then enabled to come down to the river bank and raft themselves or swim over. But alas, my beloved Gurkhas, who couldn't swim, were mostly drowned, killed or captured.

The brigadiers of both 16 and 46 Brigades swam the river and I was able to piece the story together from them and other officers. They both told me that confused fighting had at once ensued after the first Japanese onslaught, in which no one above a platoon or company commander could exercise any control. Brigadier Ekin (46 Brigade) had a hair-raising experience. He and his brigade-major were entirely cut off and hid in a patch of jungle in the middle of a Japanese battalion until, on the blowing of the bridge, they were able to escape. Brigadier Jones had managed to exercise a little more control but he was surrounded by Japs and had some narrow escapes. Had the bridge not been blown he would undoubtedly have been taken prisoner; as it was he got a well-deserved DSO from Bill Slim in the subsequent withdrawal to India.

The 1/3rd and 2/5th Gurkhas, part of 48 Brigade which had been nearest to the bridge when the Japanese attack took place, fought fiercely to try to break through the strong Japanese force encircling the bridgehead, but without success, and were nearly all killed or captured. Their story is told in their Regimental Histories.

I did not, of course, see the cables which went out from Burma Army HQ as a result of my verbal report to the Army Commander on the Sittang disaster; but their impact and meaning are clear from the writings of Winston Churchill and the despatches of General Wavell. In the fourth volume of *The Second World War*, Churchill says:

On February 20 it was obvious that a further retreat to the Sittang River was imperative if the whole force was not to be lost. Over this swift-flowing river, five hundred yards wide, there was only one bridge. Before the main body of the 17th Division could reach it the bridgehead was attacked by a strong Japanese force, while the marching columns retiring upon it were themselves beset by a fresh enemy division newly arrived, which caught them in flank.

So far, so good—except that it had been obvious to me, the commander of the division, on 12 February, not the 20th, that an immediate withdrawal across the Sittang was imperative.

Churchill continues:

Under the impression that our three retiring brigades were greatly weakened, scattered and beaten, and were in fact trapped, the order was given by the commander of the bridgehead, with the permission of the divisional commander to blow the bridge. When the division successfully fought its way back to the river bank it found the bridge destroyed and the broad flood before it. Even so 3,300 men contrived to cross this formidable obstacle, but with only 1,400 rifles and a few machine guns. Every other weapon and all equipment were lost. This was a major disaster.

As I informed Sir Winston (as he was then) in later years, he had been completely misinformed. I was not 'under the impression' that the three retiring brigades were weakened scattered and trapped. I *knew* they were. But the bridge was blown for one reason and one reason only—that the bridgehead commander could not otherwise prevent it falling into the hands of the Japanese. And the idea that the three brigades 'successfully fought their way back to the river bank, only to find the bridge blown' was a complete myth. But of such myths is history made. Even as late as 1972 Major-General Tulloch had written in his book on Wingate that Burma had been lost 'owing to the premature demolition of the Sittang bridge'.

Wavell's despatch on the operations says:

These engagements are described in General Hutton's report. It is quite clear that the enemy were allowed to gain cheap initial successes through bad handling by local commanders, lack of training, and in some cases, lack of fighting spirit on the part of the troops. The battle at the Sittang bridgehead on 22 and 23 February, which is described in General Hutton's report, really sealed the fate of Rangoon and Lower Burma. In the withdrawal from the Bilin River to the Sittang and the action east of the river, the whole of two brigades was lost.

And Wavell's 'uncensored opinion of the battle', quoted by John Connell in his biography of Wavell, adds: 'From reports of this operation which I have studied I have no doubt that the withdrawal from the Bilin River to west of the Sittang was badly managed by the headquarters of the 17th Division and that the disaster which resulted in the loss of almost two complete brigades ought never to have happened.'

Following the Sittang disaster the immediate task of the staff of the 17th Division HQ and Army HQ was to reclothe, re-arm and reorganise the 3,000 men who had crossed the river. It was now obvious that the days of Rangoon were numbered and that the Burma Army, reinforced by 7 Armoured Brigade and 63 Infantry Brigade from India, with General Bruce-Scott's 1st Burma Division, would have to withdraw to India. The staff of Burma Army therefore went full speed ahead with their preparations for the total demolition of the docks, oil tanks and so forth in Rangoon.

At the insistence of General Thompson, the Director of Medical Services, I had been forced to have a medical board earlier in the operations. I impressed on the chairman, who was my own ADMS, that I was quite fit to carry on for the time being and I insisted that I must remain in command whilst the fate of Rangoon and Burma was in jeopardy and until I had got the 17th Division across the Sittang. They agreed and passed me fit to do so provided I had two months' rest at the earliest possible moment. General Thompson fully agreed. General Hutton now recommended my application for two months' leave and General Wavell agreed to take me back to India in his plane. John Connell, in *Wavell—Supreme Commander*, writes of 'Smyth, whose illness (against which he fought with the utmost courage) was so severe that, after eight months' treatment in India, he was sent home and retired'. My division had now been much reduced in strength and I had an excellent understudy in Brigadier Punch Cowan, who took over command of the division. In any case, after a disaster, the reason for which cannot be explained to the troops, it is generally wise to change the commander. However, I had no idea at the time that Alexander was on his way out from home to take over the Army Command from Hutton. Before leaving I impressed on the General Staff at Burma Army HQ and on Punch Cowan that time was not on their side. At all costs they must not be caught in the Rangoon bottleneck when the Japs resumed their advance. Also, with thousands of naked bodies to clothe and re-arm, a young and newly arrived 63 Indian Brigade and the newly arrived 7 Armoured Brigade, a new 17th Division Commander and a new Army Commander, they wanted to avoid being caught again in an action not of their own choosing until they had been able to sort themselves out a bit.

I handed over to Punch Cowan on the morning of 2 March and motored to Rangoon to join Wavell's aircraft. He was bound first for Lashio for a summit meeting with Generalissimo Chiang Kai-shek. I was naturally much interested to meet this remarkable man about whom the whole world was talking. He was certainly an impressive personality, very quiet and still in repose, but his eyes were penetrating and he radiated vitality. He and General Wavell were closeted together for some time with an interpreter in a sort of rotunda summerhouse with open spaces for windows. As there seemed to be no security arrangements laid on I prowled round the garden looking in at them through the open windows from time to time.

So far as I could see very little was being said by either of the great men and the interpreter began to look rather harassed. Wavell was notoriously rather inarticulate and had become more so with age; and Chiang could speak little English. However, one very important thing did emerge from the conference. Wavell cabled Hutton from Lashio: 'Hang on hard—Rangoon must not be given up without battle and the most aggressive battle that our means allow on ground and in the air.' A short communiqué was also issued giving such a hopelessly over-optimistic report on the situation that it must have made the Japanese laugh.

It must be remembered that it was Chiang Kai-shek who, more than anyone else in December 1941 (with the exception of the far-sighted Sir John Dill), had realised the imminent danger to Burma and had offered two Chinese divisions, and then more, for its defence—which Wavell refused. Chiang was now very naturally deeply disturbed at the prospect of the loss of Rangoon and the cutting off of all land communications between China and the rest of the Allied world.

Next day we flew straight to Calcutta, and immediately after landing another aircraft wheeled up alongside, out of which stepped the unmistakeable figure of General Alexander, looking spick and span, calm and unruffled as always. I of course knew him very well but we were not able to have any converse as General Wavell hurried him away to the rest house. After a brief conference they emerged, and Alex boarded his plane and departed. Knowing, as I did, Wavell's views on the situation and his low opinion of the Japanese, I felt very apprehensive as to what instructions Alex had been given.

As soon as Alex's aircraft took off for Rangoon Wavell cabled the Chief of the Imperial General Staff in London: 'Have issued instructions that Rangoon is not to be given up without battle as aggressive as our means will permit.' It was these two cables, and the briefing Wavell gave to Alexander on Calcutta aerodrome, which so nearly caused the loss of the remainder of Burma Army and might even have resulted in a Japanese invasion of India.

I heard the rest of the story later from Bill Slim, Taffy Davies and others. On his arrival in Rangoon Alex had shocked them all by announcing that there was no immediate threat to Rangoon. He cancelled all arrangements for evacuating the city and moving northwards via Prome, which were already in train. On the next day Alexander attempted to stage a counter-attack against the rapidly advancing Japanese from the Pegu area, intending to use 7 Armoured Brigade and the newly landed 63 Indian Infantry Brigade—but this didn't even get started. Alexander, by then, had realised the grave danger to Burma Army which his actions had caused. He therefore ordered that the original arrangements for the withdrawal should proceed immediately. But it was too late. Both the roads leading north from Rangoon were blocked by strong Japanese forces.

General Slim wrote in *Defeat into Victory* (p 14):

General Alexander escaped from Rangoon by sheer luck. And it was that. The whole British force from Rangoon, and with it General Alexander and his headquarters, would have been destroyed had it not been for the typically rigid adherence to the letter of his orders by a Japanese divisional commander. Coming from the east, by paths through hills and jungle in a sweep on the city, he had been told to by-pass Rangoon to the north and, swinging round, to attack it from the west. To cover his flanks, as he crossed north of Rangoon, he put up a strong block on the main Prome road. He had thus completely bottled up the British force as it tried to get away. Several attacks were made on the road blocks but Japanese tenacity proved a match for British and Indian valour. The obstacle remained. All the Japanese commander had to do was to keep his road block in position and, with the rest of his troops, attack the forty-mile column strung out along the road. Nothing could have saved the British, tied as they were by their mechanised transport to the ribbon of road.

The Japanese commander, however, conforming rigidly to his orders, withdrew the road blocks, entered Rangoon from the west—and Alex escaped.

Wavell later apologised to Alexander for his hasty and ill-conceived action and the unnecessary casualties it had caused. The anxiety in Delhi and London during this fateful week was acute. I was in Delhi myself, so I knew. However, on 11 March Wavell had heard that Alexander had escaped capture in the Rangoon bottleneck and signalled to him: 'Well done. Responsibility for position in which you and troops were placed is wholly mine and I congratulate you all on determination with which you have extricated yourselves. Much regret casualties.' (Connell, *Wavell—Supreme Commander*, p 209)

Alexander was immensely loyal to Wavell. He merely says in his *Memoirs* (p 83), which were published in 1962, twenty years after the event:

> Looking back over the years with the knowledge I now have of the situation that existed when I took command in Burma in March 1942, I realise that I ought to have ordered an earlier evacuation of Burma. But at the time I was not prepared to admit defeat before I had done everything possible. This delay resulted in the whole of our forces in the south of Burma being encircled and gave the Japanese the chance to destroy them as organised formations—and they missed their chance!

This was the only campaign of Alex's in which I have heard him criticised; Slim and his staff said little about it. Nevertheless, Alex was made to look foolish and completely out of the picture at the first briefing he gave on 5 March 1942; and, being the professional soldier he was, that hurt him very much and really soured him towards this retreat, for which he could find no enthusiasm whatever.

Hutton became Chief of Staff to Alexander to start with and in this capacity he functioned with his usual efficiency. Hutton's loss over the Burma campaign was his post as Chief of the General Staff in Delhi, which he had been carrying out with great efficiency. He had never wished to be a commander in the field and had no military reputation as such. He held further administrative appointments in India and was knighted on his retirement from the service in 1944. Wavell of course returned to his post as Commander-in-Chief in India and

subsequently became Viceroy of India. He will always remain
a military hero in the hearts and minds of the British people for
his devastating defeat of the Italian Army in North Africa in
the early days of the war. In later years he had many generous
second thoughts about the Burma campaign—including my
part in it.

The subsequent fighting withdrawal of the Burma Army to
the frontiers of India is told very clearly in Slim's book, *Defeat
into Victory*. As the commander of Burcorps, 1 Burma Corps,
Slim was responsible for the tactical handling of the troops,
whilst Alexander was responsible for the strategical planning
and the liaison with General 'Vinegar Joe' Stilwell and the
Chinese. For Alexander this was, in his own words, 'an unhappy
campaign', which he referred to as 'The Burma Rescue
Operation', and he was thankful to see the last of it. He says
that the disasters of Dunkirk and Burma were 'sour experiences'
and 'It should be apparent that I recall the whole affair of
Dunkirk with extreme distaste; and there still lay ahead the
bitter pill of Burma' (*Memoirs*, pp 102 and 79). Alex hated
being beaten and loathed having to retreat—and he had more
of it in Burma than he had had at Dunkirk.

I was at some pains to discover why Alex was so unhappy as
the army commander in Burma and why the Burma Corps
thought so little of him as a commander. Slim says in *Defeat
into Victory* (p 118):

On his arrival in Burma Alexander found the decisive battle
of the campaign, the Sittang Bridge, had already been lost
and with it the fate of Rangoon sealed. The advent of the
Chinese may have roused a flicker of hope that its recovery
was possible, but the loss of Toungoo and the state of the
Chinese armies soon quenched even that glimmer. It was
then that we needed from the highest national authority a
clear directive of what was to be our purpose in Burma.
Were we to risk all in a desperate attempt to destroy the
Japanese Army and recover all that had been lost? Ought
we to fight to the end on some line to retain at least part of

Burma? Or was our task to withdraw slowly, keeping our forces intact, while the defence of India was prepared? Had we been given any one of these as our great overall object it would have had an effect, not only on the major tactics of the campaign, but on the morale of the troops. No such directive was ever received. In the comparatively subordinate position of a Corps Commander, immersed in the hour-to-hour business of a fluctuating battle, I could not know what pressures were being exerted on the local high command, but it was painfully obvious that the lack of a definite directive from above made it impossible for our immediate commanders to define our object with the clarity essential. Whoever was responsible, there was no doubt that we had been weakened basically by this lack of a clear object.

General Taffy Davies, Slim's Chief of Staff, wrote (in a letter to me dated 8 September 1972):

At the end of March Alexander had been ordered, presumably by higher authority in India or London, to withdraw part of his forces into Yunan so as to assure the Chinese of British support however badly things were going for them. Alex gave a brief description of this plan to Slim at an informal meeting on the Meiktila road. Bill Slim took strong exception to this plan. With the Chinese loss of Lashio however the plan just disintegrated.

Alexander's biographer, W. G. F. Jackson, says with regard to Slim's criticism of there never being one clear directive from the top: 'This is certainly true. There were never less than about three aims, but these were given to Alexander by Churchill and Wavell' (*Alexander as Military Commander*, p 139). If so, Alexander would certainly have said nothing about it. I think that Alexander felt that his position as an army commander—at that juncture, with a much weakened force and with a very capable corps commander in Bill Slim—was superfluous; and above all, his professional pride was hurt that he had started a most unenviable job on the wrong foot. But he did fulfil a very essential service during the long retreat. He had great prestige and he prevented Slim from being worried by orders from above and took on many very difficult discussions with the somewhat cantankerous General Stilwell, who was Chiang Kai-shek's liaison representative with the Chinese armies in Burma.

And in the final outcome Alex did get the shattered, but still gallant, Burma Army safely back to India and delayed the Japanese until the coming of the monsoon had made an invasion of India impossible. Had he failed to do so he would have got all the blame, so as he succeeded he should get the credit. But the great thing about Alex was that, at the end of this unfortunate campaign, into which he had been precipitated when defeat had become inevitable, he emerged calm and unruffled and eager to take on the next task. But the Burma campaign was something he never mentioned. It was a discordant interlude in his career which he cast out of his mind completely. Neither Churchill nor Alanbrooke ever lost their confidence in him and he went straight on with a career which brought him the highest honours of any British general in the war.

No praise can be high enough for the way Bill Slim commanded the troops in the campaign. There were two things he was determined not to do—never to under-estimate the Japanese and never to blame his own troops for their deficiencies in jungle training and equipment. And afterwards he was determined that he was not going to take on the Japanese again until he had ground forces as well trained as the Japanese and with much better equipment. Most important of all, he would insist on complete air superiority and on being supplied also with troop-carrying aircraft and supply planes so that the Japanese tactics of 'the hook' could be frustrated.

Defeat into Victory is a classic—quite the best book which has ever been written by a commander on his own campaign—though the *Memoirs of Field-Marshal Montgomery* is a very good one too.

CHAPTER FIVE

The Victorious Generals

Alexander wrote in his *Memoirs* (p 10):

> Early in August 1942 I was told to go at once to Cairo to take
> over command of the Middle East from General Sir Claude
> Auchinleck. Mr Churchill, the Prime Minister, and General
> Sir Alan Brooke, Chief of the Imperial General Staff, were
> still in Cairo when I arrived, concluding their mission which
> was to yield notable results. It is my view that the Prime
> Minister showed great powers of leadership in thus going
> out to the Middle East and making the changes which he
> believed to be essential. I know—because he told me—that
> he disliked intensely having to relieve Auchinleck. 'You
> know', he said, 'it is like killing a magnificent stag!'

On 10 August the Prime Minister gave Alexander his
directive, which was short and simple. His prime and main
duty was to take or destroy at the earliest opportunity the
German–Italian Army commanded by Field-Marshal Rommel,
together with all its supplies and establishments in Egypt and
Libya. The directive was written by Winston in his own hand
and dated 10 August 1942.

Alexander continues:

> Strangely, as I studied the directive, I remembered the queer

feeling of exhilaration which I had when I was ordered to the Middle East, a premonition that at last our fortunes were about to change. It was, no doubt about it, a completely irrational feeling. To put it mildly, the military situation did not look good. Our forces in the Western Desert had been defeated by Rommel and as far as I knew were clinging on to the last defensive positions which covered the Nile Delta. In addition, I had been through some trying and difficult experiences. For me the war so far had been nothing but defeats, rearguard actions and efforts to stave off disaster. I thought of Dunkirk and of our efforts after Dunkirk, when I commanded the South of England and had to secure, with inadequate forces and equipment, the home shores against invasion. And there had been the campaign in Burma, in which we were hard put to it to save our forces from annihilation.

Always I thought—like millions of my countrymen—that we would come through victorious in the end, even if I could not quite see how or when. But now, with my assumption of command in the Middle East, my feelings were tinged with a new confidence. Quite simply, it seemed to me that the tide in our fortunes was about to change; at last we were going to turn from defeat into victory.

Alan Brooke had accompanied Churchill for his momentous visit to the Middle East. Alan Brooke's first choice for the new commander of 8th Army had all along been Montgomery, but he said: 'I felt some very serious doubts as to whether an Auk–Monty combination would work. I felt that Auk would interfere too much with Monty; would ride him on too tight a rein.' (*The Turn of the Tide*, p 442)

And how right he was! That combination would never have worked. Monty wrote in his *Memoirs* (p 92), when he thought that he would be serving under Auchinleck in the Middle East: 'I was not looking forward to my meeting with Auchinleck. I had heard certain things about his method of command and knew that I could never serve happily under him.' He had, of course, after Dunkirk, served as a corps commander in Auchinleck's Southern Command; and he had remarked in his memoirs of this period: 'In 5 Corps I first served under Auchinleck. I cannot recall that we ever agreed on anything.' But from what Auchinleck told me then his opinion of Montgomery was similar to Monty's opinion of him. It was just one of those things. Personalities play a big part in victory in battle.

I think a great deal of credit must be given to Alan Brooke for bringing about this successful Alexander–Montgomery combination. Luck played a part in it—as luck so often does. Churchill had been in favour of 'Strafer' Gott for 8th Army and he had his way. But Gott was shot down in the air and killed before he could take up the command. 'Strafer' Gott had been one of my pupils at the Staff College and he had shown himself to be a fine, courageous battle commander. But he was quite worn out at this time, just as Wavell had been after his defeat by Rommel in the desert. His death was a tragedy but I feel sure that at this time 8th Army needed a fresh brain and new ideas. And it was these that Montgomery provided in such full measure.

But on 18 August Alan Brooke wrote: 'I pray to God that the new Alexander–Montgomery combination will be a success. I can think of nothing better.'

Alexander, of course, had a much easier task than either Wavell or Auchinleck in that he was responsible only for the much smaller Near East Command as far back as the Suez Canal and without Syria, Palestine, Persia and Iraq. It was a real brain-wave of Winston Churchill's to split the Middle East Command in this way.

Alexander had first met Monty in 1926 at the Camberley Staff College, when Alex was in his second year as a student and Monty had just come as an instructor. Monty was five years older than Alex. Then, in 1935, when Monty was a senior instructor at the Quetta Staff College he had taken some of his students to visit Alex who was commanding a brigade on the North-West Frontier. They had met again in the Dunkirk operations when Monty commanded the 3rd Division and

Alex the 1st Division. Monty had a high opinion of Alex and had urged that he should be given command of 1 Corps to conduct the final withdrawal from Dunkirk. He remarks in his *Memoirs*: 'Alex got everyone away in his own calm and confident manner.' In 1940, when Alex took over Southern Command, he found Monty commanding a corps under him and considered him 'splendid; a fine commander, a practical commander and one very keen on physical fitness'. However, he quite realised that Monty was not going to be an easy subordinate as 8th Army Commander. He says in his *Memoirs* that 'Monty wanted to have complete independence of command and to do what he liked.' But he continues (p 16):

> Montgomery is a first-class trainer and leader of troops on the battle field, with a fine tactical sense. He knows how to win the loyalty of his men and has a great flair for raising morale. He rightly boasted that, after the battle of Alamein, he never suffered a defeat; and the truth is he never intended to run the risk of a defeat; that is one reason why he was cautious and reluctant to take chances. There is, however, much to be said for his attitude when we consider that up to October 1942, we had not won a single battle since the start of the war—except Archie Wavell's operations against the Italians and some local victories against the Axis forces in the Western Desert. Monty has a lot of personal charm, yet he is unwise, I think, to take all the credit for his great success as a commander entirely to himself; his prestige, which is very high, could be higher still if he had given a little credit to those who had made his victories possible . . . Personally, I owe Monty a lot—as we all do.

And what were Montgomery's reactions when he heard he would be serving under Alexander and not Auchinleck? He was, of course, delighted. He says in his *Memoirs* (p 95): 'I soon found Alexander in the headquarters, calm, confident and charming as always. I would like to make the point now categorically, how lucky I was to have Alex as my Commander-in-Chief. I could not have served under a better Chief; we were utterly different, but I liked him and respected him as a man.'

And so began this very successful partnership between these two utterly different generals, which could never have worked if their responsibilities had been transposed, with Alex the army commander and Monty the commander-in-chief.

Churchill visited Alexander's command on 19 August 1942, on his way back from Moscow. He did not need to be convinced of the rightness of his choice of Alexander as commander-in-chief. Ever since Dunkirk Alex had been his favourite commander and he never deviated from this opinion until the end of the war—and after. He still had to be convinced, however, about Montgomery, and this visit did much to convince him that everything Alan Brooke had said of him was true.

On the afternoon of the 19th the Prime Minister, accompanied by Alan Brooke and Alex, motored out from Cairo to Monty's new headquarters on the shore near Burq-el-Arab. Winston bathed in the sea before dinner, and after dinner Monty gave them a talk about the situation which faced him as he saw it. Alan Brooke records:

Monty's performance that evening was one of the high-lights of his military career. He had only been at the head of his Command for a few days, and in that short spell he had toured the whole of his front, met all the senior commanders, appreciated the tactical value of all the various features, and sized up admirably the value of all his subordinate commanders. He knew that Rommel was expected to attack by a certain date. He showed us the alternatives open to Rommel and the measures he was taking to meet these eventualities. He said he considered the first alternative the most likely one, namely, a penetration of his southern front with a turn northwards into the centre of his position. He explained how he would break up this attack with his artillery, and would reserve his armour to finish off the attack after the artillery had rough-handled it. His armour would then drive Rommel

back to his present front and no further. He would then
continue with his preparations for his own offensive which
were already started. It would mean hard fighting and
would take him seven days to break through, and he would
then launch his Armoured Corps (his Corps de Chasse, as he
called it) which he had already formed. I knew Monty pretty
well by then, but I must confess that I was dumbfounded by
the rapidity with which he had grasped the situation facing
him, the ability with which he had grasped the essentials,
the clarity of his plans, and above all his unbounded self-
confidence—a self-confidence with which he inspired all
those with whom he came in contact.

His statement was made with such complete self-confidence
that everything would pan out just as he had settled, that
Winston took all this for granted and we shall see later on
that when, after seven days hard fighting Monty was not
through the enemy position as he had promised, a very
serious flutter resulted in the Cabinet dove-cote. After
having explained his dispositions Monty said that, on the
following day, he would take us out to see his preparations
on the ground.

I went to bed that night with a wonderful feeling of
contentment. It had not been an easy matter to get Winston
to accept Monty in command of the Eighth Army, but now
that at last he was there he was more than fulfilling the hopes
I had placed in him. I did not dare let myself think too
optimistically yet, but I had an inward happy feeling that at
last we might begin to meet with some success, a feeling I had
not yet experienced since I had taken over the duties of
CIGS. (*The Turn of the Tide*, p 478)

During the last few years of the war I was Military Adviser
to the Kemsley group of newspapers and Military Correspondent to a number of newspapers, including the *Sunday Times*
and the *Daily Sketch*. This is what I wrote about Montgomery
and Alexander *at that time* and included in a book called
Defence Is Our Business, which was published in 1944.

Montgomery is the most colourful personality of this generation, and together with Alexander, must be considered one
of the most outstanding military commanders of the present
century. Montgomery realised to the full the importance of
leadership and the human factor in modern war. He had
been insistent that the man behind the gun matters more
than the gun itself.

The First World War, with its continuous lines of en-
trenchment, had made leadership difficult.

The Second World War introduced certain conditions
which gave more opportunities for leadership. The great
improvement and increase in air power not only enabled
commanders to get about more quickly and easily, but it
meant that the commander was in the battle area—whether
he liked it or not! The greatly increased range and speed of
mechanised forces also brought the battle to the commander
and the commander to the battle. Montgomery, realising
that the importance of leadership had become greater and
not less as war became more mechanised, cashed in on his
opportunities and deliberately laid himself out to become a
real living human personality to every man in his Army.
He realised clearly that an Army Commander can exercise
little direct command in a modern battle once the troops
have become engaged; but he was determined that before
the battle was joined every man should have seen the Army
Commander, that the men should be able to recognise him
immediately and that they should know his intentions and
what was being asked of them. He set about, therefore, quite
deliberately 'to put himself across' to his troops and to the
British people. . . . Under his leadership 8th Army became
a family in which the relations of the fighting men felt
themselves included. Montgomery courted publicity for
himself and his troops on every possible occasion and in
every possible way. He realised that the people at home
yearn to know all that can be told them about the conditions
under which their men are living and fighting. They are
interested, not only in the personalities of their leaders

and their methods, but also in how they live and work.

Monty adopted a distinctive form of dress. He was the first British General to appear on all occasions in public in a beret and battledress instead of in the regulation red-banded cap and khaki tunic. When others followed his example Monty went several jumps ahead of them by adopting a mufti battle costume of corduroy trousers, high-necked polo sweater and rainproof shooting coat, with only the beret, and sometimes one medal, to mark the costume as bearing any resemblance to a military uniform. The dress the Field-Marshal adopted for his Normandy campaign was so daring in its originality and so far removed from the authorised uniform that no junior commander would have dared to copy it. It could only be approached by some of Churchill's war-time costumes.

He believed always in speaking to as many men as often as possible. These little impromptu talks were never meant to be recorded or written down. It was not what he said that mattered but how he said it and the general atmosphere in which he spoke. He cultivated certain tricks of oratory such as the repetition of sentences to add emphasis to his remarks. . . . To many people Montgomery's publicity methods appeared theatrical, un-British and altogether distasteful. But the fact remains that he captured the imagination and gained the confidence of his troops and of the British public as no other military leader has ever done before. Montgomery, however, is very much more than a colourful and popular figure. He is a great military commander—possibly the greatest of our generation—certainly the outstanding man for the biggest military adventure in our history—the invasion of Normandy and all that followed after it. He was lucky in that, after Dunkirk, he was never sent, as Alexander was, to champion lost causes at a period when lack of men and resources made their failure inevitable. Very few of our Generals survived such operations. Some went into captivity —as Percival did in Malaya and Alexander very nearly did in Burma—and others drifted into obscurity or retirement.

Montgomery escaped all this and from the time that he became an Army Commander he has always had a considerable numerical superiority over his immediate enemies on land and a crushing superiority in the air. In Montgomery we found the man the occasion demanded—and I do not believe that there was any other Allied leader who could have fitted the occasion so well.

Although his methods of leadership were novel and, to some people, distasteful, they did produce the goods—and that, after all, is the acid test. Officers and men who had served under Montgomery had the most implicit confidence in him and never wanted to serve under anyone else. Napoleon said that the moral is to the physical as three is to one; Montgomery put an even higher value on morale than that

The keynote of his leadership can be summed up in one sentence which he repeated often when talking to troops: 'We are all in this thing together; and together we will see it through.' This at once made the men feel a warm sense of fellowship with their commander. He followed this up by going to great lengths to see that every man, before an important engagement, was told the details of the plan and the Commander-in-Chief's general intention. This made each man feel that he was not just 'cannon fodder' but an important pawn in the game which was designed to check the enemy's king by a carefully thought-out combination. This inspired the fighting man to fight harder and more intelligently. Before the battle Montgomery let the men see him at every opportunity. They always saw him looking bright, fit and confident, and that made them feel cheerful and confident too. The spirit of 8th Army was a very remarkable thing. . . .

Like most great and successful commanders in history Montgomery took the greatest pains over the selection of his officers. In this matter he was completely ruthless. Many a good officer went on to the shelf because Montgomery either did not know him, had no use for him, or thought him too old. Montgomery had almost an age fetish. He was himself fifty-four when he had finished commanding a division at Dunkirk—far too old by the standards he himself afterwards applied. But he was most exceptionally fit and active, both physically and mentally, for his years. He was a teetotaller and a non-smoker and trained himself for his job as a boxer prepares for a contest in the ring. He demanded in his subordinates first youth, then physical fitness and then knowledge of their profession, combined with battle experience.

It would not of course have done if all commanders had been allowed to choose the officers they wanted, but in this respect Montgomery was a law unto himself. He gathered around himself a little band of 'Montgomery men'—young and proved corps and divisional commanders who went with him from one battlefield to another. They had implicit confidence in him and he in them. They knew his methods and fitted in with his ideas. Those who did him well received honours and promotion quite regardless of how low they stood on the promotion list. The officers who were not 'Montgomery men' came off badly—and many of them complained very bitterly. But although Montgomery's policy as regards officers had the defects of its virtues—again it produced the goods. Montgomery was not going to send troops into battle with untried commanders; nor was he going to handicap himself by having to get to know new commanders when he could take along with him his experienced generals with whom he was accustomed to work.

Although we realised the importance of team work and paid a great deal of lip service to it before the war, our system of appointments often resulted in bringing together commanders and staff officers who were not temperamentally suited nor previously trained to work with one another. It required a Montgomery to correct this defect in any formation which he himself commanded. His scheme, of course, would have failed if he had not been a good judge of men. This has been an obvious failing on the part of other British commanders in the present war—but never of Montgomery. He picked very few losers.

As regards his staff Montgomery also had revolutionary ideas. Here again he demanded much the same qualities in a staff officer as he did in a commander. He brushed aside all red tape and seniority and insisted on the best man being chosen for each particular job. But it was in his conception of staff work generally that Montgomery's ideas were novel and, in my opinion, essentially sound. He believes in the Continental method of having a Chief of Staff; that is to say, instead of having, as we do in every formation in the British Army above a brigade, a Chief of General Staff, a head of the Administrative Staff and a head of the Quarter-master General's Branch, Montgomery appoints his Chief of the General Staff as Chief Staff Officer in the formation and to him he delegates the responsibility of co-ordinating the whole of the staff work of that particular formation. This procedure gives Montgomery more time to think out his plans and to get around to see the troops. Unlike many commanders and many big men in other walks of life, Montgomery never burns the midnight oil. However important the situation, he gives himself plenty of sleep, and he always insists on having a quiet period every day when he can be entirely by himself to think. The result is that he is never rushed, never 'busy', never overworked.

From the time he took command of 8th Army Montgomery was in a position where we had superiority in numbers and it was most essential that we should not make a major mistake.

Montgomery's ideas on war and on successful command are clear cut and definite. They are based on unbroken success—which he has had, with one exception, ever since he first took command of the Eight Army; that one exception was in Italy where, once he came up against the main German position in that very difficult country south of Rome, he was unable to make any appreciable headway. Our troops, however, had a long legacy of defeats behind them, and Montgomery's method of restoring their confidence in themselves and in victory were eminently sound psychologically. He believes first of all that the air battle must be won before the land battle starts. This of course pre-supposes great air superiority, which he has always had in full measure and of which no one knows better than he how to take full advantage. Montgomery is essentially a studious and scientific commander. He studies his enemy and thinks out what that enemy is likely to do; he then makes his own plans for the battle, working out every move and looking far ahead. He believes in always imposing his own plan on the enemy and he has generally been able to accomplish that since he first did so at the battle of El Alamein.

I wrote of Alexander at the same time:

Field-Marshal Alexander, although senior to Montgomery, is actually five years younger and is a soldier of quite a different type. Alexander, like Montgomery and most of our other successful commanders of the present war, went through the mill of command from the bottom upwards. After making a considerable reputation as a promising young leader in the First World War, Alexander went through the normal routine of a successful pre-war soldier, except that he actually commanded his battalion of the Irish Guards before he went to the Staff College. At the beginning of the present war he commanded the 1st Division in the British Expeditionary Force at Dunkirk and first came to the notice of the public when he was left in charge of the final evacuation from the Dunkirk beaches. He was obviously singled out for high command and after a short period in command of a corps, he was made GOC of the important Southern Command in England, where General Montgomery was one of his corps commanders. From that time on Alexander went from battlefront to battlefront and became the hardest fought and most successful British commander of the war. His career was no bed of roses; his opponents were always Germans or Japanese and he was presented with no easy triumphs against second-class troops. . . .

In my opinion Alexander has the ideal temperament for soldiering; he remains equally poised to tackle each situation as it comes, being neither too cast down by defeat nor too puffed up by victory. He comes to the right conclusions instinctively rather than by scientific deduction as does Montgomery. He needs a particularly good staff because he gives them a very free hand and the maximum amount of responsibility. Generally speaking, he is a better commander of American troops than Montgomery as his personality and methods seem to fit in better with theirs. He abhors an office and a mass of paper and spends much of his time in the forward areas, and yet he has proved by his victory over Rommel in North Africa and his succession of victories over Kesselring in Italy that he is a fine strategist in addition to being a splendid handler of troops in battle.

Alexander's methods of leadership are entirely different from Montgomery's. He is always immaculately turned out; his manner is quiet, but he radiates confidence. He never seeks the limelight and never makes speeches when he can avoid it; but he grows on his men, on his subordinates and on his superiors and they all have complete confidence in him.

Like Montgomery, Alexander is a great believer in physical fitness but does not go to such extremes in its attainment. After over five years of war he has probably aged less than any other British commander. He is temperate in his habits, always active and interested, and he is a wonderful sleeper. A good digestion and the ability to sleep soundly whatever the situation are two very great assets in a commander, which are not always realised. I remember Lord Birdwood telling me once that his greatest asset during the trying Gallipoli campaign was a strong stomach.

This little summary of those two great men, which I wrote

so long ago, sounds as true to me now as when I wrote it. And the success which followed their appointment in the Western Desert was the first fruit of Alan Brooke's percipient insight into their characters.

To return now to that fateful visit of Churchill and Alan Brooke to Cairo in August 1942. Alan Brooke comments on Winston's wonderful vitality, his love of bathing in the sea and of the amazing way he could go to sleep at will in any circumstances. When they got into the car to drive to the aerodrome, Winston said: 'I am going to sleep.' He pulled a bit of black velvet out of his pocket, placed it over his eyes, and never woke up until they had bumped half-way down the Heliopolis runway.

The battle of Alamein went much as Montgomery had predicted. Alex says of it: 'At Alamein Rommel was utterly defeated but not annihilated. It was a decisive victory but not a complete one. Monty might have taken a bigger risk to mop up the Afrika Korps. But in the process he might have had a bad set-back.'

However, the pursuit of Rommel's beaten forces continued until, on 23 January 1943, Alexander was able to send his famous signal to Prime Minister Winston Churchill:

Sir,

The orders you gave me on 10 August 1942 have been fulfilled. His Majesty's enemies, together with their impedimenta, have been completely eliminated from Egypt, Cyrenaica, Libya and Tripolitania. I now await your further instructions.

Alex had cleverly avoided the 'cosy letters' to the Prime Minister which Pug Ismay had so unwisely advised Auchinleck to embark upon. But of course the war had reached a stage when Alex had only to write: 'You said it; I did it.' And Winston was delighted with this Napoleonic stuff. But then Winston took to Alex from the start and in his eyes the latter could do no wrong. Some critics wrote about Alex after his death that he was 'naive', 'the amateur General', 'the innocent abroad' and so on. Far from it. Alex realised the supreme virtue of simplicity in thought and deed. He had of course enormous charm—but since when has charm not been a military virtue? All the top American generals preferred to have Alex rather than any other British general—and what is more they all, from Eisenhower downwards, would have been prepared gladly to serve under Alex if circumstances had demanded.

Meanwhile, on 8 November 1942 the British 1st Army, with the American II Corps, had landed as part of the 'Torch' operation which posed a long-distance threat to Rommel's rear. Churchill, Roosevelt and the Combined British and American Chiefs of Staff met at Casablanca on 14 January 1943. They decided that Sicily was to be the next Anglo-American objective in Europe, starting in July. Eisenhower was to be in overall command with three British officers holding the executive posts of commanders of the naval, land and air forces engaged—Admiral Cunningham at sea, Alexander on land and Tedder in the air. It was also decided that these three men should assume the same commands for the final stages of the Tunisian campaign. Alexander was to take command of all the land forces in Tunisia as soon as 8th Army crossed the Libyan frontier west of Tripoli. His command, which was named 18th Army Group, comprised the British 1st and 8th Armies, under Generals Anderson and Montgomery respectively, the United States II Corps, successively under Generals Patton and Bradley, and the French Corps, under General Konig. Alexander and Tedder were both summoned to Casablanca by Churchill.

Alexander had not the same oratorical powers as Montgomery, but he painted the picture and declared his intentions with simplicity and clarity, which was particularly appreciated by the American President and by Eisenhower and his generals. Eisenhower's position as Supreme Commander was never in doubt but he had informed his own President and his own Chief of Staff, General Marshall, that, if it were considered advisable, he would be delighted to serve under Alexander in the forthcoming operations. There is no doubt that Alex was the American's favourite general.

Alexander took charge of 18th Army Group on 19 February. He expressed to his own CIGS, Alan Brooke, his main anxieties, which were the lack of any plan of campaign and the very disappointing performance of the American troops. However, Alex soon remedied the former and the Americans themselves were quick to learn and soon applied their own remedies for their rawness and lack of experience. But it was only after a lot of hard fighting that the Anglo-American forces entered Tunis and Bizerta on 7 May and then only with the assistance of two divisions and a Guards brigade from 8th Army. Throughout these early months of 1943 8th Army was fighting a succession of hard battles through Cyrenaica and Tripolitania.

The final victory in Africa resulted in the annihilation of the German Army. A quarter of a million men laid down their arms. Immense stocks of arms, ammunition and supplies were captured. Our own casualties in the final battle were less than 2,000 men. On 10 May Alexander signalled to Prime Minister Winston Churchill: 'Sir, it is my duty to report that the Tunisian campaign is over. All enemy resistance has ceased. We are masters of the North African shores.'

There is no doubt that, just as the all-important battle of El Alamein was essentially a victory for Montgomery, in which Alexander played a comparatively minor part—though he had to shoulder the prime responsibility—Tunis was an Alexander triumph. He provided the leadership, and conducted the orchestra—and saw that they were all playing the same tune, though with a number of different instruments. When he was elevated to an earldom after the war he took the title of Alexander of Tunis.

Sicily was the first large-scale amphibious operation against enemy-held beaches in World War II—with Alexander in operational command. Despite acute differences of opinion between the various Allied commanders with regard to the planning of the operation, the invasion was carried out successfully on 10 July 1943 and the heavily garrisoned and strongly fortified island was overcome in thirty-eight days. Churchill cabled Alexander on 19 August 1943:

> I am overjoyed at this new brilliantly executed achievement. I congratulate you most heartily upon all you have done. I will shortly send you a telegram for publication to your troops of the Fifteenth Army Group, but I think it better that the President and the King should send their compliments to Eisenhower first, and I am so advising.

Monty was actually very critical of the planning and was not an easy subordinate for Alex or an easy colleague for some of the American commanders. But Monty generally managed to get his own way. He was equally critical of the planning for Italy. He says in his *Memoirs* (p 190): 'If the planning and conduct of the campaign in Sicily were bad, the preparations for the invasion of Italy and the subsequent conduct of the campaign were worse still.'

However, despite the fact that Alexander had made some mistakes over the handling of the Sicilian campaign, the two senior American generals with whom he worked most closely, Eisenhower and Bradley, remained his staunchest supporters. Eisenhower wrote in his *Crusade in Europe* (p 231):

> I expressed a preference for Alexander [to command the British 21st Army Group in Europe] primarily because I had been so closely associated with him and had developed for him an admiration and friendship which have grown with the years. I regarded Alexander as Britain's outstanding soldier in the field of strategy. He was moreover a friendly and companionable type; Americans instinctively liked him. The Prime Minister finally decided, however, that Alexander could not be spared from the Italian operations.

Bradley had expressed the same preference for Alexander. Alexander himself says in his *Memoirs* (p 130):

Despite the disappointments that it brought, I never lost faith in the strategic validity of the Italian campaign, which owed virtually all its inspiration to Winston; nor did I feel any sort of regret when, because I was so close to it, he refused to release me to Ike to become his deputy in north-west Europe. I should have been more than reluctant to have taken farewell of the troops of the many nations that fought under my command in the Mediterranean. And anyway I prefer command!

Alan Brooke who, after Churchill, was the greatest power in the British military set-up, supported Churchill in his decision that Alex must stay in command of the Italian operation and that Monty should go to command the land forces under Eisenhower for 'Overlord', the invasion of Europe. Alan Brooke quite realised that Ike would sooner have Alex than Monty. Eisenhower knew that he could handle Alex, but was not fond of Monty and certainly did not know how to handle him. Alan Brooke said: 'In my talks with Alex about Command I found him, as always, quite charming to deal with, always ready to do what was requested of him, never scheming or pulling strings. A soldier of the highest principle.' (*Triumph in the West*, p 115). No one knew Alex and Monty better than Alan Brooke—who was about the only general, British or American, who could handle Monty. But I would agree with him that, from a purely professional point of view, for this particular task where meticulous planning was vital, Monty was the better man.

This whole question of the planning of 'Overlord' and the selection of the commanders and the troops who were to carry it out is one of vital interest. And it is nowhere told so dramatically and from such a high standpoint as by that greatest of all British war leaders, Winston Churchill, in the sixth volume of his historic book *The Second World War*, entitled *Closing the Ring*.

At the Quebec Conference, which ended on 24 August 1943, it was agreed that the selection of a supreme commander for 'Overlord' was urgent. As the United States had had the

African Command in General Eisenhower it had been agreed between President Roosevelt and Winston Churchill that the supreme commander of 'Overlord' should be British. Churchill had therefore proposed, with the President's agreement, the appointment of General Brooke, the CIGS, who had commanded a corps in the Dunkirk operations, with Alexander and Montgomery as his subordinates. Churchill had informed Brooke of this early in 1943. Churchill records on 19 August 1943:

> This operation was, to begin with, to be conducted by equal British and American forces and as it was to be based in Great Britain it seemed right to make such an arrangement. However, as the year advanced and the immense plan of the invasion began to take shape, I became increasingly impressed with the very great preponderance of American troops that would be employed, after the original landing with equal numbers had been successful; and now at Quebec I myself took the initiative of proposing to the President that an American supreme commander should be appointed for the expedition to France. He was gratified at this suggestion and I dare say his mind had been moving that way. We therefore agreed that an American officer should command 'Overlord' and that the Mediterranean should be entrusted to a British commander, the actual date of the change being dependent upon the progress of the war. In August 1943 I informed General Brooke, who had my entire confidence, of the change and of the reasons for it. He bore the disappointment with soldierly dignity.

Alan Brooke recalls that it was late in June 1943 that

> The Prime Minister called me in to tell me that he had been wanting to let me know during the last few days that he wanted me to take Supreme Command of operations from this country across the Channel when the time was suitable. It would be the perfect climax to all my struggles to guide

the strategy of the war into channels which would ultimately make a re-entry into France possible. On 7th July the Prime Minister again raised the matter after a dinner at 10 Downing Street for the King. He took me into the garden and again told me that he wanted me to take over the Supreme Command. He could not have been nicer and said that I was the only man he had sufficient confidence in to take over the job. (*The Turn of the Tide*, p 660)

Winston, however, entirely under-estimated the feelings of his Chief of Staff, who had served him so devotedly. Alan Brooke felt very hurt indeed and said afterwards that Winston had given in to the Americans in spite of having previously promised him the job. He records his interview with Winston when this decision was broken to him as follows:

I remember it as if it was yesterday as we walked up and down on the terrace outside the drawing-room of the Citadel, looking down on to that wonderful view of the St. Lawrence River and the fateful scene of Wolfe's battle for the heights of Quebec. As Winston spoke all that scenery was swamped by a dark cloud of despair. I had voluntarily given up the opportunity of taking over the North African Command before El Alamein and recommended that Alexander should be appointed instead. I had done so because I felt at that time I could probably serve a more useful purpose by remaining with Winston. But now, when the strategy of the war had been guided to the final stage—the stage when the real triumph of victory was to be gathered—I felt no longer necessarily tied to Winston and free to assume this supreme command which he had already promised me on three separate occasions. It was a crushing blow to hear from him that he was now handing over this appointment to the Americans and had in exchange received the agreement of the President to Mountbatten's appointment as Supreme Commander South-East Asia. Not for one moment did he realise what this meant to me. He offered no sympathy, no regrets at having to change his mind, and dealt with the matter as if it were one of minor importance. (*Ibid*, pp 706–7)

Winston, who was so sentimental about some things, was apt to be unsympathetic in cases such as this. But his decision was probably the right one. The ideal command structure for 'Overlord' from the point of view of pure efficiency would have been Brooke as Supremo and Montgomery to command the land forces. Brooke was the only general who could really control Monty. But there could not possibly have been two British generals in control of this operation, where the Americans provided the greater part of the troops. And Brooke as the top man would have been little more acceptable than Monty would have been to the American generals. They admired and respected Alan Brooke but didn't understand him. If there had to be a British general in supreme command they would have gone all out for Alex. So Winston had made the wise decision but under-estimated the heartbreak he had caused to Brooke. All credit to the latter therefore that he threw off his very great and understandable disappointment and 'soldiered on' with Winston. But the incident rankled in his mind and he recorded on 30 August 1943, on returning to London from the Quebec Conference:

Went up to the War Office at usual time, and spent a busy time with a series of interviews. Soon I shall be back at the usual grinding work, but feel badly in want of a let-up at present. The Quebec Conference has left me absolutely cooked. Winston made matters almost impossible. He has an unfortunate trick of picking up some isolated operation, and, without ever really having it looked into, setting his heart upon it. When he once gets into one of these moods he feels everybody is trying to thwart him and to produce difficulties. He becomes more and more set on the operation, brushing everything aside, and, when Planners prove the operation to be impossible he appoints new Planners in the hope that will prove the operation is possible. I wonder whether any historian of the future will ever be able to paint Winston in his true colours. It is a wonderful character, the most marvellous qualities and superhuman genius mixed with an astonishing lack of vision at times, and an impetuosity, which, if not guided, must inevitably bring him into trouble again and again.

Perhaps the most remarkable failing of his is that he can never see a whole strategical problem at once. His gaze always settles on some definite part of the canvas and the rest of the picture is lost. It is difficult to make him realise the influence of one theatre against another. The general handling of German reserves in Europe is never fully grasped by him. This failing is accentuated by the fact that he does not want to see the whole picture, especially if the wider vision should in any way interfere with the operation he may have temporarily set his heart on. He is quite the most difficult man to work with I have ever struck, but I would not have missed the chance of working with him for anything on earth. (*Ibid*, p 722)

Field-Marshal Sir John Dill might have written the same *cri-de-coeur*. But whatever differences of opinion there may be regarding the merits or demerits of the leading British commanders of World War II it would be generally agreed that none of them could have changed places with Alan Brooke as CIGS and made such a success of his colossal job. Certainly not Alex or Monty. They couldn't have burnt the midnight oil to start with, as all those closely connected with Winston had to be prepared to do. In truth the British Chiefs of Staff were a remarkable team and Winston paid this tribute to them at the end of the war.

And here is the moment when I pay my personal tribute to the British Chiefs of Staff, with whom I worked in the closest intimacy throughout these heavy, stormy years. There have been very few changes in this small, powerful and capable body of men, who, sinking all Service differences and judging the problems of the war as a whole, have worked together in perfect harmony with each other. In Field-Marshal Brooke, in Admiral Pound, succeeded after his death by Admiral Andrew Cunningham, and in Marshal of the Royal Air Force Portal, a team was formed who deserved the highest honour in the direction of the whole of British war strategy and in its relation with that of our Allies.

(Closing the Ring, p 670)

Churchill himself gave the fullest prominence and support to Mountbatten's appointment as Supreme Commander in South-East Asia and proclaimed that it had the fullest support of American and Chinese opinion. The Prime Minister, however, chafed at the delay on the part of the Americans in appointing a supreme commander for 'Overlord'. It was understood that the President would nominate General Marshall, the American equivalent to General Alan Brooke, but no official announcement had been made. Churchill addressed a letter to President Roosevelt on 1 October 1943 urging that this matter should be settled at once. He also complained at the attacks being made on Mountbatten in the American press and the campaign in favour of MacArthur for that appointment.

30 November 1943 was Winston's sixty-ninth birthday and, as he says, 'A crowded and memorable day'. A dinner was held in his honour at the British Legation in Teheran, at which Stalin repeated to Churchill the question he had posed at the Conference: 'Who will command Overlord?' To which Winston replied that Roosevelt had not yet finally made up his mind but that it was almost certain to be General Marshall. Stalin was evidently pleased at this. 'He thought that General Brooke did not like the Russians and had been very abrupt and rough with them at our first Moscow meeting.' And when Stalin supported the President's toast to Winston on his birthday Stalin repeated his attack on Brooke. The latter then rose and defended himself very vigorously. Stalin afterwards withdrew his remarks; there was much hand-shaking all round—and some final toasts.

In the talks between Churchill and Roosevelt in early December, which continued in Cairo after the Teheran Conference, the President never once referred to the urgent matter of the command of 'Overlord'. Then on 6 December, on the day of his departure, he said quite casually as he and Churchill were driving in a car to the Pyramids, that he could not spare General Marshall for the command of 'Overlord' and therefore proposed to nominate Eisenhower—to which the Prime Minister replied that he and the British had the warmest regard for Eisenhower (*Closing the Ring*, p 369).

The Prime Minister records:

The full story of the President's long delay and hesitation and of his final decision is referred to by Mr. Hopkins' biographer, who says that Roosevelt made the right decision on Sunday, 5th December 'against the almost impassioned advice of Hopkins and Stimson (Secretary of State for War) and against the known preference of both Stalin and Churchill.' (*Closing the Ring*, p 370)

It now fell to Churchill, as British Minister of Defence, to propose a British supreme commander for the Mediterranean and his choice was General Sir Henry Maitland (Jumbo) Wilson. Alexander was to command the whole campaign in Italy. Air Chief Marshal Tedder was appointed as General Eisenhower's Deputy in 'Overlord' and General Montgomery was given the all-important task of commanding the whole cross-Channel invasion force until such time as the Supreme Commander could transfer his headquarters to France and assume the direct operational control. Over and over again Churchill stressed the importance of the Italian campaign. He says:

As I saw the problem, the campaign in Italy, in which a million or more of our British, British-controlled and Allied troops were engaged, was the faithful and indispensable comrade and counter-part to the main cross-Channel operation. I was sure that a vigorous campaign in Italy during the first half of 1944 would be the greatest help to the supreme operation of crossing the Channel on which all minds were set and all engagements made.

(Closing the Ring, pp 377–8)

The American Chiefs of Staff were always lukewarm on the subject of the Italian campaign. Alan Brooke is particularly critical of General Marshall in this respect and of Stimson, the American Secretary of State for War, who supported him so strongly (*The Turn of the Tide,* p 673). The latter regarded the invasion of Sicily as an unfortunate diversion and, though he greatly admired Winston Churchill, he was most critical of him in this respect and of Alan Brooke. Stimson and Marshal completely failed to understand the importance the British attached to weakening the enemy at every point in order to prevent his transferring troops to oppose the vital—but highly dangerous—'Overlord' operation.

Brooke complains with much feeling:

When arguing with Marshall I could never get him fully to appreciate the very close connection that existed between the various German fronts. I have often wondered since the war how very different matters might have been if I had had MacArthur instead of Marshall to deal with. From everything I knew of him I put him down as the greatest general of the last war. He certainly showed a far greater strategic grasp than Marshall. I must confess however that Winston was no great help in the handling of Marshall, in fact the reverse. Marshall had a holy fear of Winston's Balkan and Dardanelles ventures and was always guarding against these dangers even when they did not exist.

(The Turn of the Tide, p 684)

But despite the great delays which had been made in the 'seats of the mighty' regarding the appointment of a supreme commander for 'Overlord', Brooke and the British Chiefs of Staff had, as far back as July 1943, selected the British troops which were to invade France. These consisted of fifteen picked divisions, five of them armoured, formed into a new command named 21st Army Group, under Brooke's former chief of staff and successor as Commander-in-Chief Home Forces, General Sir Bernard Paget. Paget, in Brooke's words was: 'A trainer of troops in the classic Light Infantry tradition of Sir John Moore. He sought, by closely co-ordinating fire-power and movement, to restore the infantry to its old pre-eminence as the cutting edge and arbiter of the battlefield.' (*Turn of the Tide*, p 657)

Paget's task was to train 21st Army Group and its supporting arms, not merely to storm Hitler's coastal fortifications but, supplied from open beaches, to fight its way forward through ideal defensive country against an army of veterans who enjoyed the initial advantage of possessing everything that ran on wheels on the Continent. It was to fight beside Allies of at first equal, and later preponderant, strength. At this time, in the summer of 1943, there was only one American field division in the United Kingdom, with about 150,000 ground-base and air personnel. But, by the spring of 1944, it was expected that at least a million American troops would be based there, including fifteen fighting divisions. Thereafter the American build-up would rapidly outstrip the British. After four years of war, with an air force which was now as large as the Luftwaffe, the world's second largest navy and nearly five million men under arms, Britain, with her comparatively small population, was more highly mobilised for war than any other belligerent.

The role of 21st Army Group was absolutely vital to the success of the whole 'Overlord' operation because if it failed to achieve its objectives then it meant the failure of the whole operation. In an amphibious operation there were certain to be two critical periods—the first in getting the first wave of the invading troops safely ashore, and the second, which might happen two or three days later, in resisting the inevitable counter-attack of the defenders. A British chief of staff, Lieutenant-General F. E. Morgan, had already been appointed to plan the whole 'Overlord' operation, with an Anglo-American planning staff under him. Much of Brooke's time that summer was spent in conference with the Chiefs of Staff Committee and with General Morgan.

Early on the morning of 24 December 1943 General Montgomery, whilst commanding 8th Army in Italy, was woken by a signal from the War Office to say he was to return to England to succeed General Paget in command of 21st Army Group. Though sad to be leaving 8th Army, he was thrilled and delighted (*Memoirs*, p 203).

Winston Churchill, who was convalescing from quite a serious bout of sickness in Marrakesh, invited Montgomery to call and see him on his way home from Italy. The Prime Minister records: 'I was gratified and also relieved to find that Montgomery was delighted and eager for what I had always regarded as a majestic, inevitable but terrible task. The General was in the highest spirits; he leapt about the rocks like an antelope and I felt a strong reassurance that all would be well.'

Montgomery had arrived at Marrakesh on the evening of 31 December 1943. He found the Prime Minister studying a copy of the plan for 'Overlord'. He asked Montgomery to have a look at it and give him his first impressions. Eisenhower had arrived in Marrakesh that afternoon. He was on his way to the United States for talks with the President before taking up his appointment as Supreme Commander for 'Overlord'. He directed Monty to act as his representative until he got to London. The Prime Minister was giving a New Year's Eve party with his staff, Mrs Churchill and Lord Beaverbrook. Knowing the party would go on late and being a confirmed early-bedder himself, Montgomery asked permission to retire after dinner to study the 'Overlord' plan. He made his remarks on it, had them typed before breakfast next morning, and took them to the Prime Minister. The latter was in bed and read them at once.

Montgomery quotes the first four paragraphs in his *Memoirs* and they run as follows:

1   The following must be clearly understood.

(a)   Today 1st January 1944 is the first time I have seen the appreciation and proposed plan or considered the problem in any way.

(b)   I am not yet in touch with Admiral Ramsey and have not been able to consult any Naval expert.

(c)   I have not been able to consult the Air C-in-C or any experienced Air officer.

(d)   Therefore these initial comments can have little value. They are merely my first impressions after a brief study of the plan.

2   The initial landing is on too narrow a front and is confined to too small an area. By D plus 12 a total of 16 divisions will have been landed on the same beaches as were used for the initial landings. This would lead to the most appalling confusion on the beaches, and the smooth development of the land battle would be made extremely difficult if not impossible. Further divisions come pouring in, all over the same beaches. By D plus 24 a total of 24 divisions have been landed, all over the same beaches; control of the beaches and so on would be very difficult; the confusion, instead of getting better, would get worse.

My first impression is that the present plan is impossible.

3   From a purely Army point of view the following points are essential:

(a)   The initial landings must be made on the widest possible front.

(b)   Corps must be able to develop their operations from their own beaches, and other corps must NOT land through these beaches.

(c)   British and American areas of landing must be kept separate. The provisions of (a) above must apply in each case.

(d)   After the initial landings, the operation must be developed in such a way that a good port is secured quickly for the British and for American forces.

Each should have its own port, or group of ports.

4   The type of plan required is on the following lines:

(a)   One British Army to land on a front of two, or possibly three, corps. One American Army similarly.

(b)   Follow-up divisions to come in to the corps already on shore.

(c)   The available assault craft to be used for the landing troops. Successive flights to follow rapidly in any type of unarmed craft, and to be poured in.

(d)   The air battle must be won before the operation is launched. We must then aim at success in the land battle by the speed and violence of our operations.

Montgomery concludes: 'The Prime Minister was intensely interested. He said he had always known there was something wrong in the proposed plan, but that the Chiefs of Staff had agreed with it and that left him powerless.'

These opinions expressed by Montgomery give a remarkable indication of his professional knowledge of military operations generally and his ability to envisage the requirements for a sea landing of these dimensions and in the circumstances which he saw so clearly would arise. The 'Overlord' plan, which had been produced by General Morgan, had been passed by the British Chiefs of Staff before the 'Quadrant' Conference at Quebec in mid-August 1943. There it had been closely discussed by the Combined Chiefs of Staff and approved in outline. They had authorised General Morgan to proceed with the detailed planning required to implement it. Montgomery had made a vital contribution to the success of 'Overlord' by his penetrating comments which resulted in major changes being made in the plan with the greatest possible speed.

Montgomery's next step was to set up the headquarters of 21st Army Group in St Paul's School, West Kensington. As soon as he had been appointed he had asked for five key officers from 8th Army. They were his chief of staff, Freddie de Guingand; General Miles Graham for administration; Brigadier E. T. Williams, Intelligence; and his senior Chaplain,

Freddie Hughes; he also asked for General Dempsey, who was commanding a corps in 8th Army, to be sent over from Italy to command 2nd Army in 21st Army Group. Dempsey, who had been one of my pupils at the Staff College, made a tremendous contribution to our final victory.

It had always been a source of considerable complaint that, when Montgomery was appointed to a new command he insisted on taking with him the key officers of his old formation. In this case the War Office refused to allow him to take Graham and Hughes. Nevertheless Monty decided 'to take Graham home with me and chance the anger in London'; and he soon managed to fix it and get Hughes and certain other people he wanted. Monty had by now become such a power in the military land that he was allowed to do more or less as he liked. The only superior officer whom he always obeyed without question was Alan Brooke.

Freddie Hughes eventually arrived at Monty's HQ at St Paul's School as Deputy Chaplain General 21st Army Group. He was not above pulling his commander's leg and enquired soon after his arrival whether, as all the Group files seemed to be marked 'Top Secret', he could mark his 'Top Sacred'.

In his *Memoirs* Monty says:

It is essential to understand that battles are won primarily in the hearts of men. When Britain goes to war the ranks of her armed forces are filled with men from Civil life who are not soldiers, sailors or airmen by profession; and who never wanted to be. The young man of today can think, he can appreciate, and he is definitely prepared to criticise. He wants to know what is going on, and what you want him to do—and why, and when. He wants to know that in the doing of it his best interests will be absolutely secure in your hands. The British soldier responds to leadership in a most remarkable way; and once you have won his heart, he will follow you anywhere. Finally, I do not believe that today a commander can inspire great armies, or single units, or even individual men, and lead them to achieve great victories, unless he has a proper sense of religious truth; he must be prepared to acknowledge it and to lead his troops in the light of that truth. He must always keep his finger on the spiritual pulse of his armies; he must be sure that the spiritual purpose which inspires them is right and true, and is clearly expounded to one and all. Unless he does this he can expect no lasting success. For all leadership, I believe, is based on the spiritual quality, the power to inspire others to follow.

Holding these views concerning the value and importance of the spiritual side, it was only natural that Montgomery should take the greatest pains to select a senior chaplain of very high quality and one whose ideas would fit in with his own. He was always a ruthless picker of subordinate commanders, and of staff officers—and therefore of padres. And he was always prepared to waive seniority to get the man he wanted. In this case, when he first got command of 8th Army in North Africa he passed over all the more senior regular chaplains to select a Territorial padre by the name of Hughes, who was at that time the senior chaplain to a division. Montgomery wrote of his choice:

I also wanted a first class Senior Chaplain. After considerable investigation we found the man I wanted in Hughes. I never regretted that choice. Hughes remained with me for the rest of the war; he then became Chaplain-General of the Army, being the first Territorial Army Chaplain to do so. He was the ideal of what an Army Padre should be and became one of my greatest friends.

On 13 January Montgomery summoned to his headquarters at St Paul's School the generals of his armies: Dempsey (2nd British), Bradley (1st United States, Crerar (1st Canadian) and Patton (3rd United States, who was not committed to the first wave). He gave them, as he put it, the 'atmosphere' in which from then onwards they would all work and fight.

During the next three months Montgomery devoted himself

to ensuring that his troops were fit, both physically and mentally, for the task ahead. He had already outlined to all general officers his views on tactical training and doctrine. He then wanted to instil confidence by one and all in the high command—which he considered to be vital. And he also wanted to see the soldiers and to have the soldiers see him. He was given the use of a special train and in it he toured England, Wales and Scotland, visiting every formation which was to take part in 'Overlord'. His method of doing this was entirely his own. He inspected groups of men, sometimes 10,000 or more at a time. They were drawn up in a hollow square and he first spoke individually to unit commanders. Then, having ordered the parade to stand at ease, he walked slowly between the ranks so that every man could see him. When this procedure was over he stood on the bonnet of a jeep and spoke to them, some-times with a loudspeaker, sometimes without. He spoke quite simply about the German soldier, never under-estimating him, but telling his audience how he could be defeated. His theme to his troops was always that he had confidence in them and that they must have confidence in him. He reckoned that in this period he inspected well over a million men who were to serve under his command—British, Canadian, American, Belgian, Polish, Free French and Dutch. And General Bedell Smith, Eisenhower's chief of staff, said how much they had appreciated his inspections.

Such was the success of his talks to the troops that the Ministry of Supply asked him to visit factories in various parts of the country which were engaged in the production of military equipment. On 22 February he addressed a represent-ative gathering of railwaymen from all over England at Euston station with the secretaries of the trade unions present. On 3 March he was asked to go to the London Docks, where he addressed some 16,000 dockers, stevedores and lightermen. Wherever he went he was recognised and welcomed by the civilian population. And, as the culmination of his campaign, he was invited on 24 March to a luncheon at the Mansion House where, with the Secretary of State for War, Sir James

Grigg, he spoke about the soldiers and reiterated his constant theme: 'We are all in this thing together and together we will see it through.'

By the end of March everything was set for 'Overlord' and the armies were on their way to their concentration areas. D-Day had been fixed for 5 June. The whole of April was taken up with exercises, culminating in a 'grand rehearsal' by all assault forces from 3 to 5 May.

On 7 and 8 April Montgomery held a two-day exercise at his headquarters in London, which was attended by all the general officers of the field armies. The object of the exercise was to put all senior commanders and their staffs completely into the whole 'Overlord' picture—the general plan and that of the Navy and the Air Force. The Prime Minister attended on the first day and spoke to all the assembled officers. During April Montgomery issued his last tactical instruction to the two armies which were to land in Normandy and on 28 April he moved his operational headquarters to Southwick House in the Portsmouth area.

On 15 May Eisenhower's Supreme Headquarters staged a final presentation of the combined plan to commanders and senior officers. This was attended by the King, the Prime Minister and General Smuts. Eisenhower opened the proceedings with a short but entirely appropriate speech. The King spoke, Smuts spoke—and finally the Prime Minister spoke. Never in the whole history of warfare has a commander launched his troops into a desperately important battle with such careful and thorough planning and preparation as Montgomery did with 21st Army Group.

It is no part of this book to describe the operations in Europe which brought victory to the Allied cause and have been the subject of so many descriptions. Suffice it to say that Montgomery came out of the cauldron, fit, fresh, vital and with a reputation which has put him amongst the great British generals of all time.

Alexander's Italian campaign, on the other hand, has been the subject of conflicting schools of strategic thought in both the Allied and the German High Commands. Alexander himself, in his *Memoirs*, poses the question:

What will be the verdict of history on the campaign in Italy? . . .

Let us consider the situation that existed in the summer of 1943. All Axis forces had been cleared from North Africa and by the conquest of Sicily we had opened up the Mediterranean to our shipping. We were in a position to strike against any part of Hitler's southern-held Europe and to bring his forces to battle. We enjoyed command of the sea and air; and we had a great number of first class fighting formations who had proved themselves on the battlefield and conquered the Afrika Korps and its Italian Allies. Of course we could have sat down in comfortable billets in Sicily and North Africa and awaited the Normandy invasion, still nearly a year ahead. But battles are not won by inactivity— nor are wars. It is inconceivable that the flower of the British and American armies, together with our French and Polish Allies, should have remained quiescent, leaving the Russians to do all the fighting until 'Overlord'. For, although we were called upon to contribute many of our best divisions to the Normandy operation, we were still left with a battle-hardened fighting force of great strength which would have withered away without action. Thus I have no doubt at all that the launching of the Italian campaign and its pursuance was a wise strategic decision. It forced Hitler to fight on three fronts. It was the Germans, not the Allies, who were contained in Italy; and as the record shows, the drain on their strength was greater than the drain on our own.

Alex wrote to me on 11 April 1945 from the office of the Supreme Commander Allied Force Headquarters when I was Military Correspondent to the *Sunday Times* in London.

I am so glad to hear that your health has progressed and you are getting back to normal. I am always anxious that the

Italian theatre of operations gets its fair share of publicity. I think the public don't always realise what a great part the soldiers out here have done in the whole strategy of the European war, and that if it hadn't been for them and our victories in the Mediterranean there would have been no D-Day in Normandy. At this very moment we are fighting 25 German divisions, all up to their War Establishment, and some of them are the best divisions in the German Army. So, even if the general public don't think the Italian theatre of operations very important, the Germans do. I think the end of the European war is now definitely in sight, although there will be a lot of mopping up to do which will take some time. But the result is quite inevitable—there can be no shadow of doubt about that. Every good wish and the best of luck.

Yours ever,
Alex

I think there is no doubt that the Italian campaign was fully justified. One of the oldest principles of war is the concentration of superior numbers at the decisive point. The decisive point was obviously Normandy, which included the perilous amphibious operation of 'Overlord'. In this operation there would obviously be a period in which the total strength of the German defence would be considerably greater than the total strength of the Allied invaders. The Allies could not use more than a certain number of troops in the initial stages. It was of vital importance therefore that the strength of the German defenders in Normandy should be reduced as far as possible by giving them unavoidable commitments elsewhere. If this could be effected—as it was by the Italian campaign—and if secrecy with regard to the main point of landing could be preserved, and if complete Allied air and sea supremacy over the landing area could be attained—then the invasion had a good chance of success. But a major amphibious operation must always be subject to many imponderable factors—as the British remembered to their cost over Gallipoli.

So the greatest possible credit must be given to the British Chiefs of Staff (including Field-Marshal Dill, who was British adviser to the American Chiefs of Staff in Washington) and most particularly to the British Prime Minister, Winston Churchill, whose dogged tenacity and far-sightedness made the whole thing possible.

The Italian campaign was fought against bitter German resistance in appallingly difficult topographical conditions of mountains and rivers, all greatly favouring the defence. I would like to refer to one of the toughest and most controversial battles in the Italian campaign—the Second Battle of Cassino, 15–18 February 1944. The Second Battle, like the First, had so nearly succeeded but there was less to show for it. In the mountains, Points 593 and 444 had been reached but could not be held. It was known after the engagement that the Germans had committed the last of their reserves during the afternoon of 18 February. The 4th Indian Division and the New Zealand Division, commanded by Generals Tuker and Freyberg respectively, had previously achieved almost unbroken success; and the 4th Division was described by General Wavell, its Commander-in-Chief in North Africa, as 'one of the greatest bands of fighting men who have ever served together in the troubled world of war and warriors'; but even they had found Cassino the toughest nut they had ever been asked to crack.

Now, how did Alexander's character and methods of command compare with those of Montgomery? General Sir William Morgan, Alexander's Army Group Chief of Staff, and formerly his GSO 1 1st Division at Dunkirk, has this to say about him:

What sort of a man was Alex? What were his qualifications, his qualities and his character? First of all he had two assets which I think are absolutely essential to good leadership; he had very good health, including a damn good digestion, and he had unbounded optimism. In fact one of his oldest friends once described him as 'a roaring optimist'—a very good description.

He had all the best qualities of an aristocrat, which of course he was. He had generosity without extravagance, tolerance, a tremendous sense of duty which remained un-expressed and which one took a long time to appreciate fully. He had great pride in his country, his family and his regiment. He had remarkable self-control and a very good temper. Of course that was part of his good manners; I only once saw him lose his temper. With his good looks and his charm he had a very large circle of friends, but he had very few intimates. I think that was because he had a natural reserve which prevented him from being too dependent on anyone.

Alex was a lazy man in that he did not like being bothered with details and reading a lot of paper. He used to go to bed quite early—ten o'clock—and I think he slept pretty well.

There is no doubt that both Alex and Monty depended very much on their chiefs of staff, but in different ways. Monty made the appreciation and the plan himself and then relied on de Guingand to see that it was carried out. Alex relied on General John Harding to a much greater extent. He relied on him to make the appreciation and the plan—up to a point where the alternatives were to be considered. Then Alex would come in and say, 'I will do this one.' And he had an extra-ordinary instinct of generally being right. Monty chose all his staff himself and kept them with him. Alan Brooke realised how important it was for Alex to have a strong and high-powered chief of staff and selected John Harding. They formed one of the most efficient and companionable military partnerships of all time.

Alexander didn't attempt, as Monty did, deliberately to make himself known to the troops; he inspired the troops through their commanders. In Italy he had a reliable and experienced 8th Army commander in Oliver Leese and a high-powered—if rather difficult—American 5th Army commander in Mark Clark. Alexander appeared to some casual observers not to be on top of his job and he had not nearly Monty's grip on detail, nor his ruthlessness in getting the things he wanted done. Nevertheless, those who served under Alex swore by him —and he made far fewer enemies than Monty.

Alex was a sensitive man. In an address to war correspondents on 3 November 1944 in Italy he said:

> When I make plans, always at the back of my mind is the thought that I am playing with human lives. Good chaps get killed or wounded and that is a terrible thing. The proudest thing I can say is that I am a front line soldier myself. I fought in the last war with my battalion of Guards and was wounded three times. So I know what it means and I do not throw away lives unless absolutely necessary.

Bill Slim is considered by many people to have been the finest commander Britain produced in the last war. He combined the best qualities of Monty and Alex. He certainly looked the part, with his square figure, strong face and powerful jaw. He was a particularly good commander of Indian troops, of which his 14th Army was largely composed. He was, of course, in the Indian Army himself, though he started his soldiering in the Royal Warwickshire Regiment. But he was also very popular with British and Colonial troops. He was a very highly trained professional soldier and a most attractive personality—being essentially modest and yet completely self-confident. And he never under-estimated the Japanese or regarded them as 'second-class troops' as Wavell did. He sums them up at the end of his Burma victory as follows:

> The strength of the Japanese Army lay, not in its higher leadership but in the spirit of the individual Japanese soldier. He fought and marched till he died. If 500 Japanese were ordered to hold a position, we had to kill 495 before it was ours—and then the last five killed themselves. It was the combination of obedience and ferocity that made the Japanese Army, whatever its condition, so formidable, and which would make any army formidable. It would make a European Army invincible.

Slim considered that the Arakan battle in May 1944 was one of the historic successes of British arms and was the turning-point of the Burma campaign. He says:

For the first time a British force had met, held, and decisively defeated a major Japanese attack and followed this up by driving the enemy out of the strongest possible natural position that they had been preparing for months and were determined to hold at all costs. British and Indian soldiers had proved themselves, man for man, the masters of the best the Japanese could bring against them. The RAF had met and driven from the sky superior numbers of the Japanese Air Force, equipped with their latest fighters. It was a victory about which there could be no argument, and its effect, not only on the troops engaged but on the whole Fourteenth Army was immense. The legend of Japanese invincibility in the jungle, so long fostered by so many who should have known better, was smashed.

Colonel Duncombe, commanding the 1st Battalion The Queen's Royal Regiment, which took part in the battle, was full of admiration for the way the Japanese constructed and used their foxholes. He told me:

These were quite simple but very well constructed. They were in fact just plain holes in the ground, from which the Japs continued to fire at an advancing enemy until the attackers were close upon them. They did not, however, withdraw but were happy to go to ground in their foxholes and let the attack sweep over them. Then, when the opportunity offered, they bobbed up again and shot any men or mules they could see. Not until every individual Jap had been killed, or become so badly disabled that he couldn't use his rifle, did he cease to function, and that always made them a great menace. The number of unwounded Japanese captured was infinitesimal and they generally killed themselves rather than surrender.

No other infantry in the world completely disregarded death as did the Japanese.

Slim never deliberately cultivated popularity as Monty did, nor was he as 'regimental' as Alex. Yet he really was trusted and beloved by his troops as few commanders have ever been—and they retained their regard for him up to the day of his death, and after. Slim was born in 1891 and was educated at King Edward's School, Birmingham. The outbreak of war in August 1914 found him a lance-corporal in the Territorial Army and teaching in an elementary school. He obtained one of the first commissions in Kitchener's Army, and was posted to the Royal Warwickshire Regiment and went with its 9th Battalion to Gallipoli in 1915. He was wounded and invalided back to England. In 1916 he went with another battalion of the Royal Warwicks to Mesopotamia where he was wounded again and awarded the Military Cross. He continued to serve in the Royal Warwickshire Regiment until the end of the war, when he joined the 6th Gurkha Rifles, to which regiment he had been posted on paper in 1916. All his life he was to be an enthusiast about the military qualities of the Gurkha.

In 1925 he passed into the Quetta Staff College and, in 1934, he succeeded me as the Indian Army Instructor at the Camberley Staff College. This was the highest and most coveted appointment which the Indian Army had to offer to an officer of that seniority and it proved a valuable start to his distinguished career. He was then selected to attend the Imperial Defence College in London. He returned to India, after almost five years in England, to take command of the 7th Gurkha Rifles.

On the outbreak of war he was given command of 10 Indian Infantry Brigade, which he took out to the Sudan and Eritrea. It took part in the first offensive against the Italians at Gallabut, where he was wounded again—for the third time in his career. He was then given command of the 10th Indian Division with which he served in Syria, Persia and Iraq. He was awarded the DSO for his service during the year. After commanding 1 Burma Corps in the second part of 1942, which I have mentioned in the previous chapter, he was appointed to command 15 Corps in India. And he had to pull the chestnuts out of the fire in the closing stages of the disastrous Arakan campaign of 1942–3. Then, towards the end of 1943, he was given command of the newly-formed 14th Army. He at once began to build up an administrative organisation, involving a highly organised air supply system, to enable a new strategy to be put into effect.

In his conversations with me, and in *Defeat into Victory* he has made it clear that an answer had to be found to the favourite Japanese tactic of 'the Hook', which they had employed on every occasion, in Malaya, in the First Burma Campaign of 1942, and in the Arakan. The Japanese used their mobility and the fact that they could live on balls of rice—and on the country—to turn the flanks of our defensive positions, or of our advances on the few occasions we were in a position to make them, and thereby force our troops to withdraw or be deprived of food and ammunition. Slim explains the problem clearly in his book (p 291): 'The Japanese had developed the art of the road-block to perfection; we seemed to have no answer to it. If we stood and fought where we were, unless the road were re-opened, we starved. So invariably we had turned back to clear the road-block, breaking through it usually at the cost of vehicles, and in any case making another withdrawal.'

Slim was quite determined that, before he took on the Japanese again in a big way he would have an air force not only superior to anything the Japanese could bring against him but which would contain transport aircraft which could enable his troops to be reinforced or supplied massively from the air when the situation required. At the same time he was also determined that his ground forces must be highly trained in jungle fighting. This training was based on a short memorandum he had drawn up, giving what he considered to have been the tactical errors of the 1942 campaign. The chief of these precepts were the following:

1 The individual soldier must learn, by living, moving and

exercising in it, that the jungle is neither impenetrable nor unfriendly. When he has once learnt to move and live in it, he can use it for concealment, covered movement and surprise.

2 Patrolling is the master key to jungle fighting. All units, not only infantry battalions, must learn to patrol in the jungle, boldly, widely, cunningly and offensively.

3 All units must get used to having Japanese parties in their rear, and, when this happens, regard not themselves, but the Japanese as 'surrounded'.

4 In defence, no attempt should be made to hold long continuous lines. Avenues of approach must be covered and enemy penetration between our posts dealt with at once by mobile local reserves who have completely reconnoitred the country.

5 There should rarely be frontal attacks and never frontal attacks on narrow fronts. Attacks should follow hooks and come in from flanks or rear, while pressure holds the enemy in front.

6 Tanks can be used in almost any country except swamp. In close country they must always have infantry with them to defend and reconnoitre for them. They should always be used in the maximum numbers available and be capable of being deployed. Wherever possible 'penny packets' must be avoided. The more you use, the fewer you lose.

7 There are no non-combatants in jungle warfare. Each unit and sub-unit, including medical ones, is responsible for its own all-round protection, including patrolling at all times.

8 If the Japanese are allowed to hold the initiative they are formidable. When we have it, they are confused and easy to kill. By mobility away from roads, surprise and offensive action we must regain and keep the initiative.

This 'tactical bible' depended of course on the troops being well trained and properly equipped for the job. It would not have been possible with the road-bound and untrained troops of the 1942 Burma campaign. Bill Slim says:

These were the lessons I had learnt from defeat and I do not think I changed them in any essential throughout the rest of the war. There was, however, one big omission. I did not mention air supply. This was intentional. Most of us had long ago recognised that air transport could solve some of our worst problems, but as yet we had no transport aircraft.

(Defeat into Victory)

Bill Slim had strong opinions on the very controversial question of the use of 'special forces'. He made it clear to me, as he did in his book, that he was not in favour of Wingate's Chindits for two main reasons; firstly, organised and well-trained formations had to be broken up to form them; and secondly, considering the losses sustained, the results were not commensurate. His evaluation of the first Wingate raid was:

About a thousand men, a third of the total force, failed to return. As a military operation the raid has been an expensive failure. It gave little tangible return for the losses it suffered and the resources it had absorbed. These are hard things to say of an effort that required such stark courage and endurance as was demanded of and given by Wingate and his men.

However, Slim acknowledges that this raid of Wingate's was worth all the hardship and sacrifice endured if only for its propaganda value. 'Skilfully handled the Press of the world took up the tale and everywhere the story ran that we had beaten the Japanese at their own game.' However, Wingate had some powerful supporters, including Winston Churchill, Wavell and Mountbatten.

Of Wingate personally, Slim says:

Wingate was a strange, excitable, moody creature but he had fire in him. He could ignite other men. When he so fiercely advocated some project of his own, you might catch his enthusiasm or you might see palpable flaws in his arguments, you might be angry at his arrogance or outraged

at so obvious a belief in the end, his end, justifying the means;
but you could not be indifferent. You could not fail to be
stimulated either to thought, protest or action by his sombre
vehemence and his unrelenting persistence.

Wingate was undoubtedly a most gallant man and the
Chindits gave splendid examples of courage and hardihood;
but Slim was strongly against the whole idea of Special Forces,
and he says:

I came firmly to the conclusion that such formations, trained,
equipped and mentally adjusted for one kind of operation
only, were wasteful. They did not give, militarily, a worth-
while return for the resources in men, material and time that
they absorbed. To begin with, they were generally formed by
attracting the best men from normal units by better conditions, promise of excitement, and not a little propaganda.
Even on the rare occasions when normal units were converted into special ones, without the option of volunteering,
the same process went on in reverse. Men thought to be
below the standards set, or over an arbitary age limit, were
weeded out to less favoured corps. The result of these methods
was undoubtedly to lower the quality of the rest of the Army,
especially of the infantry, not only by skimming the cream
off it, but by encouraging the idea that certain of the normal
operations of war were so difficult that only specially
equipped *corps d'elite* could be expected to undertake them.
Armies do not win wars by means of a few bodies of super-
soldiers but by the average quality of their standard units.
Anything, whatever short cuts to victory it may promise,
which thus weakens the Army spirit, is dangerous. Commanders who have used these special forces have found, as
we did in Burma, that they have another grave disadvantage
—they can be employed actively for only restricted periods.
Then they demand to be taken out of the battle to recuperate,
while normal formations are expected to have no such limits
to their employment. In Burma, the time spent in action

with the enemy by special forces was only a fraction of that endured by the normal divisions, and it must be remembered that risk is danger multiplied by time.

I feel convinced that Alexander and Montgomery, if faced by the same problem, would have taken the same line as Slim.

Nowhere is the story of the defeat of the Japanese in Burma told more vividly and more clearly than in Slim's own book, *Defeat into Victory*. His strategic plan for the total defeat of the Japanese armies in Burma was masterly in conception and ruthless in execution. It depended first and foremost on administration, the ability to supply large forces with food and ammunition in a country of vast distances and poor land communications. Slim realised from the outset what a treasure he had in Major-General 'Alf' Snelling, his Chief Administrative Officer. No general in the western theatre had anything like the administrative problems which Slim had.

His medical problem was also immense. In view of all the difficulties of the evacuation of casualties, the sickness rate, which can loom so large in a tropical climate, had somehow to be reduced. In the 1942 campaign where, originally, there had been no mepacrine, the malaria casualties alone were crippling. Fortunately the study of the prevention of tropical diseases had advanced immensely in the years since 1942 and the Supreme Commander, Admiral Mountbatten, had been able to bring to South-East Asia some of the more brilliant research workers in this field. Sulphonamide compounds, penicillin, mepacrine and DDT did not appear at once but they did come in time to save thousands of sickness casualties—and innumerable lives. But air evacuation of the wounded probably made the greatest difference to the casualty lists. Most important of all, however, in the reduction of the sickness rate was the stern discipline which Slim himself imposed. Mepacrine to start with was not a popular drug with the troops; it turned the men yellow and a rumour got around that it made them impotent. So a lot of the men issued with the pill didn't take it. But tests could easily show whether they had taken it or not.

Slim therefore introduced surprise checks of units. If the overall result was less than 95 per cent positive the commanding officer was sacked. He only had to sack three—and then everyone got the message.

Morale-raising in this out-of-the-way theatre of war was a big problem, until victory provided its own morale. Slim talked to a lot of the units himself and 'the Supremo', Admiral Mountbatten, talked to a lot more. Slim says of him: 'Youthful, buoyant, picturesque, with a reputation for gallantry known everywhere, he talked to the British soldier with irresistible frankness and charm. To the Indian he appealed equally. The morale of the Army was already on the up-grade, he was the final tonic.'

Admiral Mountbatten did a fine job as 'Supremo' in South-East Asia. In a type of appointment where it was easy for a supreme commander either to remain too far removed from the actual operations or to become too meddlesome in the spheres which should have been the prerogative of the military commander-in-chief, he hit the happy mean. And his forceful and combative personality made him an asset to the fighting commanders and a morale-booster to the troops. He fitted in well with Slim, relieved him of many big problems of strategic importance, and freed Slim to concentrate on beating the Japanese in battle. He also brought Slim and his army before the public eye and saw that his subordinate commanders got a fair share of the honours which they well deserved. Mountbatten continued his support of the Burma Star men and the Far Eastern prisoners of war after the hostilities had ended and continued to be a popular figure to them all—as he certainly had been whilst the war was in progress. To a greater extent than most of the commanders of troops in World War II Mountbatten campaigned for and supported the ex-servicemen who had served under him, for many of whom the wounds remained unhealed and difficulties of daily living brought their own problems.

Slim was just as insistent as Montgomery was in open warfare that the troops should be introduced gradually into jungle warfare and not thrown in head-first as the 17th Division had had to be in the 1942 campaign. This was done in a series of carefully planned minor offensive operations, carried out against Japanese advanced detachments. Japanese company positions were attacked by brigades, supported by artillery and aircraft, platoon posts by whole battalions.

The Arakan campaign of 1944 ended in the first major defeat of the Japanese forces in Burma. In the battles of Imphal and Kohima, which followed, the Japanese 15th and 33rd Armies suffered a disastrous defeat and were driven back to the Chindwin with some 50,000 casualties. In November 1944 the advance towards Mandalay began. Slim's object now was the total destruction of the Japanese forces in Burma, consisting of the 15th, 28th and 33rd Armies. He planned a great two-pronged battle for Mandalay and Meiktila, designed to cut the Japanese communications with their main base at Rangoon, to envelop and destroy the 15th and 33rd Armies in north Burma, and to isolate the 28th Army in Arakan.

The operations got going on 19 December 1944, and resulted in the capture of Rangoon and the catastrophic defeat of the Japanese armies. But before this was completed Slim had left 14th Army to command an army group known as Allied Land Forces South-East Asia, which was to carry out the reconquest of Malaya. Before the date fixed for this landing, however, the unconditional surrender of the Japanese had taken place. Slim filled many more high and important offices, but this was the end of his service as a battle commander.

I think most people would agree that the top five British generals of World War II were Wavell and Auchinleck—who were both removed from their high commands in North Africa —and Alexander, Montgomery and Slim, who were the victorious generals at the end. There is, of course, a lot of luck in generalship. The important thing for a British general is to ensure, if he can, but he usually can't, that he doesn't hold an important command in the early stages of the war when

Britain is always completely unprepared and prone to disaster. If Alexander and Montgomery had been in charge of the Mediterranean Command at the time Wavell and Auchinleck were, when the area of responsibility for the commander-in-chief was impossibly wide and the forces at their disposal impossibly weak, would they have defeated Rommel in the desert? And would they have weathered the storm of a Prime Minister demanding an early victory? Rommel had the greatest respect for Auchinleck and makes it clear that the latter's final counter-attack was the beginning of the end of his own bid for victory in North Africa. If Auchinleck had only had to command the 8th Army—and not the vast Middle East Command—would he have made as great a success with it as Montgomery? That we shall never know.

It must be remembered, however, that Wavell's early startling and audacious victories in North Africa were gained over the volatile Italians, against whom chances could be taken which would have been suicidal against the Germans. Nevertheless, if Wavell could have retired after his early victories, his place among the topmost generals would have been assured —if only from the fact that these victories had such a morale-raising effect on the hard-pressed British people. Although Wavell had no victories subsequently against the Germans in the west and the Japanese in the east, he could hardly be blamed for any of these defeats in the circumstances which then existed. Had he not been such an (excusably) tired man when the Japanese war started and had he not so gravely under-estimated the Japanese—a mistake which he freely acknowledged afterwards—the First Burma Campaign would have been much less disastrous to the British and much more painful for the Japanese.

Alexander, Montgomery and Slim were undoubtedly great battle leaders worthy to be ranked with Marlborough and Wellington. Would the two latter have been any better than the three former in modern conditions, which were so different to those of the direct command of much smaller forces and of weapons of much more limited range and destructive capacity?

Of the three whom I would rate as the greatest—Alexander, Montgomery and Slim—Alexander is the most difficult to assess. Winston Churchill undoubtedly considered him to be the greatest of all. He wrote to Alexander as follows on 29 April 1945:

> I rejoice in the magnificently planned and executed operations of the Fifteenth Group of Armies which are resulting in the complete destruction or capture of all the enemy forces south of the Alps. That you and General Mark Clark should have been able to accomplish these tremendous and decisive results against a superior number of enemy divisions, after you have made great sacrifices of whole armies for the Western Front, is indeed another proof of your genius for war and of the ultimate brotherhood in arms between the British Commonwealth and Imperial forces and those of the United States. This great final battle in Italy will long stand out in history as one of the most famous episodes of the Second World War. (*Closing the Ring*, p 461)

And later Churchill writes: 'It is right and natural that we should extol the virtues and glorious services of our most famous commanders, Alexander and Montgomery, neither of whom was ever defeated since they began together at Alamein.' But if Alexander had had to conduct the battle of Alamein without Montgomery would he have made the same success of it? And if Alexander had had to plan and conduct the momentous 'Overlord' operation, as Montgomery did, would he have done it so well? Much as I like and admire Alexander I would say that the answer to both questions would be 'No'.

So my own assessment would be that the two outstanding British battle commanders in World War II were Montgomery in the west and Slim in the east. Both were Staff College trained and battle-hardened generals with the highest qualities and qualifications. Could Slim have controlled vast, quick-moving mechanised formations against the ruthless and determined German Armies in the Western Desert and the Normandy country as Montgomery did? And could Montgomery have defeated the never-say-die Japanese Armies operating in jungle country as brilliantly as did Slim? Such questions give one furiously to think and stimulate one's efforts to re-assess the different qualities of these two great men. I myself think that Slim would have been more likely to succeed in the desert than Montgomery in the jungle. But neither would have done so well as the other in the different circumstances in which each was so successful and victorious. So I would be content to consider, as I said earlier, that Montgomery was the top general in the west and Slim in the east.

But what, then, of Alan Brooke, whom many would consider the finest British general of them all? And so he may well have been. He commanded his corps very well at Dunkirk and he was a wonderful Chief of the Imperial General Staff. But he was never tested in the crucible of continued, bitterly contested battle fighting. And that is where generals are made or broken.

Bibliography

BOOKS

Alexander, Field-Marshal Earl. *Memoirs* (Cassell, 1962)
Bryant, Arthur. *The Turn of the Tide* (Collins, 1957)
Churchill, Sir Winston S. *The Second World War*, 6 vols (Cassell, 1948–54)
Colville, J. R. *Man of Valour: Field-Marshal Lord Gort* (Collins, 1972)
Connell, John. *Auchinleck* (Cassell, 1959)
——. *Wavell—Soldier and Scholar* (Collins, 1964)
——. *Wavell—Supreme Commander* (Collins, 1969)
Evans, Geoffrey. *Slim as Military Commander* (Batsford, 1969)
Jackson, W. G. F. *The Battle for Italy* (Batsford, 1967)
——. *Alexander as Military Commander* (Batsford, 1971)
Kennedy, Sir John. *The Business of War* (Hutchinson, 1957)
Kirby, Major-General S. Woodburn. *The War against Japan* (HMSO, 1958)
Lewin, Ronald. *Rommel as Military Commander* (Batsford, 1968)
——. *Montgomery as Military Commander* (Batsford, 1971)
Montgomery, Field-Marshal Viscount. *Memoirs* (Collins, 1958)
Nicolson Nigel. *Alex: The Life of Field-Marshal Earl Alexander of Tunis* (Weidenfeld & Nicolson, 1973)
Roskill, Stephen. *Hankey, Man of Secrets* (Collins, 1970)
Slim, Field-Marshal Sir William. *Defeat into Victory* (Cassell, 1956)
Smyth, Sir John. *Defence Is Our Business* (Hutchinson, 1944)
——. *The Only Enemy* (Hutchinson, 1959)

——. *Sandhurst: The History of the RMA and the RMC* (Weidenfeld & Nicolson, 1961)

——. *The Story of the Victoria Cross* (Muller, 1963)

——. *Bolo Whistler: The Life of Sir Lashmer Whistler* (Muller, 1967)

——. *In This Sign Conquer: The Story of the Army Chaplains* (Mowbray, 1968)

——. *The Valiant* (Mowbray, 1970)

——. *Percival and the Tragedy of Singapore* (Macdonald, 1971)

DESPATCHES

General Sir Claude Auchinleck's Despatch (Middle East 1941–2) (*London Gazette*, 13 January 1948)

The Despatches of General the Viscount Gort (*London Gazette*, 1941)

Despatch of General Sir Archibald Wavell (Operations in the Middle East) (7 February 1941–10 July 1941)

Despatch of General Sir Archibald Wavell on operations in Burma (15 December 1941–20 May 1942) (*London Gazette*, 11 March 1948)

Acknowledgements

I am grateful to those many generals mentioned in this book who served with me in both world wars and other campaigns, for their example, their leadership and their courage. And also to those generals and embryo generals who, at the Staff College Camberley, were my fellow pupils, my teachers, my fellow teachers and my pupils.

I am particularly grateful to that fine fighting soldier who made valuable contributions to this book—Major-General H. L. (Taffy) Davies, CB, CBE, DSO, MC. He was Chief General Staff Officer to General Hutton and then to General Slim in the last of my many campaigns—Burma 1942. Also to my old friend, Lieutenant-General Sir Philip Neame, VC (one of my teachers at the Camberley Staff College) who kindly read my chapter 2 on the campaign in North Africa, First Phase.

I would also like to pay tribute to those who served under me in the two historic retreats—Dunkirk and Burma—the latter of which marked the end of my military career—particularly General Sir Charles (Splosh) Jones, GCB, CBE, MC, who was my brigade-major in 127 Infantry Brigade at Dunkirk and, at the time of writing, is Governor of the Royal Chelsea Hospital and President of the Royal British Legion; to the 19th (Dagger) Division which I raised in Secunderabad in October–November 1941—and for which my wife Frances designed the dagger sign

236

which the division made famous in the recapture of Burma in 1944 when commanded by my gallant friend, Peter Rees, who was one of my pupils at the Staff College; to Major-General 'Punch' Cowan, my chief of staff, who took over the ill-fated 17th Division from me in the First Burma Campaign in January–March 1942; and to my three very stalwart brigade commanders, Roger Ekin, 'Jonah' Jones and Noel Hugh-Jones, of whom only the former is still alive.

I shall always be grateful to Field-Marshal Lord Gort, who had been one of my teachers at the Staff College, for getting me home from India in 1939, where I was commanding a battalion, to command one of his brigades in the British Expeditionary Force. I was the only Indian Army officer to hold a fighting command in the operations leading up to Dunkirk.

Finally I would like to give thanks to three famous field-marshals, who were my particular friends and whom I admired beyond measure—Auchinleck, Alexander and Slim—and to the 'Supremo' of South-East Asia Command, Lord Mount-batten, with whom I have worked in so many ex-service associations and causes since World War II. How lucky I have been to have known so many of these famous fighting men!

As always, my old friend, Mr D. W. King, OBE, FLA, the Chief Librarian of the Ministry of Defence Library (Central and Army), and his capable and helpful assistant, Mrs Davies, have been towers of strength in providing me with the numerous books and other documents I required.

Lastly, I would once again like to give my warmest thanks to my wife Frances, who has typed every word of the twenty-eight books I have written and done some valuable sub-editing as well—also to my excellent secretary Jacqueline Stead who has done invaluable work on this book.

JACKIE SMYTH

Index